I0828356

Spiritual Complaint

Spiritual Complaint

The Theology and Practice of Lament

Edited by
Miriam J. Bier *and* Tim Bulkeley

PICKWICK *Publications* • Eugene, Oregon

SPIRITUAL COMPLAINT
The Theology and Practice of Lament

Pickwick Publications
An Imprint of Wipf and Stock Publishers
199 W. 8th Ave., Suite 3
Eugene, OR 97401

www.wipfandstock.com

ISBN 13: 978-1-4982-6197-5

Cataloguing-in-Publication data:

Spiritual complaint : the theology and practice of lament / edited by Miriam J. Bier and Tim Bulkeley.

xvi + 280 pp. ; 23 cm. Includes bibliographical references.

ISBN 13: 978-1-4982-6197-5

1. Laments in the Bible. 2. Laments—History and criticism. 3. Suffering—religious aspects. 4. Pastoral theology. I. Bier, Miriam J. II. Bulkeley, Tim. III. Title.

BS1535.52 B437 2013

Manufactured in the U.S.A.

This book is dedicated to the victims of the Christchurch earthquake, their families, and all those who continue to live in the broken city, facing daily uncertainty and ongoing tremors. Miriam thinks especially of the Sturgeons (Helen, Mike, Emma, and Rachael), and the Morrisons (Louise, Kris, Cora, Amy, Nathan, Faith, Miriam, and Isabella).

Contents

PART TWO: Reflections

PART THREE: Explorations

PART FOUR: Refraction

Contributors

Miriam J. Bier, Lecturer in Old Testament, London School of Theology, London, UK.

Elizabeth Boase, Lecturer in Old Testament, Department of Theology, Flinders University; Co-Director of Biblical Studies, Uniting College for Leadership and Theology, Adelaide, Australia.

Colin Buchanan, formerly the Bishop of Aston and then of Woolwich; former Principal, St John's College, Nottingham, UK.

Tim Bulkeley, Freelance Biblical Scholar teaching as Visitor at Laidlaw Graduate School, Auckland, New Zealand; and Colombo Theological Seminary, Colombo, Sri Lanka.

Stephen Garner, Lecturer in Theology in the School of Theology, Faculty of Arts, The University of Auckland, New Zealand.

Yael Klangwisan, Senior Lecturer in Education, Laidlaw College, Auckland, New Zealand.

Will Kynes, Departmental Lecturer in Old Testament Studies, Stipendiary Lecturer at St Peter's College, and Liddon Research Fellow and Tutor of Theology at Keble College, University of Oxford, Oxford, UK.

Alistair J. Mackenzie, Senior Lecturer, School of Theology, Mission and Ministry, Laidlaw College, Christchurch Campus, New Zealand.

Jeanette Mathews, Lecturer in Old Testament, Charles Sturt University, Canberra, Australia.

Donald P. Moffat, Biblical Scholar, Hamilton, New Zealand.

Robin Parry, Editor, Cascade Books and Pickwick Publications, Wipf & Stock Publishers, Worcester, UK.

Carlos Patrick Jimenez, Pastor, London, UK.

Steve Taylor, Senior Lecturer, Department of Theology, Flinders University; Principal, Uniting College for Leadership and Theology, Adelaide, Australia.

Lena-Sofia Tiemeyer, Senior Lecturer in Hebrew Bible, University of Aberdeen, Aberdeen, Scotland, UK.

Acknowledgments

This book arose out of a colloquium held under the auspices of the (then) Laidlaw-Carey Graduate School, with the support of both Carey Baptist College and Laidlaw College. We are grateful, as ever, for their support.

Acknowledgment

Abbreviations

AB	Anchor Bible
ABD	*Anchor Bible Dictionary*
AJSL	*American Journal of Semitic Languages and Literature*
AUS	American University Studies
Bib	*Biblica*
BZAW	*Beihefte zur Zeitschrift für die Alttestamentliche Wissenschaft*
CBQ	*Catholic Biblical Quarterly*
COB	Colin Ogilvie Buchanan
CurTM	*Currents in Theology and Mission*
EJIL	Early Judaism and Its Literature
Enc	*Encounter*
ErIsr	Eretz-Israel
EvT	*Evangelische Theologie*
FAT	Forschungen zum Alten Testament
FOTL	Forms of the Old Testament Literature
FTL	*Forum Theologiae Linguisticae*
FRLANT	Forschungen zur Religion und Literatur des Alten und Neuen Testaments
HALOT	*Hebrew and Aramaic Lexicon of the Old Testament*
HBT	*Horizons in Biblical Theology*
ICC	International Critical Commentary
ITC	International Theological Commentary
Int	*Interpretation*
JBL	*Journal of Biblical Literature*
JSOT	*Journal for the Study of the Old Testament*
JSOTSup	Journal for the Study of the Old Testament Supplement Series

KJV	King James Version
LHB/OTS	Library of the Hebrew Bible/Old Testament Studies
MJTM	*McMaster Journal of Theology and Ministry*
NASB	New American Standard Bible
NCB	New Century Bible Commentary
NET	New English Translation
NIB	The New Interpreter's Bible
NIBC	New International Biblical Commentary
NICOT	New International Commentary on the Old Testament
NIDOTTE	*New International Dictionary of Old Testament Theology and Exegesis*
NISB	*New Interpreter's Study Bible*
NRSV	New Revised Standard Version
OBT	Overtures to Biblical Theology
OTL	Old Testament Library
OUP	Oxford University Press
SBL	Society of Biblical Literature
SBLDS	Society of Biblical Literature Dissertation Series
SBLSymS	Society of Biblical Literature Symposium Series
SJOT	*Scandinavian Journal of the Old Testament*
SemeiaSt	Semeia Studies
ThTo	*Theology Today*
TynBul	*Tyndale Bulletin*
VT	*Vetus Testamentum*
VTSup	Vetus Testamentum, Supplements
WBC	Word Biblical Commentary
WC	Westminster Bible Commentary
WJK	Westminster/John Knox
WMANT	Wissenschaftliche Monographien zum Alten und Neuen Testament
YLT	Young's Literal Translation
ZAW	*Zeitschrift für die Alttestamentliche Wissenschaft*
ZTK	*Zeitschrift für Theologie und Kirche*

Introduction

EVERY LIFE, AND EVERY land and people, has reasons for lament and complaint. This collection of essays explores the biblical foundations and the contemporary resonances of lament literature. The editors of this book and many of its contributors have strong connections with Aotearoa, New Zealand. It is fitting, therefore, that the book begins with a lament liturgy responding to the recent Christchurch earthquake (22 February 2011). It ends with a piece considering the "Holy Land" through the eyes of the Shulamith of the Song of Songs. Between these framing laments, a variety of responses to tragedy and a world out of joint are explored. These responses arise from Scripture, from within the liturgy of the church, and from beyond the church; in contemporary life (the racially conflicted land of Aotearoa-New Zealand, secular music concerts, and cyber-space). The book thus reflects upon theological and pastoral handling of such experience, as it bridges these different worlds. It brings together in conversation specialists from different fields of academy and church to provide a resource for integrating faith and scholarship in dark places.

The biblical material in the first section (Foundations) offers new contributions to scholarship on Jeremiah, Lamentations, and Job; and ongoing discussion of the relationship between lament and penitential prayer in the Old Testament. Tim Bulkeley begins by questioning the very nature and nuance of the terms "lament," "complaint," and "confession," with reference to the book of Jeremiah. Miriam J. Bier's essay on the place of Lamentations 4 in the book of Lamentations contributes to the growing scholarly interest in the book of Lamentations, drawing particular attention to chapter 4's vital role in the book. The essays by Will Kynes and Carlos Patrick Jimenez offer detailed investigations of aspects of lament personified in Job: the relecture of Ps 22 in Job; and metaphor in Job; respectively. Lena-Sofia Tiemeyer, Liz Boase, and Donald P.

Moffat each discuss the move from lament to penitential prayer in the Old Testament. These pieces are significant for both their similarities and differences of approach and conclusions, and demonstrate that the question of the relationship between lament and penitential prayer is still a live debate.

The middle sections of the book offer a bridge between the foundations of biblical scholarship, and the contexts in which lament might be used and framed in contemporary society. The "Reflections" section pays particular attention to expressions of lament in the church. Robin Parry's reflections on possibilities for lament in the church give way to seasoned liturgist Colin Buchanan's examples of lament liturgy used in specific situations in Jersey and Japan. The third section (Explorations) offers possibilities for expressing lament into contemporary situations into which the biblical lament tradition might speak. Here settings beyond the church are explored. Alistair McKenzie and Jeanette Mathews offer reflections on lament from very different cultural contexts: Aotearoa-New Zealand; and Karen refugee camps on the border of Thailand; respectively. Stephen Garner moves decisively into the twenty-first century with possibilities for lament in a technological age, pointing out examples of lament in cyperspace. Steve Taylor and Liz Boase's joint piece explores the use of biblical lament motifs in public, secular contexts, to express communal grief at overwhelming tragedy. Taylor and Boase examine U2's handling of the Pike River coal mine disaster in West Coast New Zealand in an Auckland concert; and Paul Kelly's moving tribute to victims of the bush fires in Victoria, Australia, at a relief concert in Melbourne.

The closing "Refraction" engages, autobiographically, lament in the land of Israel/Palestine. Yael Klangwisan provides a deeply personal lament steeped in the land and literature of the Shulamith. She evokes a poetic and political world, expressive of ongoing tensions and need for lament. The collection is thus framed with laments from two lands: Aotearoa, New Zealand, fondly known as "Godzone" (God's Own Country); and the Holy Land, considered God's own land in an entirely different, and contested, way.

1

A Lament for Christchurch

Colin Buchanan

God our Father, creator of heaven and earth and all that is in them;
you have given us a fruitful and beautiful land,
and we inhabit it as your creatures, dependent upon your goodness,
and yet knowing our own frailty.

Lord, the earth has shaken, the ground has quaked,
terror has struck, and our hearts are dismayed;
our buildings are down,
and friends, neighbours, and family-members have died;
much of the city we loved is in ruins;
people are missing, families are homeless, after-shocks continue,
and our easy confidence in life has gone.

Lord and Father, we lament the city's fate before you;
we who have trodden the ground in assurance,
and built our homes, and driven our cars, and played our sports upon it,
we now mourn the city's loss, and grieve that we can trust
the ground no longer.

Yet, Lord, this is your world, and you are sovereign over it,
and even the hairs of our heads are numbered by you.

Let us learn of you, but give us space and time to do so;
help us to come to terms with disaster, and yet find your hand of love within it.

And while we grieve, we thank you for the selfless labours
of rescue workers and volunteers,
we commend to you the bereaved, the injured, the homeless
and all who suffer;
we rejoice at the unstinting help of many from far and near;
and we seek from you the will and the way for the city to recover,
for life in it to flourish, for memories to be healed,
for every loss to be made good.

Lord, deal gently with us as we mourn; and so reveal yourself to us
that we may in time put darkness and loss behind us
and walk whole and healed.

Lord, we believe: but we have staggered at this earthquake
and all that it has done;
restore now our trust in you and lead us out of darkness
into your marvellous light.

PART ONE

Foundations

2

Does Jeremiah Confess, Lament, or Complain?

Three Attitudes towards Wrong

Tim Bulkeley

The claim by Shakespeare's Juliette "What's in a name? That which we call a rose by any other name would smell as sweet" is often quoted to claim that naming is arbitrary. Yet what we call things matters. For our classifying, and hence our naming, in part defines what we can and will perceive. This chapter investigates three approaches to naming the genre present in the speeches commonly known as "the confessions of Jeremiah" in order to uncover three responses to the dark times. While these are different they also often coincide and collaborate as our spirits respond to disaster and hopelessness. I will also suggest that to read these "confessions of Jeremiah" we need to move beyond any of these neat descriptors, and perceive the interweaving of the attitudes they represent in the narrative unfolded by these texts. In doing this we will distinguish not only the literary shape or form of the texts we discuss, but also their attitude to the "wrongs" to which they respond.

Lament expresses sorrow, mourning, or regret. Such expressions are a universal response to events or situations that seem, to the speaker, wrong. The connection of this response with "mourning" is appropriate, for death and bereavement are an extreme and irreversible form of "wrongness" in our world. Furthermore (at least in the cultures that produced the texts collected in the Hebrew Bible), expressions of lament in other contexts often borrow language and imagery from the realm of death and bereavement. In particular the individual laments in the Psalter often express the psalmist's trouble as bringing them near to death.

Laments are not merely the commonest genre of psalm in the book of Psalms, but elements of lamentation are also found widely in the prophetic books. Westermann, in his study of the basic forms of speech found in the prophets, noted the "death lament over Israel" in Amos 5:1–3 to be a classic example of a form that was widespread in the prophets and particularly developed in Jeremiah.[1] Indeed, he drew attention later to the way the corpus of the Latter Prophets begins with Yhwh lamenting (in the opening chapter of Isaiah).[2] Such laments were a way of formulating an announcement of judgment. They picture the future state of the people or state being discussed as if they were dead. There are also often in these books texts that lament in ways that Dobbs-Allsopp suggests reflect the Mesopotamian genre of "city-lament" (such city-lament material is found in both the oracles against nations and against Israel and Judah in the prophetic books and most notably in Lamentations).[3] Such speech reflects the sadness of an afflicted people, rather than that of the deity witnessing the decline and punishment of a chosen people. These two movements, while both lament or mourn a loss, make use of the lament in quite different ways. In the first case the intent is to accuse, while the second is more like the psalms and appeals for divine aid in redressing the wrong.

In making this move to seeking redress of the "wrongness" this second use of lament in the prophets, like most "lament psalms," begins to move to the second of our attitudes. For in order to appeal for help and redress one must, at least by implication complain about the state of affairs to be redressed. Indeed "complaint" is one of the standard components of a lament psalm.

Within discussion of the genres of psalms often two related moves are made which recognize another attitude to disaster, very different from lament, yet closely related to it—complaint. Like lament, complaint recognizes that something is wrong, but instead of merely recognizing

1. Westermann, *Basic Forms of Prophetic Speech*, 202.

2. Ibid., 279.

3. On the prophets, see Dobbs-Allsopp, *Weep, O Daughter of Zion*, 97–153; and concerning Lamentations in particular Dobbs-Allsopp, *Lamentations*, 6–12.

and bewailing that fact, complaint goes on to lay blame, and even by implication at least to appeal for redress.

Sweeney, in his summary of the genres found in prophetic literature following standard form-critical categories, distinguishes "Communal Complaint Songs (*Volksklagelied, Klagelied des Volkes*)"[4] and "Lamentation (*Volksklage, Untergangsklage, Klaglied, Klage*)."[5] As this approach presents things, in complaints the calamity is still in prospect, thus here a plea for help is a dominant feature, while laments express sadness after the event and the plea is either subdued or absent.[6] While this before and after distinction seems to make good *a priori* sense, I want to argue that the fundamental difference between the two genres, whether in the prophets or elsewhere, is not timing but *attitude*.

The German expressions *Klage* (complaint, lament) and *Anklage* (charge, accusation or reproach) perhaps sound more similar than the words we might use in English. Indeed the German nouns are close in meaning. However, the *verbs* suggest different attitudes: *klagen* (moan, wail, or complain) suggests different mental states from *anklagen* (charge, accuse or protest). Since in this chapter I am more interested in the *functional* or attitudinal difference than the formal ones, this potentially significant difference in the German terms is of interest. For here as in most form-critically originated discussion much terminology traces itself back to German originals (as the FOTL series in which both Gerstenberger's and Sweeney's work appeared makes clear by using both German and English names for the genres discussed).

So, in contrast to this form-critically derived distinction I want to use a different one which focuses on the attitude towards the "wrong" which is expressed by the text. In this optic a lament bewails a situation that is past or more often present (as in many psalms, e.g., Pss 4–6 and some prophetic texts, e.g., Mic 7:1ff.), or one that is foreseen as a future danger (as in at least some prophetic laments, e.g., Amos 5:1–3 or appeals to lament, e.g., Jer 9:10, 17–22) whether or not that danger can potentially be averted. Again, focusing on the question of attitude, complaint suggests that the speaker believes that the one addressed has the capacity to alleviate the situation being described and (at least by implication) is appealing that they should do so. Thus Ps 80 complains that Yhwh is

4. Sweeney, *Isaiah 1–39*, 517.

5. The Earth Bible Team, "The Voice of the Earth More Than a Metaphor," 523.

6. Gerstenberger, *Psalms*, 10–14 is typical form-critical forerunner of this distinction (also in the FOTL series).

failing to act to protect or restore Israel when enemies have invaded and destroyed, much as does the psalm in Hab 3.

The third term that is important for us here, "confession," has mainly been used to describe a series of passages in Jeremiah (Jer 11:18–20; 12:1–6; 15:10–21; 17:14–18; 18:18–23; 20:7–13). These have at least since the late nineteenth century been known collectively as "the confessions of Jeremiah."[7] Since Baumgartner they have been recognized as similar in content and expression to individual lament psalms,[8] though perhaps the Babylonian work known as a *Man and his God* might offer an even stronger parallel.[9] This recognition in itself suggests that to call these texts laments is to over-simplify.

However, the traditional designation, confession, suggests yet a third and quite different attitude in response to a time of "wrong," that is an expression of trust in the one who has the capacity to right the wrong. Such confessions of trust are a commonly recognized feature of complaint psalms.[10] By "confession" in this context of literary and/or prayerful responses to times when things are "wrong" I mean the attitude which affirms or confesses confidence and trust in God despite the circumstances.[11] For in both psalms and prophets a part of the varied human response to a world out of joint has been to confess trust in God that this situation is temporary or aberrant in some way.

Although these three—lament, complaint, and confession—may well find expression together in the same piece, they represent fundamentally different stances with respect to the "wrong." Lament merely announces the wrong as wrong, complaint moves to a hope that the

7. This list is widely accepted and discussed, though some scholars add individual items (Diamond, *The Confessions of Jeremiah in Context*, 193; von Rad, "Die Konfessionen Jeremias," 227 (8:18–23); Hyatt, *Jeremiah, Prophet of Courage and Hope*, 782 (10:23–24; 17:9–10); Bright, *Jeremiah*, LXVI (4:19–21; 5:3–5; 8:18–23); Berridge, *Prophet, People and the Word of Yahweh*, 114 n. 1 (9:1–8); Holladay, *The Architecture of Jeremiah* 1–20, 152 (17:5–8, 9–10); Thompson, *Book of Jeremiah*, 88 (4:19–21; 5:3–5; 8:18–23).

8. Baumgartner, *Die Klagegedichte Jeremias und die Klagenpsalmen*.

9. Lambert, "A Further Attempt at the Babylonian 'Man and His God.'"

10. See, e.g., the list in Gerstenberger, *Psalms*, 12.

11. It is true that "confession" has been used mainly in Hebrew Bible studies to speak of psalms in which the psalmist's sin is acknowledged, however (at least since von Rad's influential work) the other meaning of "confess" to declare faith and trust in a divine being (which is the sense I intend) has been in use von Rad, *Das Formgeschichtliche Problem des Hexateuchs*.

wrong might be righted in some way, while confession moves beyond this again to a place of trust and affirmation of God even amid the wrong and even though it might not be righted.

Brueggemann offered a functional (rather than formal) classification of psalms which is widely appreciated for its pastoral and theological power. In some ways this threefold description of the attitudes expressed in texts dealing with times when life seems "wrong" is similar. It focuses on function not form, there is a measure of progression between categories.[12] The key element in the proposed classification is the attitude expressed. In "lament" mourning, sadness, regret are to the fore, while in "complaint" protest, reproach, and even accusation are the focus, and in "confession" (perhaps despite the circumstances described and even the reproachful content of the speech) trust in the one addressed or spoken about is prominent.

Turning to the "confessions of Jeremiah" and their relationship to the eponymous prophet, until the rise of form criticism and the recognition of customary elements in their expression, most studies of Jeremiah's confessions read them as outpourings of a troubled soul, and used them to reconstruct Jeremiah's thoughts and personality. Then the recognition of the conventional and social nature of "laments" suggested thinking of these texts in different ways. However, reading the book of Jeremiah as a complete and unified work and therefore reading these passages both together with each other, and also in what presents itself as in some sense a "portrait of a prophet,"[13] one is likely to perceive a narrative thread in these passages taken as a group.

This narrative thread traces a developing relationship between the speaker, Jeremiah,[14] his God, Yhwh, as well as a collection of opponents, first the men of Anathoth, later a less specific "they."

A number of features of these passages suggest their (quasi)narrative effect. The opening passage in 11:18—12:6 offers a strong narrative frame. Several features give the reader a set to understand the passage as

12. While Brueggemann's categories form a natural biographical progression the same is less true of the proposed categories of response to wrongness. While one might progress between them they each might be encountered alone, or often they succeed each other within a short composition.

13. Brueggemann, *Theology of the Old Testament*, 27–35.

14. Unless some mention in my text makes clear that "Jeremiah" refers to a putative person in Iron Age Jerusalem the term means either the book commonly known by that name, or the literary character that the book presents as its main "speaker." I am not interested in this chapter in historical reconstructions.

concerning an interaction between Yhwh (as source of revelation) and the speaker. The words "Yhwh caused me to know and I knew" suggest Jeremiah's reflection upon a past experience, while the double use of ידע also lays stress on knowing. That Yhwh is the first word of the speech is emphatic.

In the light of this set, the deictic particle אז, giving a relative time situation, reinforces sense of a narration, while the remainder of the text introduces the other parties to this story, the as yet unnamed "they." Before specifying the identity and actions of this third party, Jeremiah contrasts himself with them, note the emphatic ואני (v. 19). In likening himself to a helpless animal victim in this verse the speaker echoes a common trope of laments. By referring back to the prominent verb of the previous verse, ידע, the flashback effect is highlighted, Yhwh has caused me to know (v. 18) but back then I did not know (v. 19), further situating this text as a narration. There is no quotation formula in the middle of this verse but translators supply one, revealing that the opponents' thoughts and plans are recounted to us by Jeremiah (rather than by the narrator of the book), forming part of this narrative quasi-soliloquy.

In verse 20, however, the almost-soliloquy turns to something else. Yhwh is addressed in the second person, and thus God becomes the addressee or conversation partner in this narrative. As part of this move suddenly we are in a narrative present (rather than past) frame.

In 11:21 things become more complex, the speech is introduced by a messenger formula, and Jeremiah becomes "you" and is thus evidently a character in this unfolding conversation, rather than merely a soliloquist. The opponents are now spoken of in the present, and identified (as the men of Anathoth) and quoted. A second messenger formula (11:22) marks a change of focus in Yhwh's speech, now speaking about these men, rather than to Jeremiah directly. Despite their clear identification, as has often been noted, the contents of their judgment is surprisingly general and vague. (Perhaps a hint that in this narrative they stand as representatives of the whole nation addressed by the book in which the narrative itself stands?)

The direct address to Yhwh at the start of 12:1 marks a new beginning. However, if we read 11:18ff. as a dialogue between Jeremiah and Yhwh concerning the opponents (identified eventually as men of Anathoth) then this direct address to Yhwh seems reasonably to continue that conversation.

The next "confession," in 15:10–21, is also a dialogue with speech by Jeremiah in the first person addressed to Yhwh alternating with speech attributed to Yhwh (by messenger formulae אמר יהוה in 15:11 and לכן כה־אמר יהוה in 15:19). It has a less strongly marked narrative character but dialogue form in itself is not common in Psalms, despite claims that lament and complaint psalms might have received responses in the form of prophetic oracles. Thus the presentation here does continue the narrative thread.

The next (in 17:14–18) is the most straightforward example of the lament form, and can only be considered as part of a narrative sequence if it is considered as part of a coherent collection "the confessions of Jeremiah."

By contrast 18:18–23 begins with the marker ויאמרו (introducing words of someone else). These reported, third person, words provide a frame for the passage that follows where Jeremiah narrates his experience with opponents, and argues with Yhwh. Despite the absence of a marker in 18:19, this direct appeal to God, presented as Jeremiah's speech therefore continues the dialogue about the opponents, with this time those opponents being first given voice. On this occasion however there is no reply from Yhwh.

The final "confession" begins (20:7) with a second person masculine singular verb followed by a proper noun, clearly this serves as a vocative, and thus this passage also presents itself as a conversation. This is of course the standard form of the lament psalm and the quotation of the opponents' speech is also typical of these psalms. There is little question that in terms of form this passage is such a psalm. However, read in the context of the earlier "confessions" the narrative character implicit in these psalms becomes more evident. So how do these "confessions" trace a relationship?

In the first of Jeremiah's confessions (11:18–23) we discovered psalm-like elements encased in a narrative framework which changed the literary and rhetorical functioning of the words. So verses 19–20 with their animal comparisons, enemies who plot, threat of the speaker being removed from the land of the living, and then appeal to God (as just judge to exercise vengeance), echo the language and thought of these psalms. However verse 18 affirming that Yhwh has made the speaker (Jeremiah) aware of what an unspecified group (they) were doing, provided a narrative frame. Verse 21 provides further details, while 22–23 affirm in

Yhwh's name that he will indeed perform this vengeance. This is like the oracle of weal that is presumed to follow the complaint in the psalms.

The effect here is that, rather than merely reporting a lament or complaint, Jeremiah is confessing the God who is his redeemer-kinsman. Thus as well as changing the genre the narrative frame also changes the function and attitude of the piece. Jeremiah is the recipient of (presumably privileged) divine information (11:18), note that his dominant attribute in the book (especially in its Hebrew form) is as "Jeremiah the prophet." Through this retrospective presentation of the opponents' plans he presents himself as a harmless animal led to the butchers, or a tree to be destroyed. This imagery, and indeed all the language in 11:19–20, is thoroughly conventional and so paints Jeremiah as a "righteous sufferer." In 11:21 Yhwh's response makes all this specific, mentioning of Anathoth (known from 1:1 as Jeremiah's home) and reports his opponents' speech using an aggressive double negative: "do not prophesy in the name of Yhwh and you will not die by our hands!"

The second "confession" follows immediately (in 12:1–6) so we read it as part of the same speech. The actual complaint begins in general terms (1b–2) but in verse 3 focuses on the particular case of the speaker, who asserts faithfulness and requests vengeance (cf. 11:20, 21). Those against whom the complaint is made are simply identified as "them" and either assumed to be the guilty and treacherous people of verse 1, or the prophet's opponents in Anathoth from 11:21. The reversal of the tree motif (of 11:19b in 12:2) and application of the sheep motif to Jeremiah's opponents (from 11:19a in 12:3) together suggest strongly that these two speeches should indeed be read as one. Since 12:4 speaks in general terms of the land which is despoiled because of the wickedness of its inhabitants we assume that these local opponents of Jeremiah typify unfaithful Judah and Jerusalem.

Yhwh's answer (12:5ff.) to the prophet's plaintive questions is a sharp challenge. In terms of the envisaged oracle of weal that might have been expected to follow a lament or complaint this comes as a shock, and thus heightens the narrative drama of the passage. At first this response seems to avoid the issue by merely attacking the complainant:

> If you have raced with foot-runners and they have wearied you,
> how will you compete with horses?
> And if in a safe land you fall down,
> how will you fare in the thickets of the Jordan?

The wording here in Hebrew suggests a military and not an athletic contest: רגלי usually implied foot-soldiers, and horses are most often mentioned in military contexts. This attack suggests Yhwh has become frustrated by the complaints and lack of action of his prophet.

The next verse mentions "your brothers" and even those of your home household (בית־אב) thus linking this threatening response to the situation described in 11:21 and more directly to Jeremiah's complaint in 12:4. In doing so, since there the full weight of the military might Yhwh can command was declared against the men of Anathoth, the rhetorical questions (12:5), which seemed a threat to Jeremiah, are revealed as containing an implicit promise. How will you stand? Through my intervention! Also by linking this threat to the men of Anathoth with the blighted land of 12:4 the representative character of these opponents is underscored.

So, now reading this section as a whole, does 11:18—12:6 lament, complain, or confess? The dominant tone is clearly complaint rather than lamentation (though note 12:4 where lament predominates), but the confessional element is strong, Jeremiah both complains to Yhwh and confesses his trust that his God will redeem him. The divine response is interestingly and strangely different in the two parts. In the first it echoes Jeremiah's request and fills out details, while the second challenges Jeremiah and ends on a warning note, revealing that the God whom Jeremiah confesses is not a puppet of his spokesman, but an agent who can act independently of his prophet's wishes!

So, this passage is not a simple lament, complaint, or confession, but rather blends these three modes of speech into a developing "story" that explores theological themes in more complex ways. The section 11:18–23 on its own is coordinated against Jeremiah's opponents in Anathoth, however the more general complaint in 12:1–4 begins to give Job-like flavor to the speech and Jeremiah presents himself as a righteous sufferer. The concluding response from Yhwh comes as a correction to his prophet as well as an implied promise. Having earlier (11:21ff.) promised an appropriate end for Jeremiah's opponents, Yhwh seems to expect Jeremiah to buckle down, get on with the job, and cease whining. As with the divine speech from the whirlwind in Job 40:6ff. this is an unsympathetic response, yet if one follows the logic of the book of Jeremiah this apparent harshness of response is necessary. For 12:7ff. provide the reasons for the response, if the narrative thread is not restricted to modern scholarship's confession/lament. Admittedly, the tradition recognized a break between

12:6 and 7, however, in the language itself there is no marker, e.g., no introductory formula or other indication that something new begins, and the speaker is presumed to be the same (Yhwh).

The next "confession," in 15:10–21, is also complex. It starts straightforwardly, in verse 10, a very brief lament that the speaker has been born and an implied complaint about the monotone nature of the message he is required to deliver, with an assertion of his righteousness in fiscal matters added this reads like a (brief) typical lament psalm. However, Yhwh's response in verses 11–14, although it perhaps at first addresses Jeremiah's complaint,[15] segues into a warning to the land and its people. As in the previous text here also the prophet and the fate of the nation are linked. Together these cues suggest that these "confessions" are not meant to be read as merely personal dialogues with God, but as part of the larger theological and political picture of the book.

After divine response, the speaker then pleads to be spared this general disaster, claiming to be a faithful messenger (vv. 15–16) and to have endured trouble and pain as a result (vv. 17–18a), indeed complaining by contrast that Yhwh has been unfaithful to him! Jeremiah then calls Yhwh a liar and compares him to "waters that fail," calling to mind the "cracked cisterns" that Judah had resorted to in 2:13. The beginning of divine reply to this diatribe might sound like a call to Judah:

> If you return, I will return you to my presence and you will stand,
> if you distinguish what is precious from what is worthless.

However, the end of the short speech contrasting "you" and "them," makes clear that it applies to Jeremiah.

Once again note that the destinies of prophet and nation intertwined. The tone of Yhwh's reply to Jeremiah's protestations seems to imply that his earlier complaints were a dereliction of duty (v. 19).

Yet verses 20–21 echo the promises of Jeremiah's call and add a promise that if he does "return" then Yhwh will strengthen him and even deliver him from his enemies (v. 20). In this case the end of the passage is clearly marked by the opening of the next which is contrastive "The word of Yhwh came to me again . . ." (16:1).

Again in terms of our three modes of speech the overall impact of the dialogue is confession, yet the rhetorical stance of the speaker is complaining! Again the interplay of speakers and attitudes is complex, and the rhetorical effect may not simply reproduce the attitude attributed by

15 However, it is interesting that NET needed to address these words to "Jerusalem."

the writer to the implied speaker of the prophet's part ("Jeremiah"). For Yhwh's words must carry more weight than those of his prophet!

The "confession" in 17:14–18 illustrates how these texts are linked to each other and also into the book as a whole. The preceding verse, ending an oracle, makes reference to Yhwh as "fountain of living waters," echoing Jeremiah's complaint of 15:18. As the passage returns to the prophet's opponents (vv. 14–15a), linking his reliability with Yhwh's (v. 15b), Jeremiah's speech here compares and contrasts the three characters "them," "me," and "you." "They" are implying that the disasters Jeremiah ("I") threatened have not happened; but Jeremiah has not requested these, he has merely spoken "rightly," indeed saying what "you" (Yhwh) required (vv. 15–16). This emphasis on speaking what was known and approved by Yhwh suggests that this speech replies to 15:19, the divine appeal in the previous "confession" for Jeremiah to return to uttering what is precious and serving as Yhwh's mouth. Verse 17 then confesses Yhwh as savior, and the next verse requests disaster for his opponents (v. 18).

The tone of confession at the start, the presence of opponents, and the implications of Jeremiah's final request suggest the mood of complaint, with no real lamenting anywhere in this text. Unlike the previous passages this is a monologue (with the partial exception of the quoted words of the opponents in verse 15).

The fourth "confession" in 18:18–23 then echoes this beginning by quoting the opponents (v. 18) and the prophet's reply to them (v. 19ff.), which follows a typical complaint/lament psalm pattern:

- verses 19–20 *appeal* to God (to listen and to notice the injustice of the opponents' actions)
- verses 21–22 request *vengeance*
- verse 23 claims this punishment is just and appeals to God not to turn a blind eye to their crimes.

This is a straightforward complaint. Thus, this is the first of these poetic passages to contain simply complaint, though still perhaps in a narrative frame. Notice the opening word in verse 18 (a *vayyiqtol* introducing quoted speech "and they said")[16] has a narrative feel, also the 3mp of this verb does not obviously refer to the preceding text, so perhaps draws the

16. This form occurs frequently in narrative books and sections, but rarely elsewhere, e.g., it occurs fourteen times in Exodus 1–19, but only eight in the rest of the book, even though the legal material there is framed by narrative.

hearer's mind to previous quotations of the prophet's opponents. Previous occurrences of the quotation formula וַיֹּאמְרוּ in Jeremiah may suggest this: there is perhaps an ironic contrast between "their" planning against Jeremiah in verse 18 and Yhwh's previously announced planning against them (18:8, 11). Other verbal links to earlier "confessions" include the only use of the verb חשב (plan) earlier in the book was at 11:19 in the first "confession." This passage develops the "storyline," for while in previous confessions Jeremiah claimed that he had not desired the woeful day (17:16) now he expresses this desire clearly (18:21–23). This monologue marks a further step in Jeremiah hardening his heart against Judah.

The final text, in 20:7–13, begins with a complaint, addressed to Yhwh, not about the actions of other humans, or about Yhwh's inaction, but rather that God has "seduced" his own prophet (vv. 7–8). This develops into a sort of soliloquy exploring Jeremiah's reaction to these things (v. 9) and reporting the threats from his enemies (v. 10). The final three verses sandwich a plea (v. 12) between two segments in which Jeremiah confesses Yhwh as his savior.

So, again while there is no explicit narrative frame, and perhaps by its form the piece fits the genre of lament psalm best, this very form with its expressed addressee (Yhwh) and quotation (v. 10) from the opponents, together with the hypothetical character of verse 9, make it a quasi-soliloquy with the feel of listening to the prophet talk to himself (and his God). This nudges the reader to exercise a narrative imagination.

Jeremiah's complaint that Yhwh has seduced him is doubly ironic as he goes on to quote his opponents' hope that he might be seduced (cf. 20:7, 10), but the biggest change is more subtle, at the start Jeremiah addresses Yhwh in the second person even while accusing God of seduction, but by verse 9 he uses third person, speaking about (rather than to) his God. This adds emotional power and poignancy to his confession in verse 11 and the subsequent return to second person address in 20:12.

Traditional readings close the "lament" with the third person hymn in 20:13, but the text continues in verse 14 with a return to the motif of wishing never to have been born. Since we saw this motif in 15:10 it might well make an appropriate (if discouraging) ending here.

So in the light of this, how might the composer(s) of the book have thought of these texts? If they were "complaints" then they would function differently than if they were thought of as "laments," or if they were used as "confessions." Was Jeremiah (the eponymous character in the book, not the putative sixth/fifth century person) lamenting something, complaining to God, or confessing Yhwh to his audience in these passages?

In the light of the presentation above there is evidence in parts of these texts of each of these activities. Yet overall none of the passages really seems to fit neatly into just one of the three attitudes. Rather, each passage separately and even more all of them cumulatively seem to work best (and in most cases when each is read in their context in the book also) when read as a narrative text which portrays characters in tension. While the prophet, Jeremiah, is the primary speaker, and clearly narrates his opponents, it is less clear that "he" is narrating Yhwh. Indeed one senses that the responses of Yhwh are a challenge, and even sometimes unwelcome to "Jeremiah." In support of this I note particularly the seduction language in the last text. Thus the overall effect of the passages is not at all merely to lament or complain, but neither do they univocally confess, rather they dynamically explore the interrelationship of the three characters they present.

In view of the ways in which most of these passages are tied to their surrounding texts it seems inappropriate in fact to deal with them (as I have here) as almost isolated texts, rather perhaps they form part of a book which works in this way. Jeremiah (the book) is, in that case, closer in its poetics to Job than to a collection of "sayings." As with more obviously narrative texts the meaning is not on the surface, but in the interactions of the characters and in our responses to their "story."

These texts focus their lamenting and/or complaining primarily on the prophet and on opponents (especially the "men of Anathoth") yet even with this focus, which has been powerfully noticed by the psychologizing readers, they continually link this private personal world to the larger story of Judah and Jerusalem before their destruction by the Neo-Babylonian empire. Thus, in this larger sense, the narrated drama of Jeremiah, his opponents and his God serves to explore theological responses to this disaster, and thus serves similar functions to the lament psalms.

3

The Unique Contribution of Lamentations 4 in the Book of Lamentations

Metaphor and the Transition from Individual to Communal

Miriam J. Bier

INTRODUCTION

Lamentations 4 depicts a desolate scene, confronting its readers with a lonesome landscape that is pockmarked with pain. The chapter impresses upon readers a picture of unthinkable reversal: the impossible has occurred and everything is the opposite of what it ought to be. Gold has lost its lustre, sacred jewels are worthless, and precious gold is broken like clay pots (4:1–2). בת־עמי is cruel, suckling infants thirst, and those used to rich delicacies starve for lack of food (4:3–5). The formerly finely-clad scurry around in the muck, radiant leaders have lost their glamour, and in monstrous obscenity, women are now nourished by those they were meant to nurture (4:7–10). Enemies have entered the gates of the city, prophets are blind, and priests are defiled with an excess of blood

(4:12–16). Even the king himself has become prey instead of protector (4:19–20). All these images are impossibilities, conjuring a world that simply cannot be. Yet despite the gravity of its situation, the perfection of its poetry, and the vividness of its content, Lam 4 is not deemed as interesting or significant as the rest of Lamentations—or so the scholarly engagement (or lack thereof) would tend to suggest.

Indeed, Lamentations as a whole has, until fairly recently, been much overlooked in scholarly comment.[1] When it did receive attention, this tended to center around Lam 3, and that chapter's male figure, the גבר. The גבר's posture of repentance and trust was considered the "high point" of hope in the book, controlling interpretation of the whole. The book's message was construed concomitantly, as a call to the penitence required to reverse the suffering that the people were experiencing as just punishment for sin.[2] More recent interpreters have rightly challenged these overwhelmingly theodic readings of Lamentations by turning attention away from chapter 3 and toward chapters 1 and 2. That is, instead of reading the גבר as the pre-eminent model of penitence and patience, they turn to Daughter Zion for an alternative theological model; a model

1. There has been a recent flurry of interest in Lamentations, sparked by a series of significant works published in the late 1990s and early twenty-first century. See especially Linafelt, *Surviving Lamentations* (1997); Berlin, *Lamentations* (2002); Dobbs-Allsopp, *Lamentations* (2002); O'Connor, *Lamentations and the Tears of the World* (2002); Boase, *Fulfilment of Doom?* (2006); and Mandolfo, *Daughter Zion* (2007). Brueggemann's seminal article lamenting the loss of lament in the church must be credited with creating some of the discussion (Brueggemann, "The Costly Loss of Lament," 57–71), as must Westermann's landmark commentary (Westermann, *Die Klagelieder*). Dialogic and other literary readings of Lamentations especially have captured the imagination of a new generation of Lamentations scholars. See, for example, the following theses: Miller, "Poetry and Personae" (1996); Boase, "Dialogic Interaction" (2003); Thomas, "Poetry and Theology" (2007); and Conway, "Speaking Voices" (2008). This article is itself a revision on an early version of chapter 6 of my 2012 PhD thesis (Bier, "Perhaps there is Hope").

2. For the classic statement on the "everyman" expressing the "high point" of hope in Lamentations see Hillers, *Lamentations*, 122. For theodic readings centered upon chapter 3 see Krašovec, "The Source of Hope in the Book of Lamentations," 223–33; and more recently, House, *Lamentations*; Parry, *Lamentations*; and Longman, *Jeremiah, Lamentations*. Dobbs-Allsopp, however, cautions against valorizing Lam 3 as the theodic "center" of Lamentations, noting that "[w]hat is potentially disturbing about the privileging of this theodic construal of hope is that when left unqualified it risks transfiguring the pain and suffering so prominently displayed in Lamentations that can endow them with a false and hurtful sense of meaning and purpose. In an age after Auschwitz such a risk, even if unwitting, cannot be tolerated" (Dobbs-Allsopp, *Lamentations*, 48).

of protest and resistance, reading antitheodically.[3] Chapter 5, while not as well represented in the current literature as chapters 1, 2, and 3, is distinctive for being the most properly communal-lament-like form in the book. It draws comment for its abandonment of the acrostic form and its difficult ending, spawning various attempts to resolve or explain away the difficulties.[4] But Lam 4 has not been the subject of much interest in its own right.[5] In an ATLA search, only two articles dealing with the text of Lam 4 as a whole come to light: Mitchell's "Lamentations 4 as Historiography," and Gous' "Mind Over Matter: Lamentations 4 in the Light of the Cognitive Sciences."[6] Granted, there are studies that detail aspects of translation in Lam 4, but these studies are usually undertaken in reference to rare or difficult words that also appear elsewhere in the Hebrew text, rather than being studies of Lam 4 *per se*.[7] There are also,

3. See especially Linafelt, *Surviving Lamentations*. Linafelt identifies three biases in interpretation that have led to a focus on chapter 3: a masculine bias toward the male character; a Christian bias toward this male character as representative of the suffering Christ; and a bias toward reconciliation rather than protest (Linafelt, *Surviving Lamentations*, 5). Mandolfo also turns her focus toward Zion, arguing that Zion in Lam 1 and 2 speaks as a corrective protest to the prophetic portrayals of her found in other biblical books (Mandolfo, *Daughter Zion*). Note, though, Parry's caution that this shift in attention, while helpful in "redressing the balance," has tended toward an "unhelpful underplaying of chapter 3" (Parry, *Lamentations*, 92; cf. Thomas, "Poetry and Theology," 22). While Linafelt is right to correct the bias toward Lam 3, I suggest that both the man in Lam 3 and Zion in Lam 1 and 2; and their respective theological stances; should be considered together, polyphonically. See further Boase, *The Fulfilment of Doom?* 6–23; O'Connor, *Lamentations and the Tears of the World*, 14; Dobbs-Allsopp, *Lamentations*, 27–33; and Bier, "Perhaps There is Hope," 351–88.

4. See, e.g., Bergler, "Threni V," 304–20; and Guillaume, "Lamentations 5: The Seventh Acrostic," 2–6, for some creative proposals for imposing an acrostic upon Lam 5. Gordis surveys explanations for the ending of ch. 5 (Gordis, "The Conclusion of the Book of Lamentations," 289–93); while Linafelt provides a more recent reassessment of the question (Linafelt "The Refusal of a Conclusion in the Book of Lamentations," 340–43).

5. And has at times been passed over completely, e.g., Childs says nothing of chapter 4, aside from mentioning in passing that Gunkel assigned it, along with chapters 1 and 2, to the political dirge form (Childs, *OT as Scripture*, 591). Gottwald's "reconsideration" of Lamentations moves directly from the "special case" of chapter 3 to chapter 5, missing chapter 4 out entirely (Gottwald, "Lamentations Reconsidered," 167).

6. Mitchell, "Lamentations 4 as Historiography," 78–90; Gous, "Mind Over Matter," 6--87. These studies read Lam 4 in light of particular methodological concerns, viz., historiographical and cognitive scientific approaches respectively.

7. E.g., Salters, "Text and Exegesis in Lamentations 4:21–22," 327–37; Shaffer, "Mesopotamian Background of Lamentations 4:9–12," 246–50; Emerton, "The

of course, individual chapters dedicated to Lam 4 in those commentaries and monographs that treat the book as a whole. Following the usual lengthy discussions of chapter 3, however, these chapters can read as somewhat deflated, with commentators tackling chapter 4 almost as an afterthought, a less interesting aspect of the text to which necessary lip service must be paid on the way to the concluding chapter 5.[8]

But the fourth chapter of Lamentations is a stunning, if stark, piece of poetry that deserves some sustained attention in its own right. Further, it has a crucial role to play in the book as a whole, carrying the momentum from the first three chapters through to the communal lament of chapter 5. This paper thus brings Lam 4 into the limelight for a moment. It argues that Lam 4 has a unique position in the book of Lamentations as a transitional movement between the individual (yet representative) speaking voices of the Lamenter, Zion, and the גבר in Lam 1, 2, and 3; and the explicitly communal speaking voice of Lam 5. I show this first by demonstrating how the edges of literal and metaphorical; and individual and communal; are blurred in Lam 4. Second, I highlight the move to plural pronouns that occurs as the chapter progresses (4:17–20), prefiguring the first person plural prayer in chapter 5. Third, I suggest that the term בת־עמי ("Daughter-my-People") contributes to the shift from singular to plural, by making the female metaphor explicitly communal in a more expansive manner than the individual (yet still representative) term "Daughter Zion" has yet suggested. First, though, a brief overview of reasons why Lam 4 may not have received the attention it deserves.

WHY LAMENTATIONS 4 IS OVERLOOKED: CONTRIBUTING FACTORS

Commentators generally point to two features that contribute to the notion of "diminishment" in Lam 4, which, ironically, mirror commentators' own diminishment of interest in the chapter. First, commentators observe a diminishment in *formal* and *poetic* features. After the intensified threefold acrostic of chapter 3, the acrostic in Lam 4 returns to the more familiar pattern of chapters 1 and 2, only with two lines per stanza

Meaning of *'Abne Qodesh* in Lamentations 4:1," 232–36; Stokes, "I, YHWH have not changed," 264–76; Strong, "Verb forms of 'MM," 246–52; Tiemeyer, "The Question of Indirect Touch," 64–74; Cohen, "Lamentations 4:9," 190–91.

8. One clear exception is Dobbs-Allsopp, who includes a fine discussion of chapter 4 and its "pivotal role" in Lamentations (Dobbs-Allsopp, *Lamentations*, 129–39).

rather than three.[9] This is understood as a diminishment of the intensity of chapter 3, and a diminishment from the full three line stanzas of the previous chapters.

But aside from the shorter length and less intense acrostic, there are other formal and poetic features peculiar to Lam 4 that deserve noting and further comment. First, unlike the other four chapters (1:9c, 10c, 11c, 20–22; 2:20–22; 3:23, 42–45, 55–66; 5:1, 19–22), Lam 4 lacks any direct address to YHWH. Second, although only a brief cameo when compared with her prominent role in chapters 1 and 2, "Daughter Zion" reappears after her absence from chapter 3 (4:22). Third, the entirely new (in the book of Lamentations) metaphorical figure "Daughter Edom" appears, as a foil to "Daughter Zion." This new Daughter is now about to experience the same ignominies Zion herself has had to bear.[10] These are all points of interest unique to Lam 4.

A second factor contributing to a diminishment of interest in Lam 4 is a perceived diminishment of emotionality in the chapter.[11] Lamentations 4 is reckoned to be more *emotionally* sparse, and less personal, than chapters 1–3. The Lamenter[12] of chapter 4 is supposed to be more distant and uninvolved in the immediate situation of destruction, when compared with the intense inner emotion of the גבר of chapter 3. And this is true to a certain extent.[13] The majority of the first part of chapter

9. Dobbs-Allsopp speaks of the "formal tensions" of Lam 3 being "consciously relaxed" by chapter 4 (Dobbs-Allsopp, *Lamentations*, 129; cf. Hillers, *Lamentations*, 29).

10. Interestingly, the personification of Daughter Edom and the judgement pronounced upon her has not drawn anything like the same kind of protest as has the figure of Daughter Zion. It seems that even as commentators protest the rhetoric of the text in vilifying Zion with imagery associated with female-abuse, they are happy to accept that female nakedness and shame is appropriate when it pertains to an enemy's punishment.

11. Dobbs-Allsopp states that this "formal diminishment is mirrored by a pronounced fall off in emotional intensity" (Dobbs-Allsopp, *Lamentations*, 129).

12. I use the term "Lamenter" to refer to the opening third person speaker in chapters 1, 2, and 4, who is one of the characters constructed by the poet, along with Zion and the גבר.

13. Lanahan, "The Speaking Voice," 48; Dobbs-Allsopp, *Lamentations*, 129; Bergant, *Lamentations*, 120; O'Connor, "Lamentations," 1059. The Lamenter in Lam 1 is often similarly slated as a distant observer speaking in an "observational and uninvolved" tone (O'Connor, *Lamentations and the Tears of the World*, 59; "more matter-of-fact," Hillers, *Lamentations*, 145). While the Lamenter is clearly not distant or unemotional, on the flipside I would not describe him as effusively as Re'emi, who deems him full of love and compassion toward Jerusalem, with a "love he can only have got from God" (Re'emi, *Lamentations*, 119). Suggesting a love from God makes

4 (4:1–16) lacks any first person pronouns, apart from the pronominal suffix "my" in the epithet "Daughter-my-People" (4:3, 6, 10, בת־עמי). The Lamenter instead describes the situation in the third person, from the point of view of someone observing from the outside, suggesting to commentators that there is no self involvement on his part.[14] And yet, in 4:17–20 the Lamenter is evidently closely aligned with the city, sympathetic to her and counting himself as part of her people. The chapter, then, does not necessarily lack an emotional connection. Berlin, while noting a certain sense of detachment in Lam 4, is right to assert that chapter 4 is no less emotional than what has come before. That is, "[t]he more objective or distant stance of this chapter yields a poem no less moving, and indeed, one that is more graphic, than the earlier chapters. It is simply employing a different literary vehicle."[15] Some of the most abhorrent images in all of Lamentations appear in chapter four. Far from being emotionally removed, then, Lam 4 effectively expresses some of the horror the Lamenter has seen within a tight acrostic structure and sparse—but by no means emotionally disconnected—descriptions that skim tightly over the surface of barely contained emotion.[16] Lamentations 4 can be read, then, not as a diminishment of emotion, but as a momentary reprieve from the intense internal anguish of chapter 3, by focusing on external portraits of suffering. The external situations depicted, however, are no less excruciating than what comes before. After all, what greater horror than mothers consuming their own children (4:10)?

A further assertion sometimes made of Lam 4 is that it abandons the metaphorical, instead employing more matter of fact and literal language, and thus providing less grist for the scholarly mill.[17] But this is patently

---

little sense in a chapter which presents God as anything *but* loving and compassionate, as in Lam 4.

14. E.g., Bracke describes chapter 4 as taking a "rational and objective approach," while chapter 5, by contrast, is "an outpouring of pain and hurt" (Bracke, *Lamentations*, 235).

15. Berlin, *Lamentations*, 103, n. 1.

16. Cf. Gous, who argues that Lam 4 provides "a necessary balance between stability and adaptability by describing the chaos they experienced in a structured manner" (Gous, "Mind over Matter," 70–71). This emotion will soon burst forth like a flood in chapter 5, when the acrostic is abandoned entirely and the alphabetic takes up the urgency of staccato, single line stanzas.

17. According to at least two commentators, chapter 4 abandons the use of metaphor and personification for Jerusalem or Judah entirely (Tigay, "Lamentations," 448; Bracke, *Lamentations*, 226). One wonders if these commentators have noticed 4:21,

not the case. The metaphorical epithet Daughter-my-People (בת־עמי) recurs three times in 4:1–10 (cf. Lam 2:11; 3:48). Direct address to Daughter Zion returns in verses 21–22, along with address to Daughter Edom. Both of these terms paint metaphorical portraits of cities and nations as women. Further, Lam 4 is arguably rich with many more metaphors for the ruined city and her people. Admittedly, the boundaries between literal and metaphorical are blurred. But it is this blurring that so effectively contributes to the transition between individual and communal that occurs in Lam 4. I now turn my attention to some of these metaphors, assessing their potential as ciphers for the people of Jerusalem. While much of Lam 4 may be read metaphorically, it is precisely the very ambiguity of that metaphorical character that contributes to the blurring of boundaries between the individual and the communal in the poem as a whole. To demonstrate this blurring I highlight the literal and metaphorical aspects of three particular clusters of possible metaphors: the gold and sacred stones with which the chapter opens (4:1–2); the female בת־עמי alongside portraits of the women of the city (4:3, 6, 10); and the prophets, priests, and elders (4:13–16).

METAPHORS THAT BLUR THE BOUNDARIES OF INDIVIDUAL AND COMMUNAL

Lamentations 4:1–2: Tarnished Gold and Sacred Stones

The first image that encompasses both literal and metaphorical aspects, signifying both a distinct portion of the population and the people as a whole, is the image of blackened gold and scattered stones in Lam 4:1. Lamentations 4 opens with the exclamation: "O how the gold is tarnished!" Given that gold does not in fact tarnish, scholars seeking a literal reading surmise that perhaps this "gold" is darkened by dirt, from lying around in the dust of the streets (cf. Zech 9:3).[18] But this seeks an unnecessarily literal explanation for what is, after all, poetic language. I prefer to read with Dobbs-Allsopp, who maintains that the impossibility of gold tarnishing is "precisely to the point . . . the occurrence of the impossible

in which the metaphorical Daughter Zion is explicitly addressed, alongside Daughter Edom.

18. Berlin, *Lamentations*, 104; Ryken, *Jeremiah and Lamentations*, 759; Provan, *Lamentations*, 111.

pointedly underscores the severity of the situation."[19] The tarnishing of the untarnishable might thus be read as the first in a chapter full of impossibilities. There is no need to seek a rational explanation for tarnished gold, for in this starved and faded world nothing is rational at all. This would, I suspect, be sufficient explanation for the phrase "tarnished gold" were it not for verse 2 immediately following, in which the metaphorical character of this gold becomes apparent. In the meantime, though, alongside the tarnished gold, there is also a reference to "holy stones," another physical entity that has both literal and metaphorical aspects. Most scholars follow Emerton's philological demonstration that אבני־קדש should be understood as "precious stones," that is, as jewels or gemstones.[20] There is disagreement, however, as to whether these אבני־קדש should be understood as *literal* gemstones, perhaps stored in the temple so as to have gained the description "sacred"; or metaphorically, as foundation stones of the temple;[21] or, also metaphorically, the rubble of the entire sacred *city*, not just the temple.[22] The "precious stones" might thus refer to actual gemstones, actual stones from the ruined temple likened to gemstones because of the temple's holy status, or actual stones from the ruined city likened to gemstones because of the city's sacred status.

But a further metaphorical significance is invested in these sacred stones when it is observed that they are poured out of "at the head of every street" (בראש כל־חוצות). This phrase appears in only three other verses in the Hebrew Bible, all of which refer to children fainting or dying "at the head of every street" (Isa 51:20; Nah 3:10; Lam 2:19).[23] This is an indication that the "precious stones" being "poured out" at "the head of every street" are more than simply gemstones, temple stones, or rubble of the ruined city. They are the city's "children," that is, her inhabitants.

This metaphorical value of both terms, "gold" and "precious stone," is confirmed in verse 2 when the "precious children of Zion" (lit. "sons") are explicitly likened to gold.[24] Thus, while it may well be that literal gold and gemstones have lost their value to the extent that they are left

19. Dobbs-Allsopp, *Lamentations*, 130; see also Gordis, *Lamentations*, 188; Gous, "Mind over Matter," 81; Mitchell, "Reflecting on Catastrophe," 79; O'Connor, *Lamentations and the Tears of the World*, 61.

20. Emerton, "The Meaning of *'abnê qōdeš*," 233; cf. Hillers, *Lamentations*, 138.

21. Dobbs-Allsopp, *Lamentations*, 130.

22. Mackay, *Lamentations*, 181; Mitchell, "Lamentations 4 as Historiography," 79.

23. Cf. Mitchell, "Lamentations 4 as Historiography," 80.

24. Cf. Gottlieb, *Lamentations*, 61.

scattered in the city streets, it is the "children of Zion" who are the real concern (cf. 1:5c, 16c; 2:11–12, 19–22).[25] The tarnished gold and sacred stones in verses 1–2 can be read metaphorically, as well as literally. Further, the phrase "children" or "sons" of Zion can itself be understood metaphorically, as indicative of the inhabitants of the city Jerusalem, contingent on the metaphor of the city-woman Zion as mother.[26] Metaphor piles on metaphor so that the metaphorical "gold" and "precious stones" refer to the children. The image of the children, in turn, calls to mind the picture of Mother Zion, whose children are *all* the inhabitants of the city Jerusalem. All of these aspects, literal and metaphorical, may be in view. Gold and precious stones are worthless and scattered and fallen; precious children and a holy people lie desolate and dying at every turn in the sacred city.

Lamentations 4:3, 6, 10: Daughter-my-People

A second image that connotes a particular portion of the population, while also extending to the people as a whole, is the portrait of the city as a woman. Lamentations employs a cluster of terms for the female personification of the city, including Jerusalem (1:7, 8, 17; 4:12) Daughter Jerusalem (2:10, 13, 15); Zion (1:4; 1:17; 2:6; 4:2, 11; 5:11, 18), Daughter Zion (1:6; 2:1, 4, 8, 10, 18; 4:22), Virgin Daughter Zion (2:13), Judah (1:3; 5:11), Daughter Judah (2:2, 5), and Virgin Daughter Judah (1:15). The practice of referring to cities as "daughter" is widespread in the Hebrew Bible. There has been disagreement over whether the construction בת-(city name) should be understood as the appositional genitive "Daughter (who is) Zion,"[27] or the "Daughter (of) Zion." There is general agreement, however, that the term refers to a female personification of the city, as a woman in some particular relationship to the patron deity—in this case, Yhwh.[28]

25. Cf. Meek, "Lamentations," 30.

26. Mitchell, "Lamentations 4 as Historiography," 80; cf. Provan, *Lamentations*, 111. Mother Zion is also Daughter Zion. See further Maier, *Daughter Zion, Mother Zion*, for the way in which Daughter Zion emerges as Mother Zion across the Old Testament corpus.

27. Stinespring, "No Daughter of Zion," 133; Fitzgerald, "*BTWLT* and *BT*," 171; Frymer-Kensky, *In the Wake of the Goddesses*, 169; *NIDOTTE*, 780.

28. Galambush, *Yahweh's Wife*, 25. See further O'Brien, *Challenging Prophetic Metaphor*, 131.

The construct "Daughter (of) my People" (בת־עמי), while used once each in chapters 2 and 3 (2:11; 3:48) is especially concentrated in 4:1–10, occurring three times within the first ten verses (4:3, 6, 10). Should this be understood, like Daughter Zion and the like, as simply another term for the metaphorical representation of the people as a whole? In which case, why the change from the more usual (Daughter) Zion or (Daughter) Judah in chapters 1 and 2? Gottlieb argues on the basis of the LXX (θυγατέρες λαοῦ μου, presupposing Hebrew בנות־עמי, that is, "daughters of my people") that, at least in 4:3, only the city's women are in view in 4:3.[29] On this understanding, only the female portion of the population are highlighted; rather than the metaphorical city as woman (but note the singular θυγατρὸς λαοῦ μου in 4:6, 10).

Further, in 4:10, there is a possible chiasm:

> The hands of compassionate women
> have boiled their children:
> they have become food for them
> in the destruction of Daughter-my-People.

Read chiastically, there are the parallelisms: compassionate women//בת־עמי and children//food. Should the term בת־עמי thus be understood as בנות־עמי, *daughters* of my people, as in only the female inhabitants of the city? Once again, there is a possible blurring of the literal and the metaphorical. Perhaps the title בת־עמי does connote the female portion of the population, while still retaining the metaphorical character of a female depiction of the city to represent the people as a whole. In the literal aspect, mothers in the ruins struggle to feed their children, and perhaps even feed *upon* their children.[30] In the metaphorical aspect, בת־עמי the city-woman is unable to sustain her children, the inhabitants of the city.[31] A particular portion of the population—the women—is highlighted, while the figure of the woman representative of the city is conflated in the portrait, thus drawing in the entire population and once again blurring the boundaries between a distinct group and the whole people of which this group is a part.

29. Gottlieb, *Lamentations*, 61; cf. Provan, *Lamentations*, 112; Westermann, *Lamentations*, 200.

30. It is indeterminate whether this is simply a poetic representation fulfilling the curses of Deuteronomy; or a depiction of actual historical events. Either way, it is grotesque.

31. Cf. Dobbs-Allsopp, *Lamentations*, 131.

Lamentations 4:13–16: Prophets, Priests, and Elders

A third metaphorical portrait appears in 4:13–16. This pericope opens with reference to the sins of prophets and priests (4:13) and closes with the dishonor of priests and elders (4:16). The intervening third person plural referents, however, remain uncertain. "They" who wander the streets defiled with blood (v. 14a) could refer, at least initially, directly back to the prophets and priests who have shed the blood of the righteous in verse 13.[32] In this case, then, it is, ironically, the seers who are blind and the purifiers who are defiled.[33] But by verse 15a the identities of "they," who shouted at "them," becomes less and less certain. Who is doing the shouting, and at whom? Are the ones who are defiled (the prophets and the priests?) shouting to others to keep away, in a leper-like warning not to come near; or are the people shouting at the prophets and priests?[34] Or are *all* the people now regarded as blind and defiled, with the *nations* yelling at them all? The indeterminacy of the Hebrew third person plural pronominal suffixes allows many possibilities remain open.

The sin for which the prophets and priests are indicted—shedding the blood of the righteous—might be a metaphor for the religious idolatry of the people as a whole. It is unclear whether the accusation means the prophets and priests themselves have *actively* shed the blood of innocents themselves, or whether their standing idly by indicts them indirectly for the unrighteous acts of the people (cf. 2:14).[35]

Adele Berlin puts this sin in the context of the purity paradigm, where shedding blood is a symbol for idolatry rather than a literal act.[36]

32. On the basis of the reading of verse 13 as a conditional clause linked to verse 14 (so Berlin, *Lamentations*, 111; O'Connor, *Lamentations and the Tears of the World*, 65). Hillers, however, argues that the entire nation are the referent of "they," such that the people as a whole wander blindly, on account of the prophets' sins; and that the people as a whole are defiled on account of the priests' sins (Hillers, *Lamentations*, 142, 149).

33. Cf. Gordis, *Lamentations*, 192.

34. So Berlin, *Lamentations*, 111; Bergant, *Lamentations*, 117; Mackay, *Lamentations*, 194.

35. That is, they, "by their acts of commission or of omission, were responsible for the murder of innocent men" (Gordis, *Lamentations*, 146; cf. Provan, *Lamentations*, 117). Hillers suggests that while "the writer's idea is probably not that the priests and prophets themselves laid violent hands on the righteous, he does assert that they were ultimately responsible for it by their whitewashing of injustice" (Hillers, *Lamentations*, 149; cf. Bracke, *Lamentations*, 232; Mackay, *Lamentations*, 19; Westermann, *Lamentations*, 203; Re'emi, "Lamentations," 123).

36. Cf. Ezek 22:1–5, which reads like a both/and, rather than one cipher of the

Thus, "[t]he priests and prophets have become morally impure by shedding blood (a symbol of idolatry), a sin that defiles the land and leads to exile."[37] At the same time though, it is likely that "given the reference to priests and prophets in the previous verse, that it is crimes specifically connected with religious observance which the author has in mind here."[38] There is thus a metaphorical representation of the people as a whole within the trope of blind prophets and defiled priests, particularly if the sin for which they are indicted is idolatry. The indictees may be *both* the prophets and priests whose sins have been the city's downfall; *and* the people as a whole.[39] Just as the female image was used to indicate the failings of the entire community, now the specific failings of the priests and prophets are brought to attention, while they too are representative of the community. Further, by highlighting this cohort, the poem specifically draws out the religious aspects of the city's downfall.

There are at least three images, then, that speak of situations that could refer literally to the scene being played out in the ruins of Jerusalem, while at the same time representing particular aspects of the city's destruction metaphorically. Each image brings to mind literal aspects of the city's fall, while at the same time extending and lending their characteristics to the city and its people as a whole. In the aftermath of disaster, sacred stones and tarnished gold are scattered in the streets. Mothers are unable to nurture their children. Priests are defiled and prophets do not see. But when holy stones and priceless gold are declared worthless, a reversal in the status of God's holy people, the "children of Zion" is also latent in the metaphor. When בת־עמי is said to be cruel and unable to feed her children, so too the entire (remaining) population's desperation in the face of starvation is portrayed. When accusations are made against impure priests and blind prophets, a nation whose hands are filled with blood and that has lost sight of Yhwh is also indicted.

Other images in Lam 4 may be similarly synechdochic, with particular sectors of the population depicted to highlight both the particular plight of that group, and in doing so, representing some characteristic of

other; and Ps 106:37–40, in which there is a clear link to shedding of blood of sons and daughters sacrificed to idols; connecting the concern for children, shedding innocent blood, and idolatry (cf. Berlin, *Lamentations*, 104, 110).

37. Berlin, *Lamentations*, 104.

38. Provan, *Lamentations*, 118.

39. Cf. Berlin, *Lamentations*, 104; Provan, *Lamentations*, 118.

the whole.[40] Depictions of the rubbish-picking upper class, the wizened princes, sons, daughter, infants, and so on all demonstrate the extent to which the disaster has encompassed the whole of society. In turn, in each vignette all the people may be represented and, at times, implicated.

FURTHER FACTORS CONTRIBUTING TO THE BLURRING OF INDIVIDUAL AND COMMUNAL

The Grammatical Shift

In addition to the images blurring the bounds between individuals, or individual cohorts of people, and the communal, there is a grammatical change that contributes to the movement from individual to communal. In Lam 4:1–16 the Lamenter speaks primarily in the third person, but in verses 17–20 he takes up the first person plural in 4:17–20, explicitly grouping all together in a communal "we." The Lamenter relays the doomed hopes of the people for a helper from among the nations, and in the king who was caught. Many commentators see this as a switch from a dispassionate reporting style to a more involved first person identification.[41] But as noted above, the Lamenter is no distant observer. Rather, he is closely affiliated with this city, land, and people from the outset of the poem. There is, however, a *closer* identification with the community when he takes up the first person plural form.

The Lamenter gathers together the entire community, from the least (the infants) to the greatest (the king), identifying with them in his communal expression.[42] The community presence is now made explicit. This transition to collective voice extends the scope of Lamentations from individual (yet still representative) expressions of pain, to self conscious voicing by the entire community.[43]

40. Cf. Bergant, *Lamentations*, 112; Dobbs-Allsopp, *Lamentations*, 131; Mitchell, "Lamentations 4 as Historiography," 83.

41. Eg. Bergant, *Lamentations*, 120.

42. Cf. Hillers, *Lamentations*, 150.

43. Cf. Dobbs-Allsopp, *Lamentations*, 134; O'Connor, "Lamentations," 1064.

Naming Zion: "Daughter-my-People"

While I have commented above on the possible metaphorical aspect of the term בת־עמי, it is also worth commenting that there may be in this very name a movement toward the conflation of individual and communal. While the term still references the female personification of the city, it also makes explicit—in a way that the name "Zion" only assumes—the representative aspect by spelling out that this is not just Daughter; but Daughter-my-*People*. This is a persona in whose very name the communal is becoming ever more explicit in the progression toward chapter 5.

NRSV takes up the representative aspect of בת־עמי in its translation of "daughter my people" as simply "my people" (cf. 4:6, 10). Yet this is inadequate. While NRSV has correctly conveyed the *collective* import of the term in its translation "my people," the *femaleness* is also an important part of the trope and should not be obscured in translation.[44] One effect of the term, then, is to make the metaphor, which until now has been mostly implicit, explicitly communal.

CONCLUSION

Lamentations 4 presents impossible reversal. Gold has become dim and altered (4:1); the children of Zion, once like gold and precious jewels themselves, are now likened to everyday earthenware (4:2). Those who feasted now starve in the streets (4:5a) and the formerly purple-clad embrace the rubbish heap (4:5b). The ruling classes were beautiful and brightly colored and they are now shrivelled and black (4:7–8), compassionate women have become monstrous (4:10). Color drains away. The children, previously of so much concern, are worthless and scattered, and the Lamenter's gaze zooms out to encompass others also. Each group of people is portrayed to give an image both of the *actual* fate of various inhabitants (children, nobles, mothers, infants, elite, princes, women,

44. It is also used in prophets where, NRSV again neglects to translate the female aspect (Isa 22:4 "my beloved people"; Jer 4:11 "my poor people"; 6:26 "my poor people"; 8:11 "my people"; 8:19 "my poor people"; 8:21 "my poor people"; 8:22 "my poor people"; 8:23 "my poor people"; 9:6 "my sinful people"; 14:17 "my people"; cf. Ezek 13:17 "the daughters of your people"). Also note that of the five uses in Lamentations, three are in the construction שבר בת־עמי (Lam 2:11 "the destruction of my people" 3:48 "destruction of my people" and 4:10 "destruction of my people"). This occurs only twice elsewhere in the Hebrew Bible, both times in Jeremiah (Jer 8:1 "the wound of my people," 21 "the hurt of my poor people").

prophets, priests, elders) while at the same time symbolically representing the demise of the city and her people as whole. Everywhere the Lamenter turns his gaze he perceives the inconceivable. All these reversals of status are unthinkable, impossibilities. In this way the Lamenter graphically portrays the unbelievability of the situation that is spelt out in verse 12: how on earth could the holy city, Jerusalem, be so compromised?

In this portrayal of unthinkable reversal, Lam 4 blurs the boundaries between the individual and communal, and the literal and metaphorical, such that they are practically indistinguishable. While Lam 1–3 all do this to a certain extent, chapter 4 is masterful in its portrayal of various objects (gold, stones) and social strata (mothers, priests, prophets) that may well be *literally* in view, but could equally point to characteristics of those groups as representative of the whole people. After the intensely personal, inward looking individual focus of Lam 3 (but note the plurals there from verse 40 too), Lam 4 shifts its gaze to images that encompass the communal. Specific cohorts of people now potentially represent the whole. In each of these pictures the entire community may be in mind as each specific image draws out some aspect of the whole: reversed worth, cruelty, bloodguiltiness, and so on. Further, the first person plural in verses 17–20 prefigures Lam 5, which will be entirely spoken in the communal voice. Finally, there is within the very naming of the city בת־עמי, "Daughter-My-People" the explicit connection of the (singular) female image of the city with the (communal) inhabitants of the city. There is thus a progression, mixing and merging of individual and collective, and metaphorical and literal, to the point where Lam 5 will scoop up everyone and everything in its first person plural pronouns.[45] This gives momentum and cohesion to the book as a whole, as the individual-yet-communal portraits and pleas of Zion and the גבר yield to more explicit community representations, which will culminate in the communal prayer of chapter 5.[46]

Lamentations 4 speaks of great anguish and sorrow. The Lamenter compiles a barrage of impossibilities that demonstrate just how unthinkable it is that the city Jerusalem should be compromised. In the examples considered here, the gold and sacred stones laying in the dust bespeak the fallenness and beschmirsching of the holy people. Cruel and starving

45. But see my excursus questioning the ethics of a monolithic communal voice presuming to speak for "all" (Bier, "Perhaps there is Hope," 345–48).

46. Cf. Dobbs-Allsopp, who also comments on the way in which chapter 4 blurs distinctions between individual and communal (Dobbs-Allsopp, *Lamentations*, 135).

mothers reflect the city's inability to nurture and sustain the city's inhabitants. The priests' and prophets' religious idolatry perhaps indicates the key sin for which the people are purportedly being punished. By these and other perhaps literal, perhaps metaphorical pictures the boundaries between particular cohorts and the people as a whole become less and less defined. The chapter then moves to the communal voice in verses 17–20, bringing the tragedy together as a matter of concern for all the people. This move to communal voice prefigures the communal lament of Lam 5, which will take up the collective voice in earnest and in desperation. The blurring of literal with metaphorical; along with the progression to first person plural voice; and the naming of Zion as בת־עמי, Daughter-my-People; together indicate that the individual and communal are increasingly inextricably intertwined. In Lam 4, all the people are tarred with the same brush that taints mothers, priests, prophets. All, like the city's very stones, are reduced to dust and ashes. In this manner, Lam 4 serves as a crucial transitional movement in the momentum of the book of Lamentations, moving from individual perspectives to the communal voice. And in so doing it demonstrates, once again, that the downfall of one; or of one sector of society; is the downfall of all.

4

Lament Personified

Job in the Bedeutungsnetz *of Psalm 22*

Will Kynes

> Ps 22 ist nicht nur einer der im Neuen Testament am häufigsten zitierten Texte des Alten Testaments. Er ist schon im Alten Testament in ein umfassendes Bedeutungsnetz eingebettet, das literarische und theologische Rückschlüsse auf sehr unterschiedliche Bücher zuläßt und dem wegen der sehr dichten Intertextualität innerhalb der inner-alttestamentlichen Rezeptionsgeschichte große Bedeutung zukommt.[1]

This chapter will employ the intertextual relationship between Ps 22 and the book of Job to demonstrate the tendency toward the personification of lament in Hebrew literature. First, I will put this connection in a wider hermeneutical context by outlining five similar intertextual connections between the psalm and the wider Hebrew tradition: the life of David, other Old Testament books, the New Testament, the Midrash, and the Dead Sea Scrolls. This brief summary will demonstrate both the wide, powerful influence of Ps 22 in the Hebrew understanding of suffering and the method of *relecture* with its reciprocal effect on the interpretation of texts and events.[2] Second, I will use the lexical, thematic, and narratival

1. Bauks, *Feinde*, 11.

2. According to Brevard Childs, *relecture* is "the process by which a later biblical

similarities between Ps 22 and the book of Job to argue that its author has likewise interpreted Job's experience through the words of the psalm. Finally, I will consider the reciprocal implications of this *Bedeutungsnetz* ("meaning network") on our interpretation of these texts caught within its hermeneutical web.[3]

The second step encounters methodological difficulties that are worth acknowledging at the outset. First, though, as I will show, the lexical repetition between Job and Ps 22 is repeated and ranges across both texts, no single intertextual connection has quite the "volume," to use Richard Hays's term, to prove direct dependence.[4] Though parallels in Job to other psalms, such as the "bitter parody" of Ps 8:4[5] in Job 7:17–18 or the verbatim quotation of Ps 107:40 in Job 12:21a, 24b, may approach that level of certainty, the possibility of a third common source or an oral form informing the parallel language cannot be definitively discounted. For this reason, some scholars are reticent to affirm dependence between Job and any text.[6] However, arguments for allusion are cumulative,[7] and in this case I will propose that the evidence considered in total, including the significant narratival similarities, suggests at least a significant possibility that one text is dependent on the other, and that the repeated verbal similarities are not merely common stock language for lament, but contribute to a sustained dialogue between the texts. The rarity of the shared language elsewhere in the OT contributes to this argument, but it is primarily the way these verbal similarities correspond to the close narrative affinity between the texts that suggests direct dependence may be involved.

Even when the probability of dependence is established, the problem of priority remains. Here again, definitive conclusions are elusive. The exact dates of both Job and Ps 22 are unknown. Scholars tend to date Job between the fifth and third centuries BCE, but few commentators are willing even to hazard a guess at the date of Ps 22 beyond suggesting that

---

writer made use of an earlier writing in order to produce a new form with its one individual integrity" (*Introduction*, 514).

3. In linguistics, the *Bedeutungsnetz* of an ambiguous word is used to describe its meaning. See Würster, "The Structure of the Linguistic World," 9.

4. For Hays' criteria for identifying intertextual "echoes," see Hays, *Echoes of Scripture*, 29–32.

5. English verse numbering will be used throughout.

6. E.g., Dion, "Formulaic Language," 192.

7. Sommer, *A Prophet Reads Scripture*, 35.

vv. 27–31 are a later, possibly postexilic, addition.[8] Again, a suggestive cumulative argument is the best available. The author of Job appears to be aware of not only the lament form in general,[9] but also specific psalms, lament and otherwise.[10] These psalmic allusions contribute to the author's broader interaction with texts across the Old Testament.[11] The psalm, on the other hand, as I will demonstrate, has been a particularly attractive source for later texts describing extreme suffering.[12] So, Job shows a propensity to build on earlier texts, especially the Psalms, and Ps 22 to be a brick in later textual superstructures. Whether these tendencies hold true here is, admittedly, beyond definitive proof, but even if the diachronic relationship between the texts cannot be proven, the synchronic interaction between them is still illuminating, as it demonstrates that the author of Job has taken the lament imagery found in that psalm and a similar narrative and personalized it in his depiction of Job's experience.

RELECTURE OF PSALM 22

Some have suggested an original liturgical *Sitz im Leben* for Ps 22.[13] Whether or not the psalm actually originated in the temple, through its superscription, the text itself associates its origin with David. Brevard Childs observes that these Davidic superscriptions historicize the Psalms by drawing them into David's person and history,[14] which suggests an initial *relecture* for the psalm. The superscription's "of David," invites the reader both to interpret what follows in light of the Israelite monarch and to understand David through the words of the psalm, drawing Ps 22 into a wider intertextual relationship with the psalms attributed to David and the Davidic narratives in the historical books. Though the superscription of Ps 22 does not refer to any specific detail from David's life, other superscriptions do, and, because those incidents are generally not

8. E.g., Gerstenberger, *Psalms*, 1:112.

9. See Westermann, *The Structure of the Book of Job*.

10. See Frevel, "Theologie der Menschenwürde," 257, 262; Kynes, *My Psalm has Turned into Weeping*.

11. See, e.g., Pyeon, *Intertextuality*.

12. This would accord with Gerstenberger's proposal that its original cultic use was for "cases of extreme and prolonged suffering" (Gerstenberger, *Psalms*, 1:112).

13. E.g., Craigie, *Psalms 1–50*, 197–98; Mays, "Prayer and Christology," 323.

14. Childs, *Introduction*, 521.

royal occasions, Childs argues that the Davidic superscriptions encourage readers to interpret the Psalms as testifying to "all the common troubles and joys of ordinary human life in which all persons participate."[15] However, the psalm's hyperbolic imagery militates against either a Davidic or everyman ultimate referent as it transcends them both.[16]

Second, driven by this "extravagance of expression,"[17] interpreters look beyond David to some future referent. Even interpreters who continue to attribute the psalm's words to David place its meaning elsewhere. Rashi, for example, writes, "David composed this prayer with reference to the future [exile]."[18] The text of the psalm itself may even testify to this *relecture*. Several scholars suggest that the eschatological hymn that closes Ps 22 (vv. 27–31) is a postexilic addition when the psalm was applied to the corporate suffering of the nation of Israel by which it mediated between God and the nations.[19] This possible *relecture* of the psalm would draw it into relationship with the prophetic books, especially Isaiah.[20] Even if these final verses were written by the psalmist himself, they involve a new reading of his experience in which he points beyond himself to the community and the future.

Third, whether the result of a later addition or not, this "prophetic and universalist" conclusion, which is "rare in the Psalter," may explain the New Testament writers' affinity for the psalm.[21] Thus Calvin says: "David here speaks of himself in hyperbolical language, and he does this in order to lead us beyond himself to Christ."[22] Whether the psalm is prophetic or not,[23] the "morphological fit"[24] to Jesus' passion is undeniable, and thus it becomes the boldest hue in the evangelists' scriptural

15. Childs, *Introduction*, 521. See also Gillmayr-Bucher, "The Psalm Headings."

16. See Delitzsch, *Commentary on the Psalms*, 1:376.

17. Davis, "Exploding the Limits," 97.

18. Rashi and Gruber, *Psalms*, 257. Commenting on verse 7, Rashi explains that the psalmist "refers to Israel metaphorically as one person" (257).

19. Menn, "No Ordinary Lament," 304 n. 10. For verses 27–31 as a later addition, see, e.g., Becker, *Israel Deutet seine Psalmen*, 49–53.

20. Stephen Cook argues that lexical connections between verses 30–31 and "the postexilic, redemption-oriented texts of Ps 102:28, Isa 61:9, and 65:9," as well as Isa 44:23, support the addition's reference to Israel (Cook, "*Relecture*," 196).

21. Auvray, "The Psalms," 53.

22. Calvin, *Psalms*, 1:372.

23. Hermann Gunkel emphatically denies that it is (*Psalms*, 94).

24. Childs, "Theological Exegesis," 24. Childs is speaking of Isa 53.

palette as they depict the sufferings of Jesus.[25] Jesus' agonized quotation of Ps 22:1 in Aramaic (Matt 27:46; Mark 15:34) is the culmination of a series of allusions in all four gospels to the psalm. The casting of lots for Jesus' clothing appears in each account (Mark 15:24; Matt 27:35; Luke 23:34; John 19:23–24; cf. Ps 22:18). The mocking that pervades the psalm also appears throughout the passion narratives. Matthew's placement of jeers from the psalm in the mouths of the chief priests, scribes, and elders (Matt 27:43; cf. Ps 22:8) contributes to an array of lexical correspondences sewn through the accounts.[26] Missing from the gospel accounts but later interpreted as prefiguring the crucifixion is the phrase, "They have pierced my hands and feet" (22:16).[27] The evangelists' *relecture* of the psalm is so complete that some of the church fathers denied that it had any reference to David at all. Thus, Tertullian claimed, "David himself did not suffer this cross, nor did any other king of the Jews."[28]

Fourth, however, even if the psalm did not refer to David's experience, Jewish interpreters were unwilling to have this text wrested from their tradition. In addition to Rashi's nationalistic interpretation, the rabbis in the Midrash apply the psalm to Esther.[29] The connection begins with the words אַיֶּלֶת הַשַּׁחַר in the superscription. The first word could mean either "hind, doe," or "strength" and the rabbis apply both meanings to Esther, first, because Esther is traditionally likened to a hind,[30] and second, because David foresaw, "that 'O my Strength' was the apostrophe wherewith she would call upon the Holy One," and so David wrote the

25. See Mays, *Psalms*, 105. For an overview of various approaches to the intertextual connections between the passion narrative and Ps 22, see Tanner, *Lens of Intertextuality*, 61–63.

26. These include the "contempt" of Herod and his soldiers for Jesus (Luke 23:11; Ps 22:7), the crowds that "look on" (Luke 23:35; Luke 23:48; Ps 22:7) and "shake their heads" (Mark 15:29; Matt 27:39; Ps 22:7), the leaders that "scoff" (Luke 23:35; Ps 22:7) and the criminals that "taunt" (Mark 15:32; Matt 27:44; Ps 22:6). See Menn, "No Ordinary Lament," 333.

27. The MT here reads, "*Like a lion* [כָּאֲרִי], my hands and feet," and translators have evidently struggled to understand the verse. See Craigie, *Psalms 1–50*, 196.

28. Tertullian, *Adversus Marcionem*, 158.

29. According to Menn, "[T]he understanding of Psalm 22 as Esther's prayer dominates interpretation of the psalm in the amoraic period (third to fifth centuries CE)" (Menn, "No Ordinary Lament," 317). Jerome was already aware of this interpretation in the fourth century (Jerome and Siegfried Risse, *Commentarioli in Psalmos*, 120–21).

30. Braude, *Midrash*, 1:297.

superscription "thinking upon Esther."[31] As the commentary progresses, the lament is put on Esther's lips, and various details of the psalm are read in light of her experience.[32] For example, the opening cry of verse 1 is understood with regard to the growing urgency of Esther's fast:

> On the first day of a fast, one says: "My God"; on the second day, one says: "My God"; only on the third may one say, "Why hast Thou forsaken me?" So it was only after Esther cried in a loud voice, "What hast Thou forsaken me?" that her cry was heard.[33]

The comments on verses 9–19 construct another prayer around Esther's confrontation with King Ahasuerus. In this account, verse 16—which is translated, "My hands and my feet they made repulsive"—refers to Esther's statement, "Though Haman's sons practiced sorcery on me so that in the sight of Ahasuerus my hands and feet were repulsive, yet a miracle was wrought for me, and my hands and feet were made to shine like sapphires."[34] Further, the casting of lots for the garments of the afflicted in verse 18 is said to refer to the bystanders' desire for Esther's royal cloak as they expect her demise, though the queen is miraculously delivered.[35]

A fifth example of the *relecture* of Ps 22 was found at Qumran. Loren Fisher argues that QH 5:5–19 views an earlier disaster through the interpretive lens of Ps 22.[36] He observes that the Qumran psalmist begins, "I willingly thank thee, O Lord, for thou has not forsaken me," echoing the first words of the psalm, even as he transforms what follows from a lament into a thanksgiving psalm.[37] This theme continues as in lines 6 and 12 the author repeats the phrase, "Thou hast not forsaken me." Further, the beginning of line 11 ("But they do not open their mouth against me") adds only a negating לא to the same Hebrew phrase in Ps 22:13. Also, as Sigmund Mowinckel notes, the depiction of enemies as beasts, especially lions, which is "characteristic of Psalm 22," appears in the Qumran text.[38]

31. Braude, *Midrash*, 1:305.

32. Menn suggests that the editing of the commentary gives the impression that "the Psalm is principally about Esther" (Menn, "No Ordinary Lament," 319 n. 81).

33. Braude, *Midrash*, 1:302.

34. Ibid., 1:320.

35. Ibid., 1:321.

36. Fisher, "Betrayed By Friends," 26.

37. In this formal classification, he follows Mowinckel, "Hodayot 39.5–20," 267.

38. Mowinckel, "Hodayot 39.5–20," 270.

Finally, lines 12 and 13 have parallels to God's hearing and delivering of the psalmist (Ps 22:20, 24). Mowinckel claims the speaker is "a definite individual," whom he suggests may be the Teacher of Righteousness.[39] Whoever chose to interpret his experience of disaster and deliverance through Ps 22 in this text, his doing so testifies further to both "Israel's desire to articulate new praise to God through the mediation of older forms"[40] and the role of Ps 22 in that pursuit.

PSALM 22 IN JOB

Given this recurrent interpretation of the suffering of certain important individuals[41] through the words of Ps 22, the personage of Job is a fitting candidate to receive such a treatment. Claus Westermann has argued that Job is a "dramatizing of the lament," as its author "stands within traditions which so determine his thought and shape his questions that he cannot express himself in other than already formed linguistic structures," and thus weaves the basic motifs of lamentation together into a dramatic form.[42] By demonstrating the similarities between Job and the lament genre, which includes Ps 22, Westermann invites further reflection on this connection.[43] Westermann's reliance on form criticism results in two shortcomings for his study, however. First, he is unable to account for the prose sections of Job because they have no formal parallel in the lament psalms. Though he claims the narrative framework "simply *must* be there" because it demonstrates that "the one lamenting in the poem is a real person,"[44] he largely ignores its content. Second, he reads Job through the generic aspects of the lament, which downplays the textual details of both Job and the Psalms. Therefore, he discourages attempts to discern allusions to specific psalms in Job, instead focusing on "the relationship of the parts to one another."[45] This discussion of "parts" of

39. Mowinckel, "Hodayot 39.5–20," 269, 276.

40. Childs, *Introduction*, 515. Childs points to the Hodayot as "an excellent example" of the "growing tendency of later Israel . . . to re-use the older language" found in the Psalms.

41. Though the nation of Israel is not an individual per se, it is still distinguished in its particularity from the "everyman" interpretation.

42. Westermann, *Structure*, 12, 32.

43. See also Bauks, *Feinde*.

44. Westermann, *Structure*, 7, 8. Emphasis original.

45. Ibid., 33.

the lament is a step removed from the texts themselves and is susceptible to the generalization that haunts all form criticism, obscuring the unique features of individual texts.[46]

It is precisely the uniqueness of Ps 22 that the author of Job appears to capitalize on by applying the psalm to Job's experience. The common narrative that flows through both texts, studded with similar rare imagery, suggest that the author of Job saw Ps 22 as a primary resource for understanding his subject's suffering and redemption. This psalm is ripe for narrative analysis because "Psalm 22 has a sort of 'plot' in which something 'happens.'"[47] Precedent exists for this type of narratival connection between an individual psalm and Job. Klaus Seybold calls Ps 39 a "Hiob–Psalm" because the Job narrative illuminates the particular situation of the psalmist.[48] Douglas Green claims Job follows essentially the same "good → bad → better" narrative structure as Ps 23, in which Job 1:1–5 corresponds to Ps 23:2, most of the rest of the book corresponds to the valley of the shadow of death in Ps 23:4, and his restoration corresponds to Ps 23:5–6.[49] For Green it is the "very similar narrative patterns" shared by the texts that invite a dialogue between them and not any intertextual dependence, an issue he does not address. While Pss 39 and 23, as well as other psalms and OT texts may inform the author of Job's depiction of his hero,[50] just as several other texts are woven into the passion narrative, the distinctive narrative of Ps 22, one which pushes the lament to its limits,[51] plays a particularly influential role. The narratival similarity, far more detailed than the basic narrative structure which recurs in Ps 23 and Job (and many other texts), and shared imagery combine to form a "meta-intertextuality" between Job and the psalm,

46. Muilenburg, "Form Criticism and Beyond," 5. Because Carol Newsom addresses Job's interaction with certain genres of speech, including the lament, this tendency is also apparent in her insightful work into the dialogical nature of the book (Newsom, *Moral Imaginations*, esp. 136–38).

47. Vall, "Vox Christi," 184. He is quoting Craigie, *Psalms 1–50*, 197 and Mays, *Psalms*, 108. For more on narrative approaches to biblical interpretation, see Bartholomew and Goheen, "Story."

48. Seybold, *Die Psalmen*, 162.

49. Green, "Psalm 23 and Job," 79–80.

50. See, e.g., the possible allusion to Ps 39:13 in Job 10:20–21.

51. Mays, *Psalms*, 106–7.

which, together with the evidence of other *relectures* of Ps 22, justifies reading Job and the psalm together.[52]

Comparing the "plots" of Ps 22 and the book of Job has several advantages over Westermann's form-critical approach. First, it follows the text itself instead of creating generic categories. Second, it requires attention to the whole text as a complete presentation of the narrative. Third, whereas the form-critical approach tends to divide the psalms according to externally imposed and modernly developed categories, a narrative approach sees the differences in form as crucial turning points in a unified plot.[53]

The narratival affinities begin in the prologues to the works. The psalm's prologue is implicit, as the psalmist only provides hints at what his life was like before his affliction, which appear in verses 8–10. First, from the taunts of his adversaries (v. 8) we can conclude that the psalmist was known for his trust in the Lord and received the Lord's delight in response. In Job's prologue the same themes are prominent (1:1, 8). However, Satan, like the mockers, questions his trust and God's satisfaction with his servant (1:9–11). Second, the psalmist affirms that he has trusted in God since birth. This lifelong devotion again parallels the depiction of Job in the prologue as well as his own testimony (31:18). Finally, in the course of verse 1 the psalmist's transition from trust to lament appears. In his first words, "My God, my God," the psalmist, like Job (cf. 1:21; 2:10), expresses his faith before moving to complaint.[54]

As both move to lament, the psalmist's complaint, which has already erupted in the first verse, reflects a tangle of afflictions similar to Job's. Peter Craigie, who notes the similarity between the psalmist's expression of profound desolation and Job's lament (Job 3:1–26), provides a description of the psalmist's affliction that could apply just as well to Job: "the original cause of the distress may have been illness aggravated by the attitude of the psalmist's fellow men, as well as by his own doubts and the spiritual dilemma: God is a saving God, yet he has forsaken his

52. For "meta-intertextuality," a sustained interaction with another text that warrants reading an alluding text "against the wider context of the specific passages being alluded to," see Stead, *Intertextuality of Zechariah*, 254.

53. By labeling Job a "dramatization of the lament," Westermann anticipated this approach, although that characterization overlooks the "dramatic character of the psalm" itself (Vall, "Vox Christi," 184).

54. Calvin, *Psalms*, 1:359.

loyal servant."[55] Admittedly, the loss of children receives no mention in the psalm, but their absence is conspicuous, and this theme also receives scarce mention in the poetic sections of Job. Loss of property is also not mentioned, but the casting of lots for the psalmist's garments suggests that those are his only remaining possessions.

These multiplied afflictions lead both sufferers to lash out in lament in several directions. Job's friends reflect the psalmist's enemies, who attack instead of comforting.[56] But, in both cases, God receives the ultimate blame (Ps 22:15; cf. Job 6:4; 7:20; 10:8–17; 16:7–14).[57] While the psalmist wonders how God could forsake him when he has been cast upon God "from birth" (מֵרֶחֶם) and "from the womb" (מִבֶּטֶן) (Ps 22:10), Job rejects the life God has given him altogether, asking, "Why did I not die at birth [מֵרֶחֶם], come out from the womb [מִבֶּטֶן] and expire" (Job 3:11).[58]

Both describe their suffering with similar corporal hyperbole. The psalmist says, "I am poured out [שׁפך] like water, and all my bones [עַצְמוֹתָי] are out of joint" (v. 14). Job takes up these images in his closing lament (30:16–17):

> 16 And now my soul is poured out [שׁפך] within me;
> days of affliction have taken hold of me.
> 17 The night racks my bones [עֲצָמַי],[59]
> and the pain that gnaws me takes no rest.

These two words are nowhere else in the OT so closely connected.[60] Job's elaboration on the psalmist's words corresponds with several of his other allusions to the Psalms.[61]

Intermingled with the lament in both texts is a dialogue with the enemies. This dominates much of the book of Job, but in the psalm it appears only in verses 7–8, where the psalmist's enemies advise, like Job's friends, "Commit your cause to the Lord; let him deliver—let him rescue

55. Craigie, *Psalms 1–50*, 202, 185.

56. Bauks, *Feinde*, 109–10, see also 63. She compares Job 30:25 and Ps 22:3–8. See also Craigie, *Psalms 1–50*, 199.

57. See Schaefer, *Psalms*, 55; Bauks, *Feinde*, 28.

58. These terms appears together six other times in the OT, and, among those, Ps 58:3 similarly combines both nouns with מִן. A slightly different construction appears in Isa 46:3.

59. The ending of the word is different, but this need not invalidate the allusion.

60. They only appear in even the same chapter three other times in the OT.

61. See, e.g., Job 7:17–18 and Ps 8:4; Job 10:20–22 and Ps 39:13; Job 12:21–24 and Ps 107:40.

[נצל] the one in whom he delights!" (cf. Job 5:17–19 where Eliphaz gives similar advice and uses the same word [נצל]). The enemies' mocking advice here is unique among the individual laments.[62] Further, similar to the dialogues in the book of Job, where the earlier words of a disputant are often reused in a different way,[63] the psalmist takes up the words יהוה and נצל from the mockers and repeats them with new meaning in verses 19–20. Job implicitly charges the friends with mocking him like the psalmist's enemies when he says, "I also could talk as you do, if you were in my place; I could join words together against you, and shake my head at you [אָנִיעָה עֲלֵיכֶם בְּמוֹ רֹאשִׁי] (Job 16:4), which echoes Ps 22:7: "All who see me mock at me; they make mouths at me, they shake their heads [יָנִיעוּ רֹאשׁ]."[64] This continues several verses later in Job 16 when Job says, "They have gaped at me with their mouths [פָּעֲרוּ עָלַי בְּפִיהֶם]" (v. 10a), recalling Ps 22:13 ("They open wide their mouths at me [פָּצוּ עָלַי פִּיהֶם]").[65]

In Job's dispute with his friends a dialogue is also initiated between the book of Job and Ps 22. When Eliphaz claims, "The roar [שַׁאֲגַת] of the lion [אַרְיֵה], the voice of the fierce lion, and the teeth of the young lions are broken. The strong lion perishes for lack of prey [טָרֶף], and the whelps of the lioness are scattered" (4:10–11), his use of lion imagery to represent enemies, using three of the same words or roots, counters the threat they present in Ps 22:13 ("they open wide their mouths at me, like a ravening [טֹרֵף] and roaring [שֹׁאֵג] lion [אַרְיֵה]"). This reflects his tendency elsewhere to twist psalmic language in order to silence Job's lament (e.g., Job 15:14–15; cf. Ps 8:3–5). Westermann notes the similarities between these two passages, and claims the friends take the comparison of enemies to wild animals from the lament about enemies,[66] but, though lions metaphorically represent enemies elsewhere in the

62. According to Westermann, the other individual laments are 6, 13, 35, 38, 42, 43, 88, 102, and 109 (Westermann, *Praise and Lament*, 182). The enemies also speak in Ps 35:21, but the address is not explicit and is not advice. The nearest parallel is Ps 42:3, 10, where the enemies ask, "Where is your God?"

63. E.g., Job 18:5 and 21:17. For the importance of quotation in Job see Gordis, *Book of God and Man*, 169–89.

64. Gerald Janzen notes this similarity and claims that later in the same chapter Job conforms his speech to the lament of the innocent when he uses other images which appear in Ps 22 (Job 16:10 and Ps 22:7; Job 16:13 and Ps 22:14). See Janzen, *Job*, 122–23.

65. See Wright, *Job*, 21–22. He claims Ps 22 "represents a man whose sufferings were very similar to if not identical with" Job's.

66. Westermann, *Structure*, 85–86.

Psalms (e.g., Pss 7:2; 35:17), nowhere is the language as close. Psalm 58:7, as Westermann observes, similarly requests that God break the teeth of the lions, employing the same rare word שחל ("break"), used only seven times in the Old Testament, as Job 4:10.[67] Eliphaz may be conflating the latter passage with Ps 22:13.[68]

In Ps 22:6, the psalmist says, "But I am a worm [תּוֹלַעַת], and not human [אִישׁ]; scorned by others, and despised by the people." Only in five other passages is the word for "worm" used with that meaning, and of those, only in Isa 41:14 is it used metaphorically, but not in contrast with humanity. However, in Job 25:6, Bildad claims,

> 5 If even the moon is not bright
> and the stars are not pure in his sight,
> 6 how much less a mortal [אֱנוֹשׁ], who is a maggot [רִמָּה],
> and a human being [אָדָם], who is a worm[תּוֹלֵעָה]!

The two words for "worm" are almost identical. This form is only used in one other place, Isa 14:11, where it is not applied to humanity. Though different words are used for humans in Job and the psalm, the common contrast and the rare word for "worm" suggest an allusion.[69] Hermann Spieckermann argues that here the negative anthropological perspective of the friends is fully recognizable, as this phrase is consciously taken in isolation from its context in Ps 22 and made into the essential definition of humanity.[70]

In verses 19–21, the psalmist turns to petition, but he, like Job, does not explicitly ask to be saved from his affliction.[71] Both sufferers long for God to "answer" (ענה) (Ps 22:2; Job 31:35), and when he does finally "answer" (ענה), it is the turning point of both texts (Ps 22:21; Job 38:1).[72] The psalmist does not provide the content of this response, but the Job poet pens some of the Bible's most powerful poetry to fill this gap. After

67. Westermann, *Structure*, 86.

68. Allusions to earlier texts in the dialogue show a tendency toward conflation (e.g., Job 25:4; cf. 9:2 and 15:14).

69. Wright claims this image comes from Ps 22 (Wright, *Job*, 22).

70. Spieckermann, *Heilsgegenwart*, 250.

71. Terrien, *Strophic Structure*, 235.

72. Stolz, "Psalm 22," 144–45. Westermann observes the similarity between the narrative timing of God's answer in Job and in psalms of lamentation (Westermann, *Structure*, 106).

God's response, Job and the psalmist are alike in expressing their faith while their situation remains unchanged (Ps 22:22; Job 42:2–6).[73]

Eventually both are restored, and for both this restoration is twofold with both God and the community. God's answer and the sufferers' faithful responses demonstrate the former; the concluding verses of both texts focus on the latter. God's scolding of Job's friends is implicit in the psalm, as they disappear from the narrative. In both accounts, the community gathers and welcomes the outsiders back. They share a meal with the sufferers (Ps 22:26, 29; Job 42:11), commiserate with them (Ps 22:24; Job 42:11), and though Job does not "live forever" (Ps 22:26), he is given twice the normal lifespan (Job 42:16; cf. Ps 90:10). He lives to see four generations, presumably passing on his account of what God had done (cf. Ps 22:30–31).[74] Thus, Job, like the psalmist, is among the afflicted who will "eat and be satisfied" [יֹאכְלוּ עֲנָוִים וְיִשְׂבָּעוּ] (Ps 22:26), as he "eats" (יֹאכְלוּ; Job 42:11) and dies "full" or "satisfied" [שְׂבַע] of days (Job 42:17).

HERMENEUTICAL CONCLUSIONS

In this intertextual reading of Ps 22 and the book of Job, two conclusions implicit in the other *relectures* of the text become more explicit. First, the *relecture* of an earlier work creates an interpretive reciprocity between the two texts, which influences the exegesis of the words, images, and narrative of both works, and, second, the *Bedeutungsnetz* that repeated *relectures* create testifies to a Hebrew tendency toward particularity.

The reciprocity of *relecture* appears as the "original text is seen in a new light from the relecture of the older" and the "newer text is also interpreted from the understanding created from the comparison with the *relecture* of the older."[75] The former effect is undeniable in the impossibility of a Christian reading of Ps 22 free of the interpretive effect of its Christological *relecture*.[76] But the latter is also called for following the example of the New Testament writers who used the psalm

73. Fyall, *Now My Eyes*, 182. Further, McCann suggests the psalmist's invitation to glorify God in verse 23 "indicates renewed recognition of God's sovereignty" (McCann, "Psalms," 764). This parallels Job's reinvigorated faith in God's sovereignty in Job 42:2.

74. The last word of the second to last verse of both texts is דּוֹר ("generation").

75. Kellum, *Farewell Discourse*, 61.

76. Tostengard, "Psalm 22," 170.

as a hermeneutical context for Jesus' crucifixion.[77] Thus, this intrinsic reciprocity means the question of the ultimate referent of the psalm fundamentally misunderstands the nature of its relation to its later *relectures*. Further, if each *relecture* of the psalm affects our interpretation of it, and if its meaning affects our understanding of each *relecture*, then transitive readings between various *relectures* are necessary, especially if those *relectures* are canonically endorsed.[78] Thus, if Job is one *relecture* of the psalm and Jesus' passion is another, understanding all three fully requires reading them all in dialogue with each other.

This type of *Bedeutungsnetz* is the natural result of the Hebrew preference for particularity reflected in the way the Bible "usually refuses to postulate generalized doctrines without moving swiftly to personalized particulars."[79] In contrast to the modern predilection for propositions, an interpretative approach R. R. Reno brands "conceptual allegory,"[80] the authors of the Old Testament favored persons. Therefore, Ps 22 is not tied to the passion narrative or its other later appropriations by a common experience of "Godforsakenness,"[81] "the reality of suffering and faith,"[82] or any other abstract "theological reflection as concerning the divine *res*, not the scriptural *signa*,"[83] which has been extracted from the text and then applied to another personage, dragging traces of the psalm's language with it. Instead, the later authors use *the psalm*, the *signa* itself—its words, images, and narrative—to understand their subjects, not merely the *res* it represents. Thus, the biblical authors share the "profound personalism" of Dostoevsky, for whom "there are no ideas, no thoughts, no positions which belong to no one, which exist 'in themselves.'"[84] For the biblical authors, there is no such thing as "no-man's thoughts" which float in a vague conceptuality and may be applied to various people.

77. Mays, "Prayer and Christology," 323.

78. By this I mean that the *relecture* has been incorporated into a community's authoritative canon, which, for Christian interpreters, puts the Qumran and Midrash *relectures* in a different category.

79. Tate, *Psalms* 51–100, 445.

80. Reno, "Biblical Theology," 396.

81. Tostengard, "Psalm 22," 170.

82. Anderson, *Psalms*, 1:185.

83. Reno claims that this is the failure of Childs's exegesis (Reno, "Biblical Theology," 398).

84. Bakhtin and Emerson, *Dostoevsky's Poetics*, 31.

Instead, there are scriptural *texts*, which describe the experience of specific *persons*—"word-events" as Westermann would say.[85]

Therefore, Westermann's comments may apply just as well to the purported redactors of the psalm, the evangelists, the rabbis, or the Qumran community, as they do to the Job poet:

> For the poet of the Book of Job there is no such thing as thoughts about suffering, or reflective suffering; for him there is only real, experienced suffering. This real, experienced suffering is to be found not in abstract reflections but only in the reaction of a concrete human being to his own suffering—in a cry or in muffled silence or in the personal act of expressing this suffering, which means in a lament.[86]

However, Westermann is still too abstract, because it is not in the "*form* of the lament" but in the *words* of *actual laments*, Ps 22 especially, that the Job poet depicts Job's concrete suffering, and the evangelists follow him in this approach. It is in this and its other particularized interpretations—the irreducibly concrete *Bedeutungsnetz* of the *narrative word-events* of David, Israel, and Job—that Ps 22 informs our understanding of the passion, and not in abstract theological propositions extracted from it.[87] And the same could be said for each of those *relectures, mutatis mutandis*. And, lastly, it could be said of us, as well, to the degree that our experience reflects that of the psalm, even if only through the gut-wrenching and faith-building process of reading it and thereby entering its narrative world ourselves.[88]

85. Westermann, *Structure*, 33.

86. Westermann, *Structure*, 32. The emphasis on "the reaction of a concrete human being to his own suffering" supports my attention to narrative in the section above because this makes the character even more concrete, instead of merely disembodied words in an eternal present.

87. See Vanhoozer, *Drama of Doctrine*, 270.

88. See Anderson, *Psalms*, 1:192.

5

The Enemy Lament

A Socio-Cognitive Approach to the Metaphors of Job 16:7–14

Carlos Patrick Jimenez

INTRODUCTION

Chapters 16:1—17:16 of the book of Job contain the fifth speech of Job. Although containing a variety of themes, the main topic in 16:7–14 does not seem to be the suffering of humanity as in the previous four speeches, but the suffering of Job.[1] As in the former laments, Job argues that the main reason for his distress is God himself. However, in 16:7–14, Job pours out his complaints against God in a more intense manner, and gives by far the most merciless and severe depictions of Divine animosity in the whole book.[2] The depiction of God is such that some scholars refer to this personal lament as the "enemy lament."[3] The language of Job 16:7–14 raises some issues. Newsom observes expressions in these texts

1. Job 3:12–6; 6:1–7:21; 9:1—10:22; 12:1—14:22. See Clines, *Job 1–20*, 366–77.

2. Balentine notices that in Job, God's attacks are disproportionate (*Job*, 252–53).

3. In the I lament, Job describes his pain (16:6, 15–16), lack of vitality (17:7, 11–12), and hopelessness (16:22; 17:2, 3, 6). In the enemy lament, however, Job protests against the attacks of his enemy (16:7–14). See Clines, *Job 1–20*, 381.

that do not reflect conventional religious language used by the psalmists.[4] Unusual imagery also might cause alarm among Western readers.[5] In this chapter I will suggest that the language and imagery in Job 16:7–14 is not as unconventional as previously thought.

This chapter argues that Job 16:7–14 is better understood, and the alarm significantly diminished, if attention is paid to the way this lament is conveyed. An examination of Job 16:7–14 reveals that, out of the thirty-nine complaints made against God, thirty-three are presented as metaphors. Thus it is clear that metaphor is the core figure of speech in this text.[6] Highlighting this aspect of the enemy lament is important, because metaphor is no longer viewed as a mere rhetorical or ornamental device. Rather, it is explained by the cognitive linguistic approach: as part of our conceptual system, and as an indicator of the way we *relate, understand, experience the world,* and *interpret* our experiences.[7]

Prior to the 1980s, biblical scholarship approached metaphor mostly based on a purely linguistic methodology.[8] However, after the 1980s many of the insights of the cognitive linguistic approach were adopted, making it possible to analyze previously unexplored features of metaphor. Yet, along with these strengths biblical scholars have also incorporated one of the major weaknesses of the cognitive linguistic approach: the analysis of metaphor isolated from language and context. If the metaphors of Job 16:7–14 are overlooked, or analyzed isolated from their language and social context, we risk misreading the lament and misinterpreting its imagery. If, however, the metaphors of Job 16:7–14 are analyzed through the integration of the language, cognition, and their socio-cultural context, i.e., a socio-cognitive perspective, then the socio-cultural and cognitive gap that separates us from the Jobian world may be bridged. Such

4. Just at the point when Job should have shown repentance, turned in prayer to God, or acknowledged God as his only refuge (characteristics of lament psalms), Job depicts God as enemy, calls for avenging his blood, and for an advocate to vindicate his case in heaven. See Newsom, "The Book of Job," 456, 458; see also Clines, *Job 1–20*, 383.

5. See Newsom, "The Book of Job," 456.

6. Metaphor is important in contemporary scholarship in a range of fields (Fahnestock, *Rhetorical Figures*, 4). However, despite increasing interest in biblical metaphors, the metaphors Job, particularly in the personal laments, have been little examined.

7. See Lakoff and Johnson, *Metaphors We Live By*, 3; see also Solove, *The Digital Person*, 27–30.

8. The first book on metaphor to use a cognitive approach was MacCormac's *Cognitive Theory of Metaphor*.

an approach may also show us that beneath the seemingly blasphemous, and irreverent surface, lays a language in harmony with ancient Israelite approaches to the Divine. This paper will examine the metaphors in Job 16:7–14 from a socio-cognitive perspective, and explore hermeneutical implications of this analysis.

METAPHOR ACCORDING TO THE TRADITIONAL APPROACH: DEFINITION

Traditionally metaphor has been defined as "an implicit comparison between two unlike entities, as distinguished from simile, which is an explicit comparison signaled by the preposition like, as, as if, or as though."[9] For example:

1. עצמיו אפיקי נחושה *its bones are tubes of bronze* (Job 40:18)
2. ובית עכביש מבטחו *and a spider web is his trust* (Job 8:14)

In the examples above, *bones* and *trust* are being referred to in terms of *tubes of bronze* and *spider web* respectively. The similarity between these unlike entities is achieved by an implicit comparison,[10] i.e., metaphor assumes that the first subject (e.g., *bones*) is the second subject (*tubes of bronze*), or describes the first subject (e.g., *trust*) as equal to the second subject (*spider web*). This definition implies an important feature of the traditional approach, namely, that the structure of metaphor is made up by *two explicit entities*. In the second example, the two explicit entities are *spider web* and *trust*. Several names have been used for these two explicit entities.[11] For the purpose of this paper I will employ the terms *topic* when referring to the main subject, and *vehicle* in reference to the second subject.[12] For instance, in *its bones are tubes of bronze*, bones

9. Evans and Green, *Cognitive Linguistics*, 293.

10. As Ricoeur notes in classical rhetoric metaphor found its locus in the word (Ricoeur, *The Rule of Metaphor*, 1, 13, 74, 75).

11. E.g., "ground and figures," "target and source," "primary and secondary subjects," "topic and vehicle," "tenor and vehicle." See Black, *Models and Metaphor*, 467; Black, "Metaphor," 467; Cameron, "Operationalising Metaphor," 13; Soskice, *Metaphor*, 15.

12. Ullman argues that in the metaphor, "there are always two terms present: the *thing* we are talking about and that to which we are comparing it," while Max Black argues that "the metaphorical statement has two subjects to be identified, he calls them the *primary and the secondary subject*" (Soskice, *Metaphor*, 20; see also Cameron, "Operationalising Metaphor," 3).

would be the topic, while tubes of bronze would be the vehicle which *transports* new qualities to bones, i.e., metallic properties.[13]

In the traditional approach, metaphor is based upon *two different subjects that resemble one another*. The basis of metaphor is that the topic and vehicle look alike, or that there is a "literal (physical) resemblance between them." This type of similarity is traditionally called "antecedently existing literal similarity,"[14] i.e., they already look alike before they were compared.

Job 16:7–14: A Challenge to the Traditional Approach

The book of Job presents a challenge to the traditional approach. It contains more than seven hundred and eighty-five linguistic metaphors, and of these, less than thirty-five exhibit an A = B external structure. Out of the thirty-five metaphors in Job 16:7–14, only verse 8 exhibits an A = B structure: *You have filled me with wrinkles which is a witness.*

The rest of the metaphors of Job 16:7–14 have either no subject or one subject only. For example, in *my enemy sharpens his eyes against me* (v. 9), a topic "eyes" is mentioned specifically but the vehicle is missing. It would be senseless to say that *eyes* are being compared to a *sharpen,* rather they are compared to something that can be sharpened such as a knife or sword, but these are not mentioned in verse 9.[15]

Thirty-two out of thirty-three metaphorical expressions in this lament lack subjects. The second challenge posed by the metaphors of Job 16:7–14 is the absence of *literal resemblance* between the two subjects.

13. In metaphor, the vehicle carries meaning "beyond" the common and well known.

14. See Kövecses, *Metaphor,* 68, 76. The similarity between, say, the tubes of bronze and Leviathan's bones preexisted the comparison. It is *literal* because the similarity is not generated by the speaker's imagination, but rather is a *literal* (physical) feature of the topic (*bones*) and vehicle (*tubes of bronze*). The view that metaphors are based on pre-existing similarities is called *comparative view.* The view that metaphor generates similarity as result of comprehension, is called the *interaction view* (Way, *Knowledge, Representation, and Metaphor*, 46–50).

15. If we compare Job 16:9 with Ps 57:4, we realize that in Ps 57:4, the topic and the vehicle are explicitly mentioned, e.g., *their teeth are spears and arrows, their tongues sharp swords.* The syntactic form of Job 16:9, although equally metaphorical, does not exhibit the same structure. In the sentence *my enemy sharpens his eyes against me* (Job 16:9) we are not able to see, from a semantic perspective, to what the *eyes* of Job's enemy are being compared. In Ps 57:4 we are given vehicles such as *arrows, swords,* and *spears,* but in Job 16:9 the metaphor has only one subject: *eyes.*

Unlike the metaphors *bones are tubes of bronze*, none of the metaphors in 16:7–14 seem to exhibit physical similarity.[16] For example, it would be difficult to establish a pre-existing similarity between items such as:

3. Wrinkles and a witness (Job 16:8)
4. God and a beast (Job 16:9)
5. Eyes and knives (Job 16:9)

Furthermore, the lack of two explicit subjects would make it difficult, if not impossible, to establish any similarities in the metaphors of Job 16:7–14. For example, where are the two explicit subjects in these metaphors?

6. They strike my cheek in scorn (Job 16:10)
7. He grabbed me by the neck (Job 16:12)
8. I was at ease (Job 16:12)
9. His archers surround me (Job 16:13)

Indeed, these metaphors can be considered actual events if read out of context. The similarity suggested by Job in these examples cannot be physical, so must be perceived or created in his mind.[17] Consequently, if analyzed from a traditional perspective, most of what is considered metaphorical in Job 16:7–14 would have to be discarded. Therefore, another approach is needed in order to analyze the enemy lament.

TOWARDS A THEORY OF CONCEPTUAL METAPHOR IN JOB 16:7–14

Conceptual metaphor theory defines metaphor as "understanding and experiencing one kind of thing in terms of another."[18] In Job's case, he seems to understand his suffering mostly in terms of war. For example, to describe God's attacks on him, Job uses military terms such as: *He set me up for his target* (Job 16:12), or *His archers surround me* (Job 16:13).

Job not only understands suffering in terms of war, he also seems to experience it in such terms. Job says that he *was at ease* and God *broke*

16. See Benczes, *Creative Compounding in English*, 48; Kövecses, *Metaphor*, 68.

17. Boswell argues that metaphor suggests similarity between two *unequal* entities. The similarity is *construed* (perceived), thus metaphor invites the listener to construct the resemblance between the two subjects. This implies that the resemblance does not necessarily lie in the topic and vehicle, but in the mind of the speaker. See Boswell, *Metaphoric Processing*, 373–84.

18. Lakoff and Johnson, *Metaphors*, 5.

him in two (Job 16:12), he adds that God *slashes open his kidneys and shows no mercy* (Job 16:12).[19] These examples show that Job conceptualizes his suffering mostly in terms of organized violence by military forces on behalf of God. Job therefore gives us the conceptual metaphor, A LIFE IN DISTRESS IS A WAR ZONE. This mental association is called conceptual metaphor.[20] The capitalized letters indicate that the wording A LIFE IN DISTRESS IS A WAR ZONE is not mentioned explicitly but implied. This begs the question, if the subjects are not explicitly mentioned how can we identify A and B, for a linguistic metaphor consists of *two explicit subjects* represented by the A = B schematic formula.[21]

Similarly, the structure of a conceptual metaphor is formed by the association of two domains. A domain is any logical set of experiences we have coherently organized information about, e.g., GOD and ARCHER. Let us identify A and B in the expression: *He set me up as his target* (Job 16:12). Here we have a topic explicitly mentioned: *he,* i.e., GOD; but no vehicle is mentioned. The vehicle, however, is inferred in the behavior God is exhibiting, namely, *setting* Job *for a target.* So we can deduce that Job is conceptualizing God as an archer, thus ARCHER is our vehicle.

Therefore, from the sentence *He set me up as his target,* we can identify the conceptual metaphor GOD IS AN ARCHER. In this case God is the topic, A, and ARCHER is the vehicle, or B.[22] I will discuss some of the conceptual metaphors implied in the language of the enemy lament. Note the intensity of Job's lament, and the severity with which he depicts God's attacks against him:

10. *God has worn me out*: GOD IS A WRESTLER
11. *He has shriveled me up:* GOD'S IMPOSED AFFLICTION IS PHYSICAL COMPRESSION
12. *He has desolated all my company:* GOD IS AN INVADING ENEMY

19. Following the conventions of Lakoff and Johnson (*Metaphor,* 454).

20. See Benczes, *Creative Compounding in English,* 48.

21. When considering the traditional view in the following examples: זכר כי־רוח חיי, remember that my *life is breath,* (Job 7:7), and כי צל ימינו עלי־ארץ *because our days on the earth are but a shadow* (Job 8:9), *life* and *breath, days and shadows* are considered the two pairs of subjects.

22. In the case of A LIFE IN DISTRESS IS A WAR ZONE, both topic and vehicle are implied from the imagery, e.g., setting Job for his target (v. 12), sending his archers to shoot Job (v. 13), ambushing him (v. 13), sharpening tools (v. 9), etc. See Evans and Green, *Cognitive Linguistics,* 295.

13. *My leanness has risen up against me and testifies to my face:* EMACIATION IS AN ANTAGONISTIC WITNESS
14. *He has gnashed his teeth at me:* GOD IS A THREATENING BEAST
15. *He sharpens his eyes against me:* GOD'S HATEFUL LOOK IS A CUTTING KNIFE
16. *They have struck me insolently on the cheek:* VERBAL ABUSE IS PHYSICAL HARM
17. *God gives me up to the ungodly:* GOD IS A TRAITOR
18. *He seized me by the neck:* IMPOSED EMOTIONAL DISTRESS IS STRANGULATION
19. *He set me up as his target:* GOD IS AN ARCHER
20. *His archers surround me:* AFFLICTIONS ARE ENEMY SOLDIERS
21. *He pours out my gall on the ground:* IMPOSED SUFFERING IS A WAR CRIME

Almost all elements of war crimes are present in Job's accusations against God in this lament.[23] This brief presentation shows that the conceptual metaphor theory offers philosophical underpinning explaining where meaning comes from, how meaning develops and how it is expressed.[24]

Neither Hebrew nor context were taken into account when identifying the conceptual metaphors of Job 16:7–14. This is due to the fact that although context and language are alluded to by Lakoff, Johnson, and Turner,[25] these elements play only a small part in conceptual metaphor theory.[26] Metaphorical meaning therefore, is assigned mostly based on the intuition of the researcher, as well as on cognition and bodily

23. E.g., murder, "he dashes me to pieces," the ill-treatment or deportation of civilian residents of an occupied territory, the wanton destruction of cities, towns, and villages and the unjustified devastation by military or civilian necessity. See Solish, *The Law of Armed Conflict*, 301–3.

24. See Lakoff and Turner, *More Than Cool Reason*, 59; Szlos, "Body Parts as Metaphors," 186, 195.

25. See Lakoff and Johnson, *Metaphors*, 3, 5, 63–64, 116, 142–43, 146, 154.

26. Stern, *Metaphor in Context*; Zinken et al., "Discourse Metaphors" 363–86; see also Evans and Green, *Cognitive Linguistics*, 324.

experiences.[27] This translates into a lack of empirical rigour. Without taking into account the language and context in which these metaphors emerged, we risk misreading the metaphors and imagery.

I am not claiming there is only *one specific* meaning for each metaphor; most words making up the metaphors here are polysemantic. The word *neck* in verse 12, has at least three different meanings, i.e., the front neck or throat, the nape and the top of the head or crown. Above, I *assumed* that God is strangling Job, but we might never know if Job is saying that God is asphyxiating him, dragging him by the hair, or taking him by the nape, unless the act of being *seized by the neck* is analyzed in light of its socio-cultural premises.[28] Therefore, language and context may be the only elements that will enable us to better understand the way the man of Uz is conceptualizing his lament.

JOB 16:7–14: TOWARDS A SOCIO-COGNITIVE APPROACH TO METAPHOR

In this section I argue that the language of Job 16:7–14 reflects concepts of the divine influenced by specific socio-cultural and cognitive premises, which create a gap between Job and us. If this gap is to be bridged, then the linguistic, socio-cultural, and cognitive phenomena of this lament must be considered during the process of interpreting its metaphors.

27. See O'Neil, *Interactive Media*, 147; Lakoff and Johnson, *Philosophy in the Flesh*; Lakoff and Johnson. *Metaphors We Live By*.

28. In that respect the word עֹרֶף, *neck* in Hebrew is usually translated as "back," i.e., the back of the neck or nape especially in military contexts. The idiomatic expression "to give the neck" has been translated as "*to flee*" (from the enemy). For example: "O Lord, what can I say, now that Israel has turned their backs (necks), to their enemies!" (Josh 7:8), "Therefore the Israelites are unable to stand before their enemies; they turn their backs (necks) to their enemies." (Josh 7:12), "I will make all your enemies turn their backs (necks) to you." (Exod 23:27). Thus "*to give the neck*" has been translated as "*to turn the back*." 2 Chr 29:6, Ps 18:40; Jer 2:27; 32:33. The imagery of the enemy lament is predominantly military as we will see, and Job is conceptualizing God as an enemy, so it is possible that Job is seeing himself as a defeated soldier who ran for his life but whose enemy was faster and finally caught him.

A Socio-Cognitive Approach: Definition and Assumptions

To date, an integration of language, cognition, and context has been suggested in metaphor research.[29] It would seem however, that such an approach has not yet been systematized. Accordingly, I am suggesting the following definition: A socio-cognitive approach to metaphor describes a method in which the contextual, cognitive, linguistic, and bodily properties of metaphor are taken into account when interpreting it.[30] This approach considers that all these properties are reciprocally connected, and essential for accurate interpretation of metaphor, especially ancient metaphor.

This paper suggests three main steps. First, the identification of any lexical items that are being used metaphorically. Second, the investigation of the socio-cultural sources that may be nurturing the metaphor. Third, the identification of the concept implied in the metaphorical language.

To identify the linguistic metaphors, I will use the procedure called MIP (metaphor identification procedure), for identifying linguistic metaphors in text and speech.[31] The linguistic identification is used here in order to avoid arbitrary decisions and biases in the identification of metaphor,[32] and to avoid confusions between linguistic and conceptual metaphors.[33] When identifying a metaphorical item, MIP suggests four stages. One: read the whole text. Two: establish which lexical items are being used metaphorically in the discourse. In this stage I identified at least thirty-nine items being used metaphorically in Job 16:7–14.[34] For

29. Cameron, "Operationalising Metaphor," 4–5, 8, 10, 12.

30. The socio-cognitive model should not be confused with the social-cognitive approach. The difference is that a socio-cognitive approach would see the metaphors of the enemy lament as the result of Job's exposure to his culture, language, society, religion, bodily experiences, and cognition (the way Job thinks and perceives things). On the other hand, a social-cognitive approach would argue that the metaphors of Job 16:7–14 are directly related to the observation and imitation of social practices and interactions in Job's society. See Miller and Dollard. *Social Learning and Imitation*; Bandura, "Social Cognitive Theory." See also Bandura et al., "Transmission of Aggression through Imitation," 575–82.

31. Pragglejaz Group, "MIP," 3.

32. Krennmayr, "Linguistic Metaphor Identification," 97–115.

33. The MIP, a reliable procedure for identifying linguistic metaphor, prevents researchers from seeing "concrete manifestations of conceptual metaphors everywhere." See Krennmayr, "Linguistic Metaphor Identification," 100.

34. "Job", "God," "worn me out," "desolate," and "company" (v. 7). "Shrivelled me up," "witness," and "testifies" (v. 8). "Torn," "wrath," "hate," "gnashes," "teeth,"

the time being I will limit the analysis to one metaphorical expression in Job 16:12, *he dashes me to pieces.* Three: compare the contextual meaning of the identified lexical item with its basic meanings, e.g., contextually, Job uses the phrase ויפרפרני, *he dashes me to pieces,* to say that he is overwhelmed with pain and suffering.[35] On the other hand, the more basic meaning of the verb פרר is *to break* in the sense of to make void, violate, or nullify a contract or covenant.[36] Once we have compared the contextual and the basic meaning of the lexical item, the researcher should ask the two following questions: does the contextual meaning of פרר, *to break,* clearly contrast with the basic meaning? If so, can these meanings be understood in some form of comparison?

The answer to the above questions is yes. This is because the contextual meaning (breaking Job in pieces), and the basic meaning (say, breaking the covenant), clearly contrast, yet they still can be understood in some form of comparison, as shown in the following examples: the earth is broken (Isa 24:19), the covenant can be broken (Lev 26:44), the law can be broken (Ps 119:126), and a person can be broken (Job 16:12). In fact, the verb פרר, *to break,* was mostly used figuratively, and occurs in around fifty different contexts with the predominant sense of "break."[37] Given the fact that although the meanings contrast, yet they can be understood when compared, the lexical item פרר, *shattered* or *break in pieces,* in Job 16:12 can be classified as metaphorically used.[38]

Having identified ויפרפרני as a lexical item used metaphorically, we will proceed with the *second step:* investigate what socio-cultural, linguistic or bodily sources are nurturing this sentence. In Job's case, the socio-cultural influences that shape the metaphor, *he shattered me to pieces,* are predominantly mythological, i.e., combats between Yhwh and the forces of chaos, battles against dragons, battles in or against the sea, battles

---

"adversary," "sharpens," and "eyes" (v. 9). "Smitten," "cheek," and "mass themselves" (v. 10). "Pushes," "hands," and "turns me over" (v. 11). "At ease," "broke me in two," "he has seized," "by the neck," "dash me to pieces," "set me up," "set," and "target," (v. 12). "His archers," "surround me," "slashes open," "kidneys," "spare," "pours out," and "gallbladder" (v. 13). "Breaks me," "breach upon breach," (v. 14a). The lament finishes with a simile: He rushes at me like a warrior (v. 14b).

35. See Renn, *Expository Dictionary*, 143.

36. Lev 26:44; Isa 33:8; Ezek. 17:16; Ps 119:126; 2 Sam 15:34; Ps 33:10; Job 5:12; Prov 15:22; Isa. 44:25.

37. See Renn, *Expository Dictionary*, 142

38. See Pragglejaz Group, "MIP," 3; Krennmayr, "Linguistic Metaphor Identification," 100.

between gods, etc. In these battles, Yhwh uses tools such as a powerful hammer to *shatter his enemies to pieces.*[39]

Once the possible sources have been identified, *the third step* is to identify the conceptual metaphor: Job conceptualizes his suffering in terms of severe physical damage, i.e., *shattered to pieces.* However, God did not shatter him physically, thus Job must be referring to emotional and psychological damages. Therefore, the underlying concept is EMOTIONAL ABUSE IS PHYSICAL DAMAGE.

This is the way I am suggesting for bridging the socio-cognitive gap between the Jobian world and ours. I am aware of the fact that the analysis of concepts falls out of the domain of the linguistic and contextual analysis of metaphor. This is because what may have motivated Job to apply the vehicle PHYSICAL DAMAGE, to the topic EMOTIONAL HARM, is to be found, not as result of a linguistic or contextual analysis, but at a level of concepts.[40] However, concepts do not exist independently of socio-cultural factors; on the contrary, they are limited and shaped by them. In that respect Lakoff argues that "human concepts are not random or arbitrary, they are highly structured and limited, because of the limits and structure of the brain, the body, and the world."[41]

Similarly, in his socio-cultural theory of human learning, Vygotsky argues that social interaction plays a fundamental role in the development of cognition.[42] Vygotsky's experiments showed that speeches are extremely sensitive to social factors. That is, speeches are socially and environmentally oriented, so development in thought, he concluded, is not from the individual to the society, but from the society to the individual.[43] If society plays such a remarkable role in the formation of speeches and concepts, then that implies that the meaning given to a metaphor can be as distinctive as the socio-cultural setting from where it emerged.[44]

39. See Clines, *Job 1–20*, 384; see also Newsom, "The Book of Job," 459; *HALOT* 2, 954.

40. See Leezenberg, *Context of Metaphor*, 251.

41. Lakoff and Nuñez, *Where Mathematics Comes From*, 1.

42. See Vygotsky, *Mind in Society*, 57; see also Wertsch, *Vygotsky and the Social Formation of the Mind*, 60–61.

43. See Emerson, *The Outer World and the Inner Speech*, 131.

44. Different cultures metaphorize body parts in different ways. For example, ancient China and ancient Israel conceptualized the heart as the centre of cognition, i.e., the heart thinks. See Yü, "The Chinese Heart as the Central Faculty of Cognition," 131–68; Mumford, "Emotional Distress in the Hebrew Bible," 92–97, and Pritzker, "Thinking Hearts, Feeling Brains," 251–74. Likewise, both ancient civilizations

Here lies the reason for the alarming reactions towards the metaphors, and the mode of expression, in the enemy lament: if the metaphors are analyzed apart from their language and socio-cultural setting, they will be misread, and arbitrary meanings will be given to their imagery.[45] If, as Vygotsky suggests, speeches are environmentally oriented then the imagery, as well as the mode of expression used to approach the Divine in Job 16:7–14, is being molded by ethnic, cultural, and social influences. So, what may seem irreverent or blasphemous in our society, might have been acceptable in Job's.[46]

In fact, lamenting has a cultural dimension as well. This is shown in that searching for God, and arguing with him, is manifested in cultural expressions, mediated by an ancient Israelite socio-religious context, and nurtured by non-Israelite cultures.[47] Therefore, premises alien to the worldview of the ancient Hebrews, may not be helpful in achieving a serious understanding of the place, and role of this language, in their religion.

---

conceptualized the gallbladder in terms of a container of emotions. In ancient Israel, however, the gallbladder was a container of bitterness, while in ancient China it was a container of courage. See Yü, "Metaphor, Body, and Culture," 13–31; see also Clines, *Job 1–20*, 384–85.

45. See Gunton, *The One the Three, and the Many*, 212. A social unit is an indispensable aspect of semiotic activity. See Emerson, "The Outer World and the Inner Speech," 125.

46. Socio-cognitive elements facilitate the Jobian mode of addressing the Divine. For example, ancient Israel have a *wider repertoire of concepts* for God (zoological, military, domestic, positive and negative, etc), hence a larger set of metaphors for the Divine. Also according to Frank, for ancient Hebrew *God is by nature argumentative*. The Hebrew Bible depicts him arguing with Abraham (Gen 18), changing opinion after an argument with Moses (Exod 32:13–14), challenging Job to a verbal duello (Job 38:1–42:6), and inviting humans to enter into an argument with him (Isa 1:18). Another element that may explain why Job can interact with God in such a manner is that the ancient Israelite assumes that *God is good*, and not malevolent or distant. See Frank, "Arguing" 73–74; Tidwell, "Holy Argument," 486–87; Laytner, *Arguing with God*, xix–xx; Lefkowitz, *Greek Gods, Human Lives*. See also Grady, "Image Schema and Perception," 35, 44; Gentner, *Metaphor is Like Analogy*, 207.

47. Sperling, "Israel's Religion in Ancient Near East," 8–12; Green, "Introduction," xviii; Tisdell, *Exploring Spirituality*.

THE ENEMY LAMENT

Lastly, I will apply the steps suggested above to the metaphors of Job 16:7–14. As we consider Job's portrayal of God, it will become clear why this text has been called *the enemy lament*. Job begins his depiction of God by saying: *you have made desolate all my company.*[48] Here God is conceptualized in terms of a physical force, a desolator who ravaged and killed Job's family, thus leaving him isolated and afflicted.[49] This term was primarily applied to places or settlements that could be literally "deserted" or "inhabited." By using the term השׁות *desolate*, Job gives us the first conceptual metaphor: GOD IS AN INVADING ENEMY. Once he is left without support, Job's conceptual world changes from a disaster zone, to a court room. Verse 8 introduces two witnesses who come forward to speak against him: *wrinkles* and *leanness*. Here, Job personifies his chronic emaciation and skin disease as witnesses who tell everyone that he is a dreadful sinner.[50] The sores and the wrinkles are the evidences that Job sinned against God.[51] In this sense, A CHRONIC DISEASE IS A HOSTILE PERSON.[52]

48. Job 16:7. Delitzsch argues that Job "means to say that he stands entirely alone without any support, and completely shut up to himself" (Keil and Delitzsch, *Job*, 282).

49. One application of שׁמם was "to be removed from contact with other people because of deprivation or affliction" (as in 2 Sam 13:20; Isa 54:1), *HALOT* 2, 1564. A second word in verse 7 is עדתי, *my company*. Its contextual meaning is generally understood as "my closest family members and friends"; its basic meaning has cultic implications: עדה, was used to refer to "congregations" of the children of Israel, but here is used as a metaphor for Job's close ones (*HALOT* 1, 789–90). This metaphor introduces the theme of Job's involuntary social isolation. See Driver and Gray, *Job*, 144. Newsom suggests that this topic introduces the themes of personal isolation from the community of support, which are developed later on in 17:1–2, 7–9 and 11–14; Newsom, "The Book of Job," 458.

50. His wasted emaciated appearance, *told him to his face*, in other words, accused him, not merely behind his back, but boldly and directly, as if he were a convicted criminal (Keil and Delitzsch, *Job*, 282, 283).

51. The thought belongs to that complex of ideas in which fatness signifies prosperity, which in turn signifies divine pleasure (21:23–24; 15:27), and thinness signifies what is dried up, devoid of life. Clines argues that the psychic sense of being dried up, has previously come to expression in 13:25, and 14:7–9. See Clines, *Job* 1–20, 382.

52. According to *HALOT* 2, 1108–9, קמט has the sense of to seize, hold fast, press and depress. All the meanings suggested imply physical contact between God and Job. In relation to the same verse, כחשׁ *leanness* is conceptualized in terms of a biological failure (Ps 109:24; Isa 58:11). ובשרי כחש משמן, *and my flesh faileth of fatness* (KJV). The use of *failure* or *lie* used to describe an infirmity may be another metaphor used to conceptualize the origin of leanness, namely "to let someone down acting falsely. This

In verse 9, a more dangerous character joins the scene: אפו, *his anger*, which Job conceptualizes in terms of a savage animal who tears Job's flesh, and gnashes its teeth at him. Basically אפ means *nose,* and is used interchangeably for both the organ as well as the emotion, anger.[53] The term טרף, *tears,* denotes the savage and disproportionate attacks of God on Job.[54] Its basic sense is "to pull or seize forcibly and to tear in pieces."[55] The earliest usages of טרף were applied to beasts and wild animals.[56] However, the metaphorical net was extended to humans, and even to God himself.[57]

The beast חרק *gnashes,* or threatens Job. According to Clines, the grinding of the teeth of this beast is a sure threat to the prey of its imminent devouring. The basic sense of חרק is "a strong and violent rage or fury that can boil into an all-out attack, usually physical at any moment."[58] The zoological imagery implies that Job is being savaged and mauled by God's anger.[59] The intention of the beast is not to wound Job, but to kill him. The beast ילטוש *sharpens* his eyes against Job. This conveys a sense of hatred: "a piercing look with murderous intent."[60] The primary meaning of the verb לטש is to hammer, to sharpen, or to whet swords, knives, axes

in turn may imply that the infirmity (leanness) is a person that has *failed* or *let down* the rest of the body by not fulfilling its biological part" (*HALOT* 1, 469–70).

53. The term אף anger, is used to refer to the nose of humans (Gen 2:7; Num 11:20) or of animals (Job 40:24); for the anger of men (Prov 22:24; 29:22), and the anger of God (Deut 32:22; 29:19; Job 36:13).

54. This may depict superhuman abilities to harm, and death threatening assaults (Balentine, *Job*, 252–53; Clines, *Job* 1–20, 382).

55. The verb טרף *to tear,* is related to the behavior of wild beasts (*HALOT* 1, 380).

56. Gen 37:33; 44:28; 49:27; Exod 22:12; Deut 33:20; Ezek 19:3–6; *HALOT*, 1, 380.

57. In this sense, great personal loss or collective catastrophes were seen as God *tearing apart the flesh* of the sufferer, but the imagery is also used to represent the violence of the enemies against the sufferer and the weak (Gen 37:33; 44:28; 49:27; Deut 33:20; Ps 22:14; 50:22; Hos 6:1; Nah 2:14). The term is used as a metaphor for anger, Job 16:9, 18:4, and conceptualizes God as a beast, see Job 50:22; Hos 1:6; Exod 22:15; Jer 5:6; *HALOT* 1, 380.

58. See Ryken, *Dictionary of Biblical Imagery*, 847; *HALOT* 1, 356.

59. חרק is never applied to animals in the Hebrew Bible, its first use is in Job 16:9, elsewhere the subjects are the wicked and the psalmist's enemies (Clines, *Job 1–20,* 382; see Job 16:9; Pss 35:16; 37:12, 112:10; Lam 2:16; Acts 7:54).

60. Clines, *Job 1–20,* 38. Balentine describes it as a "murderous focus," (*Job*, 252). Delitzsch comments that the intent of the look is to pierce Job through (*Job*, 283).

etc.[61] *Eyes* cannot be sharpened like a knife or a sword, so the phrase is understood as the description of a hateful look.[62]

I would like to clarify who is being bestialized in verse 9. The singular noun אף *anger,* has a third person masculine singular suffix, אפו, literally, *his anger.* This implies that anger is the subject of the sentence, and it is carrying out the *tearing, gnashing and sharpening*.[63] The implication is that God is not being bestialized as in Lam 3:10–11, but it is *his anger* that is being personified, thus implying the conceptual metaphor: GOD'S ANGER IS A SAVAGE BEAST. There are other conceptual metaphors implied in verse 9 which will be better identified if I divide the verse into smaller units:

22. *His anger has torn me*: GOD'S ANGER IS A FEROCIOUS BEAST
23. *and hated me*: GOD'S ANGER IS A HOSTILE ANIMAL
24. *He has gnashed his teeth at me*: GOD'S ANGER IS A THREATENING BEAST
25. *my enemy:* GOD'S ANGER IS A FEROCIOUS OPPONENT
26. *Sharpens his eyes against me:* GOD'S ANGER IS A BEAST WITH MURDEROUS INTENTS

The metaphor also implies God, in the sense that he is the owner of this animal. Yet while this animal clamped its sharp teeth around Job's body, God stands by and does nothing to stop this protracted and vicious attack. Thus, in verse 9, GOD IS AN INDIFFERENT MASTER. When the animal is done with Job, a mob joins the scenario, and starts beating him up with their hands, probably while he still lies half dead on the ground.

61. See Gen 4:22; 1 Sam 13:20. It was also used in relation to an evil tongue (Pss 52:2; 64:3; 140:3). The verb is used in relation to "brandish a sword and "to sharpen an edge" (*HALOT* 1, 528). This look in the eyes of a beast may indicate hatred towards *Job* in Job 16:9 (Ryken, *Dictionary of Biblical Imagery*, 56).

62. Out of the five times לטש *to sharpen* is used in the OT (Gen 4:22; 1 Sam 13:20; Job 16:9; Ps 7:12; 52:2; Job 16:9) only twice it is applied to members of the body (Ps 52:2; Job 16:9).

63. And not "in his anger," which would imply that Job portrays God in terms of a wild animal as rendered by the KJV and NRSV, but rather like in the case of Gen 39:19; Num. 11:1; Deut 13:18; Josh 7:26; etc., where אפו, is translated *his anger.* Hence, *His anger has torn me and hunted me down* (NASB). Anger performs or does the actions described in the verbs, "torn," "hate," "gnash," "look," and receives the transferred epithet "my enemy." See Balentine, *Job*, 252.

The phrase *they struck me on the cheek*, הכו לחיי in verse 10b describes the mockery and humiliation Job was submitted to. The basic sense of נכה, the hiphil, is "to strike, to hit or injure and to pierce."[64] Thus Job conceptualizes the verbal humiliation he went through in terms of a physical beating. Accordingly, Clines suggest that since slapping the cheek is the insult בחרפה *with scorn*, must refer to derogatory words that accompanied the insults.[65] So, the blows here seem to be inflicted more for the sake of humiliation, than physical injury.[66] This expression depicts words in terms of blows, thus implying the conceptual metaphor VERBAL ABUSE IS A PHYSICAL BEATING. In verse 11 God steps in, not to stop the beating, but to negotiate with the wicked: יסגירני *he gave me up to the ungodly*, Job laments, i.e., God *handed over or betrayed* him.[67] Basically he סגר *delivers* or *surrenders* Job, knowing the outcome will be negative for him.[68] Once the transaction is over, God *pushes him* into the hands of the wicked. God's push ירטני was harsh and rude, destined to precipitate Job to destruction.[69] Thus, in verse 11, GOD IS A TRAITOR and BETRAYAL IS VIOLENT PRESSURE AGAINST THE BODY.

64. See *HALOT* 1, 697–98.

65. בחרפה also means *with abuse, scorn, disgrace*. See Ezek 21:33, 1 Sam 25:39; Clines, *Job*, 383. This is probably why Habel suggests that "the action of smiting the check, jaw (10b) may be carrying the image beyond the domain of wild beast, and implying ritual gestures of disgrace" (1 Kgs 22:24; Mic 4:14, [5:1E]; *The Book of Job*, 272).

66. Slapping the cheek is a human gesture, hence the imagery is not returning to the metaphor of the wild beast. Contextually this gesture has been understood as disdain, emotional pain caused by social humiliation (Hartley, *The Book of Job*, 261).

67. Job is being handed over into the hands or the control of, the wicked. The idiom, "to give into the hands of" is used to speak of exercising authority, e.g., Gen 9:6; 1:26–28; Num 33:1; Josh 2:24; 6:2; 8:1; Judg 3:28 etc; see Ryken, *Dictionary of Biblical Imagery*, 361. Now Job who is being delivered into the hands of the wicked, and God is conceptualized as a traitor. See Clines, *Job 1–20*, 376.

68. The term *to give up* also means to "withdraw support, care and attention from someone," and to give up and hand over to a third party, to be handled as he/she pleases. In 1 Samuel it is used with the sense of betrayal (1 Sam 23:11,12; cf. Deut. 23:16). In the Hiphil, "to give into someone's power," "hand over," "deliver," (1 Sam 23:11; Deut 23:16; Amos 1:6); "surrender someone," (Deut 32:20); "to arrest," (Job 11:10); "to separate and seclude," (Lev 13:4–54); "Isolate," (Lev 14:38, 46). See for example Job 2:6; 9:24, 16:11; 24:14; *HALOT*,1, 185. See also Muraoka, *A Greek-English Lexicon*, 433–34.

69. ירט *to push*, not only means to throw (*Gesenius's Hebrew and Chaldee Lexicon*, 368), but also "to fall defeated or exhausted in battle" (Gen 49:17); "by the sword" (Hos 7:7; 16; 14:1; Amos 7:17); referring to casualties in battle field (Judg 2:8); "killed" (Lev 26:7); casualties not specifically in battle field (Exod 19:21, 32:28); to collapse a building or part of it (Amos 3:14; 9:11). See Keil and Delitzsch, *Job*, 285; Muraoka, *A Greek*

While the mob takes him away Job remembers that once he "*was at ease*." In verse 12 the adjective שׁלו means "untroubled or unaware of danger."[70] The early uses of this word are related to political and military contexts.[71] Clines suggests that the thought is reminiscent of Judg 18:7–27, where the people inhabiting Laish are said to have been "*at ease*" and "*unsuspecting*" before they were attacked by the Danites. Thus, by awaking the memories of Laish Job conceptualizes himself in terms of a city and God in terms of an army.[72] Hence, AN UNSUSPECTING HEART IS A VULNERABLE CITY and GOD IS AN ENEMY ARMY. After surprising him, God *breaks* Job *in two* and *dashes him to pieces* (v. 12). These sentences "indicate the fierceness and savagery of God's attacks on Job."[73] The basic meaning of ויפרפרני from פרר is "to break up entirely, crush and crumble in pieces."[74] The primary meaning of the intense form ויפצפצני, from פצץ, is *to brake in pieces.*[75] This duplicated pilpel is also used in the context of battle. When compared, these two meanings give the idea that Job is being beaten savagely or dismembered by God.[76] Hence, EMOTIONAL DISTRESS IS MILITARY BRUTALITY. The merciless beating

English Lexicon, 458; *Gesenius's Hebrew and Chaldee Lexicon*, 368; *HALOT* 1, 438.

70. According to Balentine the basic sense of *I was at easy*, basically is "tranquil and unsuspecting" (*Job*, 252).

71. Clines obverses, that שׁלו, "to be quiet or untroubled," occurs sometimes in military and political contexts (1 Chr 4:40; Zech 7:7), and is said of a land or a city, differently in Dan 4:1[7]. The phrase can be translated as *"quiet and at ease,"* continually quiet or continually in luck, (Jer. 49:31; Zech 7:7; Job 16:12; 21:23; 1 Chr 4:40; Sir. 41:1; *HALOT* 2, 1505).

72. Clines, *Job 1–20*, 384.

73. The attack is "disproportionate, savage and forceful" (Balentine, *Job*, 252). Delitzsch calls the act of grabbing Job by the neck, raising him on high in order to dash him to the ground with all his might "the enraged of God against Job" (*Job IV*, 285), see also Hartley, *The Book of Job*, 261.

74. The Pilpel ויפרפרני, of Job 16:12 means "to savage," or "to break in two," "tug or shake someone about," "to break to bits," "shatter to split," "divide" (*HALOT* 2, 975).

75. The LXX translated the corresponding intense form ויפצפצני, as *dietilen* literally: "he has plucked me," a metaphor for, "he has taken all I had." However, it also means "*He has shattered me,*" and "*he has dismembered me.*" Driver translates it as, "he has mauled me." See *HALOT* 2, 954.

76. According to Clines, these duplicated Pilpel forms, probably interactive or intensive in force, are used in the context of combat, (Ps 74:13, 24:19) and likewise פצץ, (Hab 3:6; Jer 23:29; *Job*, 384). Newsom argues that these verbs not only denote shattering into pieces, but are also used elsewhere to describe God as a divine warrior, "breaking open" (פרר Ps 74:13), the chaotic sea, and "shattering" (פצץ Hab 3:6) the mountains ("The Book of Job," 459).

continues in verse 12 as God ואחז בערפי, *seized* Job *by the neck*. The term אחז, "seize," indicates Job's vulnerability and subjection, the basic sense "being bound or seized" by the neck depicts capture and subjection; in a military context, עֹרֶף, *neck* usually denotes the back of the neck, i.e., the nape.[77] Delizsch argues that by "taking him by the neck, God raises him on high in order to dash him on the ground with all his might."[78]

In verse 13 it is said that *God sets Job for his target*. The basic sense of קום "to set" in the hiphil is "to arise one (thing or person) that is fallen down."[79] Once more, God picks him up from the ground, but this time puts him in a particular place, and starts practicing aiming and shooting,[80] hence, GOD IS AN ENEMY ARCHER. Soon God's archers join the shooting and surround Job, the sentence יסבו עלי רביו *his archers surround me* (v. 13), contextually implies that Job has been ambushed by a numerous enemy troop, or God's band of soldiers.[81]

The primary meaning of סבב is "to march or walk around," thus; military personifications depict Job's enclosure on all sides.[82] This implies another change of conceptual scenery in which JOB IS A BESIEGED

77. In Scripture the act of taking some one by the neck is performed only against enemies (Gen 49:8), usually in military contexts the enemies are taken by the nape. (Exod 32:27; Josh 7:8, 12; Ps 18:40). This comparison is evoking imageries of combat, but in this case it is Job's neck that is being grabbed and not that of an enemy, and by someone he considered a closed friend before. See Ryken, *Dictionary of Biblical Imagery*, 591–92.

78. Keil and Delitzsch, *Job*, 285.

79. See Deut 22:4; it also means "to lift up the afflicted," (Job 4:4; Ps 41:11); "to set up a tent," (Exod 26:30); "a statue," (Deut 16:22); "an altar," (1 Kgs 16:32); "towers," (Isa 23:13); "to set up again a tent that has fallen down," (Amos 5:11); "to cause to stand," (Ps 40:3); "to cause to stand still or restrain," (Ps 107:29; see *HALOT* 1, 1086–88).

80. As suggested in the Hiphil *caused him to arise*, erect or build Job as a target. Clines argues that, קום, *to set*, evidently means to mark something or somebody as a target (*Job 1–20*, 384).

81. The concept implied in the term רב, involves arrows, and those who are throwing them at Job. Although the versions differ in their translations of רב, *many*, in Job 16:13, I will be adopting the translation, *his archers*, as suggested by scholars such as Clines and others considered above (*HALOT* 1, 1173–78). Among those who translate רביו, as "his archers," are Balentine, *Job*, 253, Habel, *Job*, 273; Clines, *Job 1–20*, 384; Driver and Gray, *Job*, 106; Newson, *Job*, 459.

82. It also means "go partly around," "circle about or encircle," (2 Kgs 8:21; 2 Chr 21:9; Ps 118:10–12); "surround," (2 Sam 22:6; 1 Kgs 5:17, 7:15–23; 2 Kgs 6:15; Jer 52:21; Hos 7:2; Ps 17:11; 18:6, 13–17); "encompass." In a hostile sense, Eccl 9:14, also followed by אל (also 2 Kgs 8:20 Judg 20:5; Gen 37:7; and Job 16:13; see *HALOT* 1, 738–40).

CITY, GOD IS A MILITARY COMMANDER, and UNFORTUNATE EVENTS ARE ENEMY SOLDIERS.

During the shooting, *God shows no mercy*, and inflicts a fatal wound on Job.[83] The arrows split כליותי, *Job's kidneys,* and the bile from his מררה, *gallbladder,* is spilled out on the ground. The basic sense of יפלח is "to cleave" (Piel from פלח "to split open, to pierce through").[84] This sentence seems to depict deep emotional harm as כליה, *kidneys,* represent not only a vital organ, but also the center of one's emotions and passions.[85] Hence, a deep emotional wound is conceptualized in verse 13. Job must be deeply disappointed in God for everything that is happening in his life, so he concludes that EMOTIONAL OR PSYCHOLOGICAL HARM IS PHYSICAL DAMAGE TO VITAL ORGANS. The other organ that is affected by God's arrows is the gallbladder, the secretion of the liver, which God ישפך, *pours out*[86] on the ground as he punctures this organ with his arrows.[87] The gallbladder, or bile, has been always known as something bitter. The term is derived from the stative verb מרר, "to be bitter," so bitterness seems to be spilling out from Job's inmost parts

83. Some ancient versions render רביו:, as "his darts," "his arrows or projectiles," (*BDB*, 912–13; *HALOT* 1, 1173; Keil and Delitzsch, *Job,* 285–86. *HALOT* 1, 738–40, 753). Hartly does not make reference to "archers," when commenting on Job 16:13; he says that it is God who "taking careful aim, shoots at the target without relenting" (*The Book of Job,* 261). If the translation is taken to mean his arrows, as Delitzsch proposes, then the arrows are images of divine decree against Job (*Job*, 286).

84. See Prov 7:23; Job 16:13. It also means "to cut into slices or pieces" (2 Kgs 4:39); and "split the mouth of the womb," as a metaphor for "giving birth" (Job 39:3; see *HALOT* 1, 930).

85. Balentine, *Job*, 253. Kidneys are part of a sacrificial animal (Exod 29:13–22; Lev 3:4, 10, 15; 4:9; 7:4; 8:16, 25; 9:10, 19; Deut 32:14; Isa 34:6) and symbolic of the "innermost or most secret part"; *kidneys* is parallel to heart in Jer 12:2; Pss 73:21; 139:13; Job 16:13; 19:27; Prov 23:13. Kidneys provide a metaphor for the interior of the wheat grain (Deut 32:14; see *HALOT* 1, 479), and the "*inmost mind,*" as the seat of the desires and affections (Jer 11:20).

86. The primary uses of שׁפך *to pour out* are related to the shedding of blood (Gen 9:6), water (Exod 4:9), dust (Lev 14:4), bowels (2 Sam 20:10). It is also used in a cultic sense, to pour water before the Lord (1 Sam 7:6), a drink offering (1 Sam 57:6); also as a metaphor "to pour out anger" (Jer 6:11); his spirit (Ezek 39:29); one's evil (Jer 16:14); to pour one's heart (Ps 62:9); symbols of speaking one's mind (1 Sam 1:15). The word implies the deliberate act of killing, with the exception of the acts of vengeance, it is considered a criminal act (*HALOT* 1, 1629–30).

87. Delitzsch argues that although Job is speaking figuratively here, the imagery is disturbing (*Job*, 286).

(kidneys and gallbladder), as a result of his disappointment.[88] Thus, BITTERNESS IS A LIQUID SUBSTANCE THAT FLOWS FROM A BROKEN CONTAINER.

The city is besieged, the enemy is down, but one last obstacle stands in God's way, hindering him from taking over it. This last obstacle is implied in the metaphorical phrase: *he breaks through me with breach after breach.*[89] In this case, Job uses the verb פרץ *to break through*, which is used to describe the breaching or tearing down of walls, and the breaching of cities. Job also uses the noun *breach.*[90] This is an example of a metaphor rooted in military operations, specifically warfare and combat techniques. Breaching or drilling walls was a common practice among enemy armies when taking a city.[91] Consequently, Job is conceptualizing himself in terms of a walled city, while God is being conceptualized as a battering ram.[92] This sentence implies the conceptual metaphors: A PERSON IN DISTRESS IS A BREACHED WALL, and GOD IS A BATTERING RAM.

88. In Exod 15:23 and Num 33:8 the term is applied to the bitterness of the waters, the word has also been translated as "sorrow or sadness of spirit," (Gen 26:35); מרר, and grief (Prov 14:10; see *HALOT* 1, 633). If the affections and sympathies have been assaulted, it is bitterness that spills out (Clines, *Job* 1–20, 384–85). This word is also used when referring to Divine mistreatment, harshness and calamity (Ruth 1:21). Thus, the terms used refer to "bitter emotions," caused by suffering as result of a bad experience, hence the embittered heart (*HALOT* 1, 629).

89. This imagery evokes the breaking of Job (Newsom, "The Book of Job," 459). Delitzsch argues that this breaking is due to the arrows or battering-rams of God (*Job*, 286; cf. *HALOT* 1, 971–72)

90. פרץ is used generally to mean "to breach or burst out" (Gen 38:29; 2 Sam 6:8); "to make a breach in a wall" (2 Kgs 14:13); "to breach a city" (Prov 25:28); "breaches" (Neh 2:13); "to tear down a wall" (Isa 5:5); "break into a house" (2 Chr 24:7); "break through" (Mic 2:13); "break out among or against" (2 Kgs 5:23). Thus Job compares himself to a wall that was repeatedly broken through (Keil and Delitzsch, *Job*, 286). The singular noun פרץ, indicates "ruptures and death," and it is used in the context of making a breach (2 Sam 5:20; 1 Kgs 11:27), "rupture of a woman in childbirth" (Gen 38:28); "rupture of relations between tribes" (Judg 21:15); "and death" (Ps 144:14); "to make a split," "to make a breach," "to break through," "breach," "gap," etc. (*HALOT* 1, 971–73).

91. One of the ways of taking a city was by breaking or breaching the city walls. See 2 Kgs 14:13; 2 Chr 25:23; 26:6. See also Ryken, *Dictionary of Biblical Imagery*, 923.

92. The battering ram had a metal point on the end, and was used to batter a hole in the wall. This did not take long, given that the walls were more often than not made of mud-brick. See Rocca and Hook, *The Fortifications of Ancient Israel and Judah*, 47. See also Gabriel, *The Military History of Ancient Israel*, 48.

Finally, the wall is breached, God seizes the opportunity, penetrates the city and *rushes* towards Job כגבור *like a mighty warrior.* However, God is not coming to Job's aid as expected from the Divine warrior in the Hebrew Bible,[93] but rather to single combat, probably to settle the issue between the two, as was the custom in antiquity.[94] When the word רוץ, "rushes," is followed by אל or על (as here ירץ עלי) it denotes a hostile manner.[95] So in the last scene, God is seen running towards Job getting ready to inflict the final blow. Before he reaches Job however, the curtains come down, and we are left to imagine what happened next. In such an enigmatic fashion finishes the portrayal of God according to the man of Uz.

CONCLUSION

This paper has considered the role of metaphor in conceptualizing the Divine in Job 16:7–14. It has demonstrated the limitations of previous approaches to metaphor, and highlights reasons for using a socio-cognitive approach. Metaphor is not a mere rhetorical ornament but, as in the enemy lament, is an indicator of how we understand and experience the world, and how we interpret those experiences.[96]

The paper also analyzed the effect of integrating language, context, and cognition in the analysis of metaphor, and suggested the steps to be taken into account if this integration was to be systematized, and its results assessed. Returning to the hypothesis posed at the beginning of this paper, it is now possible to suggest that the advantages of approaching the

93. In every other passage where God is called גבור, *mighty warrior,* salvific power is being hymned (Isa 42:13; Jer 20:11; Zeph 3:17; Ps 24:8; 78:65). Here in a shocking reversal of Israelite piety, he has the character of the enemy of the psalmists, namely, the "mighty man" that boasts of mischief against the godly. See Ps 52:3[1] cf. 124:4, where the warrior is specifically an archer. See Balentine, *Job*, 253; and Clines, *Job 1–20*, 385.

94. See 1 Sam 2:12–17; 21:15–22; 23:20; as Tsumura notes, biblical as well as extra-biblical evidence portrays the champion "as a man who steps out to fight between the two lines," like David and Goliath in 1 Sam 17, and here in Job 16:14 (Tsumura, *The First Book of Samuel*, 440).

95. Cf. Job 30:14; Ps 80:13[12]; 89:41[40]; Amos 4:1; 1 Kgs 11:27; Isa 5:5; Neh 3:35,[4.3]. First, God acts like an overwhelming army, inflicting one breach on another upon the city's walls. The attack of the city has one man's defeat as its object: Job is both the city, and its lone inhabitant. The flow of the imagery mirrors the onward rush of the invader.

96. See Lakoff and Johnson, *Metaphors We Live By*, 3. See also Solove, *The Digital Person*, 27–30; and Black, *Models and Metaphor*.

metaphors of Job 16:7–14 from a socio-cognitive perspective are clearly supported by the fact that this approach bridges the gap that separates us from the Jobian world.

This is because the integration of language, cognition, and context, unearths ancient social and linguistic phenomena, which clarifies what otherwise may be obscure concepts and blurred imagery. The hermeneutical implications of analyzing the metaphors of Job 16:7–14 from this perspective were seen in the wider repertoire of the imaginary characters, conceptual sceneries, military weapons, and mythological events that make up Job 16:7–14. The implications were seen in broader and more accurate identification of conceptual metaphors. It was also pointed out that laments have a cultural dimension. Thus to argue that Job is blasphemous, or irreverent, in the way he laments, is to overlook the fact that the motivational basis for the way he addresses God, and argues with him, is mediated by the ancient Israelite socio-religious context, the same elements that make up the metaphors. Therefore, our worldviews may not be helpful in achieving a serious understanding of the way Job interacts with the Divine in this lament. Finally, approaching the language of the enemy lament as it is, metaphorical, and researching these metaphors from a socio-cognitive perspective, will lead not only to a more accurate interpretation of the language, imagery, and the theology therein, but also to a better understanding of the way ancient Israelites lamented before the Divine.

6

Blurring the Boundaries

The Rhetoric of Lament and Penitence in Isaiah 63:7—64:11

Elizabeth Boase

The affinity between Isa 63:7—64:11 and the psalms of communal lament has long been noted.[1] Similarities with the book of Lamentations, and the penitential prayers of Ezra 9 and Neh 9 have also been identified.[2] Discussion as to the relationship between these texts has frequently been based within the methodological framework of form and/or tradition criticism,[3] however, within this chapter, Isa 63:7—64:11 will be discussed from the perspective of the rhetorical and ideological climate of the exilic and post-exilic period, drawing on the literary framework of Mikhail

1. See, for example, Westermann, *Isaiah 40–66*, 386; Hanson, *Isaiah 40–66*, 235; Blenkinsopp, *Isaiah 56–66*, 61; Childs, *Isaiah*, 522; Seitz, "Isaiah 40–66," 526.

2. E.g., Seitz, "Isaiah 40–66," 524; Bautch, *Developments in Genre*; Williamson, "Exilic Lament?" 48–58.

3. See Bautch, *Developments in Genre*, 1–12 for an overview of recent research. Bautch notes that source criticism has also been important in the literature. One of the purposes of Bautch's study relates to intertextual sources and allusions, in part in the service of relative dating, but also in order to map the development of the genre in the post-exilic period. Bautch's focus is not on how the communal lament was lost in the post-exilic period, but rather has a more positive perspective of tracing the transformation in the tradition.

Bakhtin.[4] The chapter seeks to argue that Isaiah 63:7—64:11, through its participation in and modification of the communal lament genre, enters into an ongoing dialogue between the ideological/theological framework of the communal laments and the emerging, dominant Deuteronomistic/Priestly (Dtr/P) framework so strongly evident in the penitential prayers of Ezra/Nehemiah.

In order to explore the rhetorical engagement of Isa 63:7—64:11, the nature and function of genre will be explored, followed by a discussion of the broad rhetorical context of the text. This will lead to a more detailed examination of the way this particular text both reflects and engages with the changing rhetorical environment in the post-exilic period.

FROM FORM CRITICISM TO GENRE THEORY

Isaiah 63:7—64:11 is a key text in studies that trace the development of penitential prayer in the exilic and post-exilic periods. Using form-critical analysis, it has been argued that penitential prayer replaces lament as the dominant communal prayer form in response to crisis within this period.[5] It has been noted that the two prayer forms have in common many structural elements, and on this basis it is argued that penitential prayer develops out of, and may even replace, the communal lament.[6]

Many of these studies have been classificatory in nature, working within a framework of genre which might define its purpose as the identification of "a group of written texts marked by distinctive recurring characteristics which constitute a recognizable and coherent type of writing."[7] Although form criticism and genre studies have much in

4. Rom-Shiloni, "Socio-Ideological Setting," 51–68, does consider the rhetorical and ideological environment which led to the emergence of the penitential prayer, but does not do so from a dialogical perspective.

5. Westermann, *Praise and Lament*, 171. For a summary of the history of form criticism in relation to penitential prayer see Boda, "Form Criticism in Transition," 181–92.

6. Early discussions suggested that in the emergence of penitential prayer replaced lament (see, e.g., Brueggemann, "The Costly Loss of Lament," 67–81). There are differing perspectives, however, on whether penitential prayer "replaced" lament or not. Bautch has demonstrated that lament does occur beyond the exilic period ("Lament Regained," 83–99), and Boda argues that lament is itself regained through penitential prayer ("The Priceless Gain of Penitence," 51–75).

7. Newsom, "Spying Out the Land," 20. In his opening address to the SBL consultation on Penitential Prayer, Werline offers a definition of penitential prayer in the hope

common, recent trends in genre studies have seen a significant shift away from this analytical/classificatory task.[8]

Christine Mitchell identifies that, historically, genre theory has moved through four phases;

1. *Genre as rules*: genre is understood to be the basis of textual production, thus placing the meaning of genre in the intention of the author.
2. *Genre as species*: the meaning/importance of genre is seen in its ability to classify texts and to trace the history of development and growth through time.
3. *Genre as patterns of textual features*: genre is understood as a means of identifying the patterns of textual features and forms, thus placing the meaning of genre in the text itself.
4. *Genre as reader conventions*: late twentieth-century theory locates the meaning of genre in the readers of texts as opposed to its location in the intention of the author, in the literary history of the text, or in the literary features of the text.[9]

Mitchell notes that much of biblical form criticism lies within the third stage, although studies that seek to trace the development of genres lie very much within the second stage.[10] Much of the recent work on Isaiah 63:7—64:11 falls within this stage, emerging as it does from a series of studies concerned with the development of penitential prayer within the second temple period.[11] Mitchell also identifies, however, that outside of biblical studies, literary genre theory has entered into yet a new phase

that it "enhance not inhibit our ability to speak clearly and concisely to one another (i.e., the participants in the consultation), and it should assist in making distinctions and comparisons between penitential prayer and what we see as related phenomena: various psalms, hymns, liturgies, litanies, confessions, and so forth. We can offer a definition of penitential prayer because a number of prayers exhibit a similar form and contain similar formulaic expressions" (Werline, "Defining Penitential Prayer," xiv).

8. Boda ("Form Criticism in Transition," 191) notes that the investigation of the development of penitential prayer from a form-critical perspective needs to be supplemented with rhetorical synchronic methodologies.

9. Mitchell, "Power, *Eros*, and Biblical Genres," 31.

10. Ibid. The seminal work Westermann, *Praise and Lament*, demonstrates this concern with the evolution of the psalms of lament. Westermann identifies that his investigation of the lament form works from the assumption that "*the lament has a history*" (168, italics original).

11. Boda, "Form Criticism in Transition," 185.

"that locates genre both in the text and in the reader, in text and in context, and in the combination and recombination of genres and fragments with each other."[12] This understanding of genre within the nexus of text, reader, and context is important for the current study. Rather than seeing genre as a means of classifying a given text in order to determine the "group" of texts to which it might belong, genre is considered as a more fluid, dynamic, entity. Genre is a means of communication and an instrument of meaning not a tool for classification.[13]

Genre plays an important role in the transmission of meaning, but does so in conjunction with content. Form and content cannot be separated. The Russian literary theorist Mikhail Bakhtin argues that form (genre) is the means by which the author and the reader can interact with the content of an utterance.[14] Genre, for Bakhtin, not only transmits meaning, but can reflect and shape social construction and social context. "The meaning of a text does not lie in the particular combination of devices but in the ways in which the text is produced, interpreted, transmitted and used."[15] Genre is "part of the discourse-network that constructs and constrains all social discourse."[16] A genre expresses a certain worldview.[17] To read a text within its genre is to "learn to think in that genre's terms."[18]

If genre is part of a discourse network, then there is a historical dimension to the understanding of genre. Central to Bakhtin's understanding of text is that every text is a reply to what has gone before. Extending from this, every genre is a response to every other instance of that genre, and is a reply also to other genres. This dialogic relationship "carries forward the ever changing configuration of the genres."[19]

12. Mitchell, "Power, *Eros*, and Biblical Genres," 31.

13. Newsom, "Spying Out the Land," 20–21.

14. Mitchell, "Power, *Eros*, and Biblical Genres," 33.

15. Coleby, cited by ibid.

16. Ibid., 34.

17. See Morson, "The Aphorism," 410–11, for brief discussion.

18. As cited by Mitchell ("Power, *Eros*, and Biblical Genres," 34). Medvedev states: "Every genre has its methods and means of seeing and conceptualizing reality, which are accessible to it alone. . . . The process of seeing and conceptualizing reality must not be severed from the process of embodying it in the forms of a particular genre. . . . The artist must learn to see reality with the eyes of the genre." (Cited by Newsom, "Spying out the Land," 29).

19. Newsom, "Spying Out the Land," 28.

Extending the importance of genre further, Bakhtin has argued that changes in genre reflect changes in social life.[20] Similarly, Opacki states

> Every literary trend—or phase of it—has underlying it certain defined socio-historical factors, which shape a specific attitude towards the world and a certain sphere of interests and problems. In turn, this brings with it the creation of a specific system of poetics, an ensemble of means of expression, of ways of structurally linking them, which—growing out of the "extra-literary" environment of the trend—carry in them historically specific meanings and functions.[21]

Genres are the expressions of worldview, and as such, not only represent the rhetorical environment, but are ideological instruments through their very representation of worldview.

If genre expresses a worldview, and is responsive to changes in the rhetorical environment, then an understanding of genre as a means of classification becomes even more problematic because classification assumes that genre is a fixed entity. Bakhtin argues that texts do not *belong* to a genre, but rather *participate* in them, and in this participation change the genre itself. A text can participate in a genre "by conformity, variation, innovation, or antagonism."[22] Genre is not static. Bakhtin captures this sense in his oft quoted paradoxical formulation "a genre is always the same, yet not the same, always old and new simultaneously."[23] Growing out of this assertion, Bakhtin refers to genre memory—"a genre lives in the present, but always remembers its past, its beginning. Genre is representative of creative memory in the process of literary development."[24]

If we take seriously the intersection between genre, context, and meaning, and also the fluid nature of genre, then it follows that changes in a rhetorical environment should be reflected within texts. In relation to the emergence of penitential prayer in ancient Israel, it is often noted that penitential prayer, in relation to the lament form, became the more dominant prayer in the post-exilic period. In the discussion that follows, Isa 63:7—64:11 will be viewed from the perspective of its participation in

20. Bakhtin, "The Problem of Speech Genre," 88.

21. Opacki, "Royal Genres," 119.

22. Newsom, "Spying Out the Land," 21.

23. Bakhtin, *Problems of Dostoevsky's Poetics*, 106.

24. Ibid.

the communal lament genre in the midst of a changing rhetorical context and as being reflective of a changing social discourse.

THE RHETORICAL CONTEXT OF ISAIAH 63:7—64:11

In order to discuss how Isa 63:7—64:11 engages in its rhetorical environment, it is first necessary to consider the possible dating of the text. Isaiah 55–66 is most commonly dated to the first century of Persian rule (ca. 522–422 BCE).[25] The dating of Isa 63:7—64:11 is more difficult to establish, with suggested dates ranging from the early post-destruction period,[26] through to as late as 302/1 BCE.[27] In support of an earlier date, Williamson has argued that the text was composed for liturgical recital at the site of the ruined temple, alongside Ps 106 and Neh 9:5–37.[28] Blenkinsopp argues, however, that the "structural and metrical irregularity of the composition and its close connection with the passage that follows could with equal plausibility favour the hypothesis of a purely literary work that imitates the language and themes of lament."[29] Broadly, the earliest likely date of this text is in the exilic period, most probably post-dating the book of Lamentations through to the first century of Persian rule.

The rhetorical context of the exilic and post-exilic period is dominated by the destruction of Jerusalem and the temple in 587 BCE and the need to understand why this fate should have befallen Israel/Judah. Issues of theodicy were central. A key text for understanding the rhetorical environment of the exilic period is Lamentations. A number of studies on the book of Lamentations suggest that various viewpoints existed within the community in relation to the questions raised by the destruction.[30] Different theodic solutions are explored within Lamentations, primarily from the perspective of retributive (e.g., Lam 1:5, 8, 9, 14,

25. Blenkinsopp, *Isaiah 56–66*, 43.

26. Westermann, *Praise and Lament,* 247; Westermann, *Isaiah 40–66*, 386; Tiemeyer, *Priestly Rites and Prophetic Rage*, 79. Note that Bautch (*Developments in Genre,* 89) suggests that the lament elements in Isa 63:7—64:11 are redactions whose "origins reach back generations." More specifically, Bautch argues that 63:15–19a and 64:4b–6 significantly predate the final form of the prayer (98).

27. As proposed by Odil Steck (cited Blenkinsopp, *Isaiah 55–66*, 43). Few would advocate such a dating.

28. So Williamson, "Exilic Lament?"

29. Blenkinsopp, *Isaiah 56–66*, 259.

30. Boase, *The Fulfilment of Doom*; Dobbs-Allsopp, *Lamentations.*

18, 20, 21–22; 4:6, 16; 5:16) and educative (3:25–30; 34–39) theodicies.[31] These theodic solutions are not, however, the only perspectives within the book, with complaint and protest, which raise questions about divine culpability, also evident. F. W. Dobbs-Allsopp also argues that there are anti-theodic elements in Lamentations, that is, elements which refuse to "to justify, explain or accept as somehow meaningful the relationship between God and suffering."[32]

Blenkinsopp considers the rhetorical context of Trito-Isaiah itself, arguing that the long term crisis of faith evoked by the Babylonian conquest was still being felt, with the dominant frame of mind being "disorientation and disillusionment." This is especially evident in Isa 59:9–15a and 63:7—64:11.[33] We know from the Psalms that lament was the most dominant response to experiences of disorientation within the pre-exilic period. Lament provides a language through which loss and vulnerability can be embraced.[34] Inherent in the lament is a theology of covenant in which both parties (God and humanity) are able to call the other to account, a dimension evident from the human perspective in the accusations directed at God. In the Psalter, confession of sin is rare. An understanding of retributive theology is evident in the imprecations, but protestations of innocence are the more common response from the supplicants. Israel's suffering is not automatically equated with its sin.[35]

In response to the questions raised in relation to the Babylonian exile, the confession of sin, which preserves divine righteousness through a retributive theodicy in which sin and punishment are linked, becomes increasingly dominant.[36] This theological framework finds early expression in the confessions in Lamentations (Lam 1:8, 18, 20, 22; 3:42; 5:7, 16). Confession is present in Isa 63:7—64:11, but is much more developed in the penitential prayers of Ezra 9 and Neh 9. It has been argued that penitential prayer is a development of, or polemic against, the lament,

31. Boase, "Constructing Meaning," 449–86; Dobbs-Allsopp, *Lamentations*, 28–29.

32. Dobbs-Allsopp, *Lamentations*, 29.

33. Blenkinsopp, *Isaiah 56–66*, 77–78.

34. Brueggemann, "Necessary Conditions," 26

35. Burnett, *Where is God?* 131, notes that in most lament psalms, "divine absence, divine retribution, and human sin do not necessarily correlate."

36. Boda ("Form Criticism in Transition," 190) has identified that "the legacy of the destruction of Jerusalem and the exile of the people is seen in the size of its impact on the prayer forms of Israel from this point forward."

with both genres sharing many common features.[37] The balance between the elements is, however, radically changed, as is their underlying anthropology and theodicy. Penitential prayers draw on orthodox character credos about God (e.g., Exod 34:6–7) emphasizing the covenantal faithfulness and grace of God, only occasionally or implicitly emphasizing the anger of God.[38] The theological influences on these prayers include the Priestly and Deuteronomistic theologies of penitence, and the prophetic theologies of judgment.[39] The Priestly and Deuteronomic theologies are commonly identified with exilic and post-exilic explanations of the disaster of 587 BCE. Both have a theodic flavour, attempting to explain the destruction and suffering in a way that allows for the continued identification of the community with God. At the core of the penitential prayer, is an "acceptance of the rightness of divine judgment."[40] The confession of sin "serves as the reflex of repentance in a theological sequence of sin-punishment-repentance-salvation."[41] They express a retributive theodicy, assuming human culpability as the root cause of suffering.

In the exilic and post-exilic periods, then, a theological and ideological shift can be argued in the movement from lament to penitential prayer as the dominant communal expression in times of distress. In the discussion which follows, it will be argued that Isaiah 63:7—64:11 enters into the rhetorical environment in which this theological and ideological shift was emerging. It engages dialogically with that environment through its participation in the genre of the communal lament in a way which anticipates the penitential prayers. The engagement is evident in both the form and the content of the text.

37. For the argument that penitential prayer is a development of the lament form see Westermann, *Praise and Lament*, 206; Bautch, *Developments in Genre*; for the view that they are a polemic against lament see Rom-Shiloni, "Socio-Ideological Setting."

38. Boda, "Gain of Penitence," 84. Boda notes that this transition occurs alongside a decline in emphasis on Zion theology, that is on the election of Jerusalem and the understanding of the temple as "the unique place of rule and worship and the choice of the Davidic line as vice-regent" (96).

39. Boda, "Confession as Theological Expression," 49–50; Rom-Shiloni, "Socio-Ideological *Setting*," 52; Bautch, *Developments in Genre*.

40. Bautch, *Developments in Genre*, 5.

41. Ibid., 21.

ISAIAH AND THE ENGAGEMENT OF GENRE

In his study on the development of penitential prayer in the post-exilic period, Bautch notes that Isa 63:7—64:11, Ezra 9:6–15, and Neh 9:6–37 are expressive of the form-critical ideal of the communal lament, but satisfy the psalmic criteria only partially and unevenly. The prayers use the literary conventions of lament, petition, and confession of sin, but differ most significantly in relation to the recital of the past relationship between God and Israel, a history marked by Israel's moral failure, and in their theological framework.[42]

Bautch is primarily concerned with tracing developments in genre, however, in the discussion which follows, I want to reshape the nature of the discussion, focusing instead on the way that Isaiah 63:7—64:11 participates in the communal lament genre, and in doing so, how it dialogues with that genre in a way that enables the introduction of different dialogic voices. Isaiah 63:7—64:11 incorporates familiar lament elements but at the same time modifies the genre, with the lament functioning as a scaffold which allows for the introduction of differing ideological and theological voices.

Isaiah 63:7—64:11 shares with the communal laments a number of common structural elements, thus marking its participation in this genre.[43] The text can be structured as follows[44]

42. Bautch, *Developments in Genre*, 3–4, 137.

43. A range of communal laments have been discussed in relation to Isa 63:7—64:11, including Pss 44, 75, 78, 79, 89, 106, with Ps 106 identified by Williamson ("Exilic Lament?"), as structurally and thematically closest.

44. There is, on the whole, relative uniformity amongst commentators as to the structure of Isaiah 63:7—64:11. See, for example, Bautch (*Developments in Genre*, 86), who structures the text: 63:7–14—historical recollection; 15–19a—lament; 63:19b—64:4a—appeal; vv. 4b–6—confession of sin; vv. 7–11—appeal (asserts confidence vv. 7–8; second lament vv. 9–10, conclusion v. 11); or Blenkinsopp (*Isaiah 56–66*, 257) who structures 63:7–9, 10–14, 15–19a, 19b—64:6, 64:7–11. Westermann (*Isaiah 40–66*, 392) isolates 63:15—64:11 as "the most powerful communal lament in the OT, dividing it into 63:15–16—introductory prayer; vv. 17–19a—lament; 19b—64:4a—prayer that God intercede by an epiphany; vv. 4b–6—confession of sin; v. 7—confirmation of confession; vv. 8–10 prayer that God return with reason and lament for Zion; v. 11—concluding question.

63:7–14	Historical recollection
vv. 15–19a	Petition and Lament
v. 15a	Petition
vv. 15b–17a	Lament
v. 17b	Petition
vv. 18–19a	Lament
63:19b—64:4a	Petition
64:4b–6	Confession of sin[45]
vv. 7–11	Petition and lament
vv. 7–8	Petition with reason
vv. 9–10	Lament
v. 11	Concluding lament question

Two aspects of the Isaiah text highlight its particular rhetorical/ideological engagement—the historical recollection (63:7–14) and the confession of sin (64:4b–6). While these elements are not unknown within Israel's traditions, their use in this particular context highlights the theological and ideological shift that was occurring in the late exilic/post-exilic period in relation to the divine human relationship and the theodic explanation of the disaster of 587 BCE.

In lament literature, the recollection of God's past deeds emphasizes the saving acts of God, often functioning as a motivation for God to act in the present.[46] The audience of the recollection is God, as it is God who must act. Psalm 44 is a helpful exemplar. The psalm opens with a recollection of God's past saving deeds (vv. 1–8). Divine warrior language is used (reference to God driving out nations [v. 2], to God's right hand and arm [v. 3], to God as a King who commands victories [v. 4]), with God portrayed as one who acts on Israel's behalf against Israel's enemies. There is no recognition of past failure on Israel's behalf. The recital concludes with the claim that the people have boasted in God continually

45. Although I have identified these verses as confession of sin, this view is not universally held. Those who support this being interpreted as confession include Westermann, *Isaiah 40–66*, 392, 396–97; Whybray, *Isaiah 40–66*, 264. Blenkinsopp, *Isaiah 55–66*, 264; Hanson, *Isaiah 40–66*, 239–40; Seitz, *Isaiah 40–66*, 529; Pioske, "Isaiah's Lament," 18–21; Bautch, *Developments in Genre*, 39. For the argument that these verses should be read as part of the lament, see Tiemeyer, *Priestly Rites and Prophetic Rage*, 102–9; So also in Tiemeyer's essay in the current volume. This view is also held by Blank, "And All Out Virtues," 149–54.

46. Confession of sin is generally absent from these recollections. An exception is Ps 106, in which the recollection is also associated with identification of past failures.

and given thanks to God, a claim that leads directly to an accusation that God has rejected the people (44:9–16) and a protest of innocence (17–22). The declaration of innocence includes the statement that the people have not forgotten (שכח) God, or been false (שקר) to the covenant. The concluding petition (vv. 23–26) calls on God to act in light of the lament, the recollection of God's past saving deeds and the protest of innocence. The cause of the current distress is understood as God's rejection of the people, with direct accusation occurring in verses 22 (*Because of you we are being killed all day long*) and 24 (*Why do you hide your face? Why do you forget our affliction and oppression?*). The implied theodicy is that the innocent people suffer through the negligent action/inaction of God. The recollection of God's past actions calls on the character of God, providing the basis on which God's future action is to be expected. The psalm emphasizes that the people, not God, have been the faithful partners within the divine human relationship.

In Isaiah 63:7—64:11 the rhetorical function of the historical recital differs, standing closer to those of Ezra 9 and Neh 9.[47] Isa 63:7–14 opens with praise of God's graciousness, mercy, and steadfast love (v. 7) followed by a statement placed in the mouth of God (v. 8) which paves the way for the recollection of Israel's past unfaithfulness (*For he said, "Surely they are my people, children who will not deal falsely"* שקר). Whereas in Ps 44 the people protest that they had not been false to the covenant, and, by implication, that God had, Isa 63 both anticipates (v. 8) and then describes (v. 10) the unfaithfulness of the people. As with Ps 44, Isa 63:7–14 uses military imagery now, however, with God acting against the people as a direct result of their unfaithfulness. The current plight of the people is then named through questions about God's absence (v. 11, *Where is the one who brought them up out of the sea with the shepherds*

47. Morrow, "The Affirmation of Divine Righteousness," 113, notes that "historical retrospectives occur in a number of community laments (e.g., Isa 63:7—64:11; Pss 44:2–4; 60:8–10; 74:2; 80:9–12; 83:10–13; 89:20–39). They also occur in Dan 9:7–17; Ezra 9:7–13; and Neh 1:7–9; 9:6–31. A comparison of the two groups shows that retrospects in the psalms emphasize the experience of exodus, conquest of the land of promise, and the gift of the Davidic dynasty. There is no mention of the bestowal of divine commandments on the nation as part of the descriptions of salvation history. The closest to this theme is the retrospect in Ps 89:20–38, which mentions the precepts and laws given to the Davidic dynasty (v. 31). In contrast, the historical retrospects of biblical penitential prayers all mention the gift of the commandments and divine instruction to the nation in its early history (Dan 9:10; Ezra 9:10–11; Neh 1:7; 9:14).

of his flock? Where is the one who put within them his holy spirit?).[48] The passage, however, lacks the accusatory tone of Ps 44 given the acknowledgment of sin in verse 10.[49]

Although structurally on par with the communal laments, the recollection in Isa 63:7–14 contrasts God's acts to Israel's failures. The relationship between God and Israel is marred by Israel's failure (63:10), which led to God's enmity against the people. This shift is particularly significant given the absence of any expression of confidence in the text.[50] This combination—recollection of past failure and absence of expressions of confidence—points to different theological and ideological assumptions about the causes of the present plight of the people. A retributive theodicy is presented, echoing exilic and post-exilic Dtr theology.[51] Causality has shifted from divine absence to human failure, reducing certainty as to whether God will act again on behalf of Israel.

It is significant to note that recollection of God's past saving action is all but absent in the book of Lamentations.[52] In the early period after the destruction of Jerusalem, this absence suggests a devastating collapse in the community's confidence as to the ways of God in the world. While earlier psalmists could petition God on the basis of God's past deeds, the recalled memories in Lamentations are grounded in the immediate past, a past dominated by the perception of God as relentless enemy. The one exception is the dialogic voice of Lam 3:22–39 which evokes a sense

48. Note that there are some significant textual issues in 63:11. See Blenkinsopp, *Isaiah 55–66*, 256.

49. Williamson ("Exilic Lament?" 35), citing Whybray, states that "the purpose of the historical survey is not, as in Ps 44, to reproach Yahweh with his recent neglect of an innocent people, but to express penitence and to appeal for another chance." Williamson goes on to say "indeed, we might add that Ps 44 includes a protestation of innocence by the psalmist, which is quite unlike anything in our passage. Moreover this aspect of penitence removes the passage even further from such psalms as 66; 68; 105; 107; 135; and 136, where historical recital is used for praise of God alone" (55).

50. Blenkinsopp (*Isaiah 56–66*, 41) notes the omission of the essential element of "assurance of a hearing."

51. Westermann, (*Isaiah 49–66*, 386) argues of the historical survey in Isa 63:7—64:11, "It was surveys of this kind , summing up the whole thing with a confession of guilt sub-joined, that contemporaneously called the Deuteronomistic history into being."

52. Lam 3:22–39 does reflect on the character of God, thus providing an element of hope within the book, however, this is a long way short of a recollection of God's past deeds as seen in both the communal lament psalms, in Isa 63–64 and Ezra and Nehemiah.

of hope based on the character of God. This hope is not sustained, and Lamentations closes with there being no certainty of a divine response (5:20–22).

Isaiah 63:7—64:11 has moved beyond Lamentations in that God's past saving acts are expressed, and, in conjunction with the petitions, there is some hope. As with Lamentations, however, the possibility remains open that the relationship between God and Israel might be permanently fractured. This doubt is inherent in the linking of the past recollection with Israel's failure, and is strengthened in the conclusion of the passage. In phrases reminiscent of Lamentations, especially 5:20–22, Isa 64:7–11 raises the possibility that God's mercy may be withheld. The concluding questions (*After this will you restrain yourself, O Lord? Will you keep silent, and punish us so severely?*) raise the same doubts as Lam 5:20–22 (*Why have you forgotten us completely? Why have you forsaken us these many days? . . . unless you have utterly rejected us, and are angry with us beyond measure*). The allusions to Lamentations are strengthened through the reference to God's exceeding (מאד עד) anger (קצף) in Isa 64:8 and Lam 5:22, and also references to God's anger in (1:12; 2:1 (x2), 2, 3, 4, 6) and the description of Zion as a wilderness (Isa 64:10; Lam 4:18).

Although Isa 63:7–14 modifies the lament's recollection of God's past deeds by the identification of Israel's sin as the cause of God's enmity, the accusation against God has not entirely disappeared. Isaiah 63:15–19a contains a lament section more typical of the communal lament psalms. Verse 15 opens with a petition followed by two questions which seek to evoke a response from God, and suggest an element of divine causality in the ongoing suffering (*Where are your zeal and your might? The yearning of your heart and your compassion?*). Further lament questions occur in verse 17, again in an accusatory tone (*Why, O Lord, do you make us stray from your ways, and harden our heart, so that we do not fear you?*). The exodus traditions are evoked here, particularly the Priestly account of the interaction between God and the Egyptians (e.g., Exod 14:4). In evoking the P traditions, the text aligns itself with the movement towards penitential prayer, which draws on both Priestly and Deuteronomic theologies, however, a dialogic tension is created in the use of this theology in the service of a lament element more typical of the communal laments. The accusation that God has hardened the hearts "amounts to a protest of innocence."[53] The text negotiates its way through

53. Bautch, "Lament Regained," 88.

competing viewpoints as to the causes of the current plight, with genre and form coming together to create a space in which contrasting voices concerning divine or human causality can be heard.

Further suggestion of this dialogic tension is found in the confession of sin in Isa 64:4b–6. In 64:4b divine causality is grappled with (*but you were angry, and we sinned; because you hid yourself we transgressed*). A causal relationship between the anger of God and the sin of the people is suggested, with God's anger being prior to the sin. The people sinned because God was angry. God's hiddenness led to the people's transgression.

Commentators have long grappled with the causal nexus suggested here, and various solutions to the theological issues have been suggested.[54] Given that Isa 63:7—64:11 exists at a point of tension between the theological perspective of the communal lament, which accuses God of failure to maintain the divine human relationship and attributes the cause of suffering to God, and the theological perspective of the Dtr/P shaped penitential prayer traditions where human sin is the primary cause of suffering, this causal link is perhaps not as difficult as it may first appear. The text evokes a dual causality, placing responsibility for the suffering both in the hands of God and in human sin. The suggestion that the people transgressed because of God's anger and hiddenness represents the theological tensions of the day.

The confession of sin itself moves Isa 63:7—64:11 towards the penitential prayer traditions.[55] Boda defines the penitential prayers in Ezra, Nehemiah and Daniel as "prayers that represent the penitential cry of the community for relief from their enduring predicament brought about by the fall of Jerusalem, the exile of the people, and the loss of national autonomy."[56] These prayers have in common several elements with lament psalms including 2ps address, the use of a vocative, request and motivation, complaint, description of internal anguish and external predicament, and the use of historical overviews.[57] The prayers differ in

54. See Blenkinsopp (*Isaiah 55–66*, 256) and Tiemeyer, (*Priestly Rites*, 102–9) for an overview of the issues.

55. There is also a dialogic engagement with the book of Lamentations in the confession of sin in Isa 63:7—64:11, including references to sin in terms of a menstrual cloth (Isa 64:6 and Lam 1:9), however this moves beyond the present discussion of genre.

56. Boda, "Form Criticism in Transition," 183.

57. Ibid., 184.

that there is no accusation of God, with divine righteousness being upheld and human sin confessed.

Both Ezra 9:5–15 and Neh 9:5–37 contain historical recitations, and, like Isa 63:7—64:11, these occur in the context of confession. In Ezra, the recitation is dominated by the confession. Ezra's prayer opens with an expression of present shame and embarrassment, followed by confession of sin leading into the recollection of the past interaction between Israel and God which brings the repeated sins of the people to the fore. Rhetorically, Ezra's prayer is exhortatory and directed to the worshipping community, despite its "prayer" form. Sin and suffering are linked (v. 7),[58] and God's mercy is portrayed as occurring despite Israel's sinfulness. Rather than pleading for God to act, the prayer serves as an exhortation for the people to confess and then to act appropriately in relation to marriage to the people of the land (vv. 13–14).

The prayer in Nehemiah is itself identified as a confession ([the people] *stood and confessed their sins and the iniquities of their ancestors*).[59] The historical recital spans creation, the ancestral period, the exodus, the giving of the law, the conquest of the land, and the Babylonian destruction. In a manner typical of DtrH, Israel's history is characterized as a cycle of disobedience, punishment, and mercy. The pinnacle of the prayer is the declaration of God's righteousness and a lament, laced with confession, as to the current plight of the people alongside a petition for God to act (vv. 32–37).[60] Like Ezra 9, the recollection of past history does serve to shape the worldview of the community towards a recognition of their sinfulness, however, the petition in 32–37 is clearly addressed to God and in this way seeks to evoke divine response. Unlike Isa 63:7—64:11,

58. "From the days of our ancestors to this day we have been deep in guilt, and for our iniquities we, and our kings, and our priests have been handed over to the kings of the lands, to the sword, to captivity, to plundering, and to utter shame, as is now the case."

59. The resemblance between Neh 9 and Isa 63:7—64:11 has been well argued by Williamson ("Isaiah 63,7—64,11: Exilic Lament?" 57). As well as noting similarity in the use of various traditions (God's spirit associated with the wilderness period, events from the exodus period singled out as having made for him/you [i.e., God] a name) and various lexical items, Williamson notes that Isa 63:7—64:11, Neh 9, and also Ps 106 share a similar structure. He argues that all passages derive from a Palestinian origin during the exilic period, and that, taken together, the historical recitals within these three texts shed "light on the liturgical concerns of the late exilic period."

60. Williamson, *Ezra-Nehemiah*, 306 notes that verse 32 marks the beginning of a new section which is much closer to a communal lament than the remainder of the passage.

there is no divine accusation present, with God's righteousness emphasized throughout (vv. 8, 17, 31, 32, 33). A retributive theodicy is clearly present.[61]

BLURRING THE BOUNDARIES

Isaiah 63:7—64:11 speaks into and engages the rhetorical context of its time. The above discussion has identified that this text participates in both the communal lament genre and the penitential prayer genre known from Ezra-Nehemiah. In the way it utilizes different generic elements, Isa 63:7—64:11 draws into dialogue voices which are expressive of the changing theological and ideological tensions of its day. This tension revolves around issues of theodicy, that is, the relationship of God to the suffering experienced by the community, both in the events surrounding the destruction of Jerusalem and in the ongoing plight of the community following the return from exile.

The text provides a space in which both human and divine causality for the suffering is expressed. The naming of divine causality is reminiscent of the communal lament psalms, while confession of sin and attribution of causality to the community aligns the theology of the material closer to that of the penitential prayers. Human causality is evident in the historical recital which recounts God's saving acts as well as Israel's unfaithfulness, and also in the confession of sin itself. Divine causality can be found in the lament sections of the text, but also within the confession of sin. In this way, two opposing theological frameworks are integrated into the one text.

The presence of these competing voices is reflective of the changes of the social/theological discourse of the post-exilic period. The most dominant theological understanding of the destruction was that God acted against Israel in response to its sins. But this viewpoint stands in contradiction to the tradition in the communal lament psalms which accused God of a failure to uphold the terms of the covenant agreement.

61. Morrow ("Affirmation of Divine Righteousness," 105), who suggests that the audience of the prayer is the people and not God, argues that the function of the recollection is to motivate the people to confess that sin and to recognize their dependency on divine grace. It is the people rather than God who need to be reminded of the divine human relationship, with petition emerging out of the people's confession of their sin and thus calling again on the divine righteousness. Divine righteousness is never doubted.

Through the combination of form and content, these viewpoints are held together in Isa 63:7—64:11 incorporating as it does elements from both the communal lament and the penitential prayer traditions.

Arguably, however, this text does more than simply hold two opposing viewpoints together. Much of the recent research on penitential prayer argues that as a response to the Babylonian destruction, it was a relatively new innovation. Texts such as Isa 63:7—64:11, which hold both the theological framework known from the communal lament together with a theodicy which names human sin as the cause of the destruction, provide a space in which to negotiate the competing voices. Isaiah 63:7—64:11 is thus both innovative and familiar, reflective of a changing theological framework, and in its dialogue with the rhetorical context helps provide a platform through which theological/ideological reform could be raised.

7

The Profit and Loss of Lament

Rethinking Aspects of the Relationship between Lament and Penitential Prayer

DONALD P. MOFFAT

LAMENT AND PENITENTIAL PRAYER are closely related. Both are responses to suffering and crisis yet the ways in which they address God and the assumptions they make about the relationship and the allocation of responsibility are quite different. In the light of recent research on penitential prayer I want to re-examine aspects of the relationship between such prayers and the laments. In the process I want to look again at the implications for theology and Christian practice that were highlighted in seminal work by Claus Westermann and Walter Brueggemann.[1]

TRANSITION AND IMPLICATIONS

Westermann pointed out that prayers prompted by suffering and crisis transitioned from lament to penance.[2] He noted that lament—that is, complaint that God has wrongly allowed or unjustly caused suffering—played a significant role in Old Testament theology but was removed

1. Westermann, *Praise and Lament*; Brueggemann, "The Costly Loss of Lament," 52–71.

2. Westermann, *Praise and Lament*, 204–13.

from post-exilic prayers, which replaced it with penance. This transition has been traced by a number of scholars, most notably in recent work by Mark Boda, Rodney Werline, and Richard Bautch.[3] Bautch, who rejects the idea that penitential prayer is a separate category from lament, nevertheless identifies significant changes. His form critical study of Isa 63:7—64:11, Ezra 9:6–15, and Neh 9:6–37 traces the changes in form and content from the classical lament to the penitential prayer of Second Temple Judaism.[4] The change is mediated by prophetic texts like Isa 63:7—64:11, Jer 14:1—15:4, and Lam 3 which retain the major features of classical laments but introduce penitential features.[5] It is this transition that has resulted in a group of prayers (Ezra 9:6–15; Neh 1:5–11; 9:6–37; Dan 9:4–19) with its own distinctive features. While the debate about whether lament and penitential prayer are distinct genres continues, their differences are clearly significant. Boda concludes, "[w]hether we talk about this shift as a new form or a major transformation within an older form, one must admit that there is a difference between a prayer of request that is dominated by complaint (lament) and a prayer of request that has an absence of complaint and dominance of penitence."[6] Lament and penitential prayer are related responses to suffering and crisis with distinct emphases.

Boda warns that we should not think about a tidy transition from one form to the other but rather of a continuum of prayer styles where prayers with penitential features come to dominate. There are clearly mixed type prayers particularly in the exilic and early post-exilic era.[7] That mixing is also evident in the later Hellenistic and Roman era when lament elements return and the historical review changes from a catalogue of cumulative sin to a review of the faith of ancestors.[8] Nevertheless, penitential prayer styles dominate the Second Temple era. That domination is highlighted by those prayers that address the suffering of the righteous. These are cases where penitential prayer seems inappropriate and lament is surely

3. Boda, *Praying the Tradition*; Bautch, *Developments*; Werline, *Penitential Prayer*.

4. Cf. also Werline, *Penitential Prayer*; Boda, "Form Criticism in Transition," 181–92.

5. Bautch, *Developments*, 29–63, 165–66; Boda "From Complaint to Contrition," 179. See also the essay by Boase in this volume.

6. Boda, "Form Criticism in Transition," 188.

7. This is illustrated by the papers by Lena-Sofia Tiemeyer and Elizabeth Boase in this volume.

8. Bautch, *Developments*, 137–61.

the better option. Yet in cases like Tobit (3:2–6) and the Prayer of Azariah (an apocryphal addition to Daniel) we find penitential prayers used by righteous sufferers. These prayers certainly have more elements of lament but they are penitential prayers.[9] For Second Temple Judaism penitential prayer is the appropriate response to suffering, whether deserved or innocent.

Westermann claimed that the replacement of complaint by penitential features had some negative implications theologically and followed that by expressing concern about the absence of lament from Western Christianity. Brueggemann, following Westermann's lead, identified two problems caused by the loss of lament from the liturgical life of a faith community, namely the loss of genuine covenant interaction and the stifling of questions about theodicy.[10] On the first point he argues that a focus on praise renders the human partner of the covenant voiceless because there is no place to challenge God about divine faithfulness. Using psychological theory about the development of the ego he claims the dependent partner needs to have an independent voice to which God responds in order to develop a strong faith that is able to genuinely praise God.[11] Lament calls on God as a partner in covenant and refuses to be intimidated by the divine nature of the senior partner.

On the second point Brueggemann argues that the Hebrew Bible is "more committed to questions of justice than to questions of God."[12] The human covenant partner needs to be able to call the divine partner to account when suffering is intolerable,[13] even if the only court is in fact the court of the God who stands accused. Brueggemann presumes a social situation analogous with the monarchy where the religious institution is closely aligned with the political power. A key point in Brueggemann's analysis is that lament embodies the voice of the suffering masses against the political powers who gain their legitimation from the central religious

9. Werline, *Penitential Prayer*, 161–89.

10. Brueggemann, "The Costly Loss of Lament."

11. Boda questions Brueggemann's use of social and psychological theory as the basis for the analysis ("The Priceless Gain of Penitence," 51–75).

12. Brueggemann, "The Costly Loss of Lament," 62.

13. Ibid., lists four features of lament that respond to theodicy. The attitude of God's obligation to the complainant as covenant partner is explicitly stated in the last one and is presumed in the others. That is an area where penitential prayer displays a significantly different attitude. See below.

institution.[14] Ultimately God is responsible for the system and lament is a means to demand a change.

The features of lament that Brueggemann highlights as essential to a healthy relationship with God are the very features that appear to be lost in the transition to penitential prayer. Brueggemann offers some valuable insights here and pointers to social application that have increasingly been heeded in a world more open to acknowledging mourning and disaster. However, I have questions about both the claimed loss that founds the theological concern and the assumption that penitential prayer closes off questions of theodicy. On the first point, lament is not really lost from the worship of Second Temple Judaism. True, it is not present in the prayers uttered in times of crisis but it was still part of worship. Complaint prayer was relocated rather than lost. Second, the contexts of the two forms of prayer are quite different. The exile had an enormous impact on the life, beliefs, and practices of Second Temple Jews. That changed context, particularly the changed place of the cult in relation to crisis prayer had a profound effect.

RELOCATED LAMENT

The foundation for Westermann's and Brueggemann's lament about Western Christianity was that its worship mirrored the loss of complaint prayer from Judaism and was therefore impoverished by that loss. While both scholars were undoubtedly right in their analysis of a problem in the Western church the link they make with Second Temple Judaism is based on a narrow selection of its worship practice. Their contention that prayers which protested suffering were lost only relates to official prayers uttered in response to crisis. Westermann acknowledges that lament continued to occur in the literature of the Second Temple but it was significant to him that it existed independently of prayer.[15] Yet this does not make lament absent from Jewish worship. More recent research

14. While Brueggemann makes this point in "The Costly Loss of Lament" it is more forcefully made in other examples of his writing. See for example, Brueggemann, "Theodicy," 3–25; or Brueggemann, "Embrace of Pain," 395–415.

15. Westermann, *Praise and Lament*, 206–13. He points to several examples of lament that are separate from any formal prayer: Bar 4–5; 1 Macc 2:6; *Pss. Sol.* 2, 8; 2 *Bar.* 10–12. On the other side Bautch argues that the element of confession waxes and wanes in Second Temple penitential prayers and so questions whether penitential prayer should be regarded as a separate category from lament. See Bautch, *Development*, 160.

reinforces the notion that complaint prayer was not lost to the thinking and practice of Second Temple Judaism. William Morrow notes that while lament prayer is absent from official worship, it continued to find expression in popular piety at times of crisis. He points to a "practice of informal protest prayer that continued to assert itself in expressions of popular piety."[16] It is also important to note that elements of lament returned in later penitential prayers.[17] In addition we need to account for the book of Psalms. Lament is the most common form of Psalm, comprising some 40 percent of the book. If the standard scholarly assumption that Psalms is the song book of the Second Temple is correct then laments continued to have a significant role in Second Temple worship. As Patrick Miller has observed, wherever there is suffering there is a need to cry out to God.[18] The Second Temple era provided plenty of examples of suffering. The cry of the innocent sufferer may have been displaced but it was not silenced in Jewish worship.

CHANGE OF CONTEXT

Complaint continued to find a place in Jewish worship. Yet it is striking that penitential prayer predominates as the response to crisis in Second Temple prayer liturgy. What complaint exists in the literature was, for a period at least, separate from prayers uttered at times of community crisis. Lament was lost from penitential prayers because the context had changed. Changed circumstances forced a change in outlook on life (*Ausblick aufs Leben*), which in turn demanded a change in ideology.[19]

Brueggemann's concern is about theodicy and the need for worshipers to call God to account in the face of suffering. Penitential prayers do not question God's faithfulness. In fact, one of the recurring features of the prayers is a review of history that identifies Yhwh's covenant faithfulness and Israel's unfaithfulness. Neither do penitential prayers question

16. Morrow, "Affirmation of Divine Righteousness," 103. He lists 1 Macc 2:7–13; 3:50–53; 2 *Bar* 3:1–9; 1 *En.* 84:2–6; 2 Esd 3:28–36; 5:28; 6:55–59.

17. Werline, *Penitential Prayer*, 161–89.

18. Miller, "Heaven's Prisoners," 15–26.

19. Boda, "Form Criticism in Transition," 181–92. Boda's comment is that form criticism can only take analysis of lament and penitential prayer so far. He suggests that progress will come from those methodologies that pay closer attention to the context of the prayers. He therefore indicates a need to focus on the *Ausblick aufs Leben* rather than the *Sitz im Leben* of form criticism. Note also Boase's essay in this volume.

God's righteousness or faithfulness, quite the opposite. One of the most consistent features of penitential prayers is the declaration of God's righteousness (אתה צדיק), which particularly refers to covenant faithfulness.[20] These prayers represent suffering as the result of evil at work in the world not the actions of an angry or negligent God.[21] The penitent relies on God, characterized by righteousness and faithfulness to the covenant, to respond by rescuing the oppressed. In the demise of these two features lament was indeed lost from prayers offered in suffering and crisis.

Community lament is a mode of prayer designed for the people of Israel gathered in the temple in the face of national disaster. It presumes that the suffering is both an affront to God (Ps 79:12) and the result of divine anger (Ps 79, 80) or neglect (Ps 44). The covenant relationship is understood but the emphasis is on divine obligations to the nation rather than on the people and their obligations.[22] As Westermann notes, lament is founded in the exodus and the understanding that when the people call out in distress God hears and responds.[23] The psalmist relies on God's חסד, that divine faithfulness, goodness, and mercy that will compel divine response in the face of the people's distress. While the lament may acknowledge community sin, it is hardly a determinative factor in the encounter with God. Rather the lament prayer presumes that the community needs to survive, if only for the sake of God's reputation and the continuance of proper worship. The issue of sin was not addressed through lament, instead sin was addressed through specific cult practices. Lament presumes an active cult that dealt with the issue of impediments in the relationship between the supplicant and God. In essence, lament presumes national election, covenant relationship, functioning cult, and a God whose nature would not allow the nation to be destroyed.

This assumption of the role of the cult in dealing with impediments to the relationship with God is hardly surprising when we think about the historical context of lament. While, as I have noted, lament continued to be used in Second Temple worship, its primary context was the

20. Boda, *Praying the Tradition*, 6–64.

21. Penitential prayers that have a stronger element of lament often point to the excesses of a human agent as the reason for the suffering. In that sense they hold on to the idea that God is responsible for giving the powerful their role but absolve God of direct responsibility by invoking the free will actions of the agent.

22. Rom-Shiloni, "*Setting* or *Settings*?"

23. Westermann, *Praise and Lament*, 259–61. Cf. Miller's argument that lament is imbedded in the human divine relationship ("Heaven's Prisoners," 15–20).

monarchic era. The laments in the book of Psalms originated in the pre-exilic era and thus presume an active royal cult. Likewise the book of Lamentations stems from the early exilic period when the patterns of the monarchy were still assumed, although the cult had been interrupted if not halted by the second Neo-Babylonian conquest. Transitional passages like Isa 63–64 show the change in context and ideology where the cult was not so accessible. Penitential prayers fully reflect a situation where the cult is not operable or is inaccessible, a situation that remained even when the Second Temple was established. It was not accessible to the Diaspora and some residents in Judah may have found their access restricted.[24]

Penitential prayer shares some of lament's features but it also has distinct features born out of its different historical and ideological context. The *Sitz im Leben* of community lament is prayer offered in the face of national crisis in the context of the cult. Two examples will illustrate the point. When the Israelites were defeated at Ai, Joshua fell on his face "before the ark of the LORD" and prayed a lament (Josh 7:6–9). Similarly Hezekiah's response to Sennacherib's letter was to enter the temple in mourning (2 Kgs 19:1–4). Penitential prayer was also uttered in the face of crisis, yet the temple, even when functional and accessible, was not the place where the prayer was spoken.[25] The prayers in Ezra 9 and Neh 9, both set in Jerusalem after the temple was rebuilt, take place in public spaces. Nehemiah 1 and Dan 9 are uttered in exile in Susa and Babylon. In post-exilic practice penitential prayers were spoken outside the temple even when the pray-er was present in Jerusalem. Penitential prayer, unlike lament, is not dependent on a functioning cult. Indeed it

24. The threat of the ban against non-compliant families in the mixed marriage controversy in Ezra 9–10 indicates active policing of access to the temple and it is possible that dissident groups, which passages like Isa 63:16 hint may have existed, also faced restrictions.

25. Note also Tobit, Baruch, and the Prayer of Azariah. The one arguable exception is 3 Macc 2 where Simon the high priest prays in the temple before the sanctuary. The location is hardly surprising when the prayer is about a desecration of the temple by the Greeks. Probably written in the early first century BCE the prayer evidences other changes from the penitential prayers in the canonical texts. The historical review in this prayer is not a catalogue of past sin and the prayer pleads with God not to punish Israel for the Greek defilement of the temple. Thus, while it does confess sin like other penitential prayers, it also evidences characteristics which reflect still more change in context and ideology. Yet even in this case the prayer is uttered because the temple has been compromised and therefore was temporarily unfit for its function.

presumes that the temple is not accessible and that the prayer functions even if the cult is not.

Penitential prayer's altered relationship with the cult is highlighted by the two roles it had in relation to sin. It either *supplemented* the cult or it *substituted* for the cult. The supplementary role can be seen in Ezra 9 where the prayer paved the way for the guilt offering which confirmed the repentance of the guilty and their renewed obedience to the law. Part of the function of penitential prayer was to move sin from the realm of the unforgivable to the place where the cult could deal with it. This is based on the priestly view of repentance where remorse and confession transfer deliberate sin to a place where, according to Jacob Milgrom, it can be dealt with. Milgrom argues that the sins listed in Lev 5:20–26 (Eng 6:1–7), described as מעל, "unfaithfulness," are deliberate and therefore not forgivable through sacrifice.[26] However, they are made forgivable by the אשם "guilt" sacrifice after confession. It is this priestly idea of repentance by remorse and confession that is the basis for penitential prayer's role in supplementing sacrifice.[27] Penitential prayer by confession and expressing remorse therefore played an important role by changing the status of the sin from that with which the cult could not deal to that with which the cult could deal. One could argue that the sin of mixed marriage in Ezra 9–10 was inadvertent because it arose from a new application of the law. However, the sin is described as מעל (Ezra 9:2; 10:2) and is linked to the past sins of the people that led to the exile. It therefore required confession as preparation for the guilt offering. In contrast to lament, which makes no attempt to deal with sin but relies on the cult, penitential prayer aids the cult in dealing with sin.

More radically penitential prayer was part of a process that could substitute for the cult. It was not the prayer alone but associated factors such as contrition and suffering that made the penitentiary act a substitute for cultic actions. This role is evidenced in Dan 9 where the prayer and mourning are effective without any cultic action. This substitutionary role seems to be a response to the inaccessibility of the cult.[28] This is

26. Milgrom, *Cult and Conscience*, 17–21; Milgrom *Leviticus 1–16*, 375–78. Good summaries of Milgrom's arguments are given in Werline, *Penitential Prayer*, 48–50, and Falk, "Scriptural Inspiration," 133–39.

27. Milgrom, *Cult and Conscience*, 126–27. "Thus remorse (*'sm*) for inadvertencies and remorse plus confession for deliberate sins constitute the Priestly doctrine of repentance."

28. In his examination of regularized penitential prayer used by the Covenanters at

not necessarily because the cult was not operational but simply because it was inaccessible, whether through geography, such as Daniel's location in Babylon, or ideology, in the case of the Qumran Covenanters, for whom the Temple was compromised.[29] In a world where sufferers could not rely on access to the cult in order to rid the community of sin, the notions of repentance and confession rooted in both Deuteronomy and Priestly texts enabled penitential prayer along with suffering to substitute for cultic sacrifice. In this way the sufferer could clear the ground of any impediments in the relationship with God that might contribute to the suffering.

Lament arose in a context where the cult apparatus dealt with the effects of sin on the relationship between God and the people. Penitential prayer arose to deal with sin in a context where the cult could not be relied upon. It either paved the way so sin could then be dealt with through sacrifice, as exemplified in Ezra 9, or, in the absence of the temple and sacrifice, the prayer and suffering substituted as a means of restoration, as exemplified in Dan 9.[30] It is interesting to note that penitential prayer continually acknowledges the cumulative aspect of community sin.[31] This is a factor that, according to many texts in the Hebrew Bible, led to the exile and arguably was not dealt with effectively by the cult. In short lament and its evolutionary child penitential prayer respond to suffering with emphases dictated by different environments that produced different outlooks.

In further contrast to lament, penitential prayer does not rely on divine election and the honor of God's name, represented in the existence of the nation, being enough to prompt redemptive action. The exile was stark evidence that God was willing to risk his reputation and utilize another nation to discipline a people who flouted their obligations to the covenant. That meant that the political authority over the community

---

Qumran, Falk urges caution in attributing this substitutionary role to lack of access to the cult. While he acknowledges that regularized prayer took place at times of sacrifice and came to have the same significance as sacrifice he argues that the use of penitential prayer at Qumran rests as much on the theology of repentance and atonement as it does on inaccessibility to the cult. See Falk, "Scriptural Inspiration," 127–57. However, one wonders how much the lack of access to the cult impacted on the theology.

29. An example of the Covenanter's ban on entering the temple is CD 6:11b–14a.

30. Hogewood, "The Speech Act of Confession," 69.

31. Note that penitential prayer presumes the cumulative nature of sin over generations, a priestly notion, not cross-generational accountability for sin noted in Deuteronomy. See Boda, "Confession as Theological Expression," 34–39.

was not its own king, also in covenant relationship to Yhwh, but a foreign ruler. This negates the social protest aspect that Brueggemann argues is such an important function of complaint prayer.[32] Complaint prayer was a means to protest suffering and call to account those who claimed legitimacy through divine election.[33] Penitential prayer operated in a different environment. The ruling figures were foreigners co-opted by God rather than kings in covenant relationship. The suffering was seen as the result of those authorities overstepping the boundaries rather than a king failing his responsibilities. As social protest lament was irrelevant in the post-exilic context, at least until the Maccabean era. At this level lament was not a loss to the post-exilic community because the social function was made redundant by the circumstances. Penitential prayer was a suitable replacement because it addressed the altered social situation.

One further difference that is worthy of note is the difference in the psychology of the people. Laments have a confidence that God will act in redemption based on the special relationship the nation of Israel had with their God and their role as witnesses of divine benevolence. The exile shattered that confidence and placed human faithfulness to the covenant at the top of the agenda. The extent of the trauma made it natural, when suffering reached crisis point, that the first question the community asked was about how their behavior may have influenced the situation.[34] The exile changed the community psychology and focused the question of responsibility for suffering in a different way.[35] In this

32. Brueggemann, "The Costly Loss of Lament."

33. There is a tendency methodologically to keep communal and individual laments separate. I note, for example, that Miller, "Heaven's Prisoners," 18, brackets out communal laments when he offers a theological application of lament to contemporary worship. He argues that lament is the voice of private pain. However, penitential prayer is also used in a context of individual suffering, though admittedly not in the canonical text, which suggests that the comparison between lament and penitential prayer should not be restricted to communal prayer. Even private pain was an issue for the immediate community of the sufferer in the biblical world and I will suggest below that both prayer forms have a role in community worship today.

34. I do not adhere to the notion that the Neo-Babylonian invasion had a relatively minor affect on the people of Judah. The archaeological evidence indicates significant devastation and a massive decline in population after the invasion. See Lipschitts, *Fall and Rise*. Further the dramatic changes in ideology and the indications of profound suffering expressed in the text argue that the trauma must be taken seriously. See Smith-Christopher, *Theology of Exile*.

35. Bautch, *Developments*, 171–72. William Morrow suggests this is the result of the transformation of thinking of the Axial Age ("The Affirmation of Divine Righteousness," 101–17).

sense penitential prayer met the psychological needs of the community by dealing with its greatest fear. It enabled a restoration of the relationship with God so that the community could have confidence in a divine response to relieve their suffering.

In the sense that penitential prayers are fit for their historical context, I do not think that the loss of complaint from prayers offered at times of community crisis was a loss of the opportunity to question God's role in the crisis as Westermann and Brueggemann claim. Rather the question about God's role in suffering had moved. Penitential prayers accepted that excessive suffering was not the direct result of divine action but the result of human sin, either in unfaithfulness or, in the case of the punishing powers, by overstepping boundaries. The prayers eschew the easy option of pushing the blame for evil on heaven and accept its earthly origins. Affirming God's righteousness did not close down the question of theodicy but refocused it around how God might respond to human suffering at the hands of other humans.[36] Confession removed any grounds for divine anger so that mercy could prevail. It put the penitent in the position to maintain genuine covenant interaction. Lament lingered in different forms in the post-exilic era and responded to a different set of motivators which perhaps focused more on the suffering of the faithful as "collateral damage" in the consequences of national failure. Not all those who suffered under the Babylonians, for example, were unfaithful yet all suffered.

THEOLOGICAL IMPLICATIONS

Dalit Rom-Shiloni has argued that the move from lament to penitential prayer is not so much a transition as a theological debate.[37] She notes that both forms are present in the Persian era and claims that laments articulate a "nonorthodox" theology while penitential prayers respond with an "orthodox," that is, Deuteronomic, theology. This is an interesting suggestion and, coupled with Katherine Hayes' argument that prophetic laments may have been a necessary step in leading people to recognize failure and to respond with repentance, it has some merit.[38]

36. It is interesting to note that the theodicy question in Job results from a series of predominantly natural disasters. This is a somewhat broader situation than the suffering addressed by penitential prayers.

37. Rom-Shiloni, "Socio-Ideological Setting or Settings?"

38. Hayes, "When None Repents," 119–43.

Nevertheless the idea of a theological debate has some deficiencies that caution against accepting it as the only or even primary factor in the differences between lament and penitential prayer. First, we need to note that differences in relating to God are not necessarily an indication of ideological conflict. The fact that laments dominate the book of Psalms while penitential prayer dominated Second Temple era response to crisis should warn us that both forms had their place and may not have been seen as contradictory.[39] Second, as noted above, the context of the two forms is different. Penitential prayer responds to an era when the cult could not be presumed to deal with sin in the way that lament presumed it did. Third, characterizing penitential prayer as championing Deuteronomic orthodoxy is rather too narrow a focus on its ideological basis. Boda's study has shown that penitential prayers arise out of a context of reflection on past traditions and that the prayers themselves evidence strong Priestly as well as Deuteronomic influence.[40] Penitential prayers are an amalgamation of Deuteronomic and Priestly ideas that reflect the merging of ideologies in the post-exilic era rather than the assertion of one pre-exilic perspective.

While theological debate may not be the primary reason for the relationship between lament and penitential prayer, the notion that they may interact or complement each other has its attractions.[41] Both forms of prayer appear to be operative in the Second Temple period. It is unlikely that laments would have been such a prominent part of Psalms if the issue of theodicy had been closed off by penitential prayer. Job indicates that the relationship between retributive theology and innocent suffering was a live issue. Thinking about lament and penitential prayer as complementary modes of response to crisis raises some interesting theological reflections.

The different contexts and perspective between lament and penitential prayer must have some bearing on how they are appropriated theologically and, as a result, on how they influence contemporary faith practice. Biblical scholars do not always make the transition well, nor does theology always grasp the biblical text well. As Mark Boda has observed in a recent reflection on commentaries with theological application, the task might be better tackled by collegial co-operation rather than left in

39. See also Lena-Sofia Tiemeyer's essay in this volume.

40. Boda, *Praying the Tradition.*

41. Balentine, "Afterword," 196–98.

the hands of the individual.[42] With that in mind I will offer some pointers which others may wish to follow up.

There are some implications for theological application from the supplementary and substitutionary role of penitential prayer in relation to the cult that are worthy of note. While penance is a normal part of many Christian liturgies it is often individualized and its relationship to suffering is rarely recognized. Penitential prayer should remind us of the damaging effect of personal and corporate failure and of the cumulative effect of unacknowledged sin. Churches, particularly in a Western individualized society, can be very slow to recognize, own, and confess corporate failure, particularly its historical elements. Recent scandals, particularly of historic abuse, have shown how slow churches are to address significant corporate wrong. A second implication here is the relationship between suffering and sinful failure. Too often any retributive theology is rejected as simplistic and crude. Reasons for suffering are complex and blaming the victim can do much harm, yet there is also a place for close self examination in the face of persistent difficulties. There is a healthy aspect, particularly where corporate suffering is involved, to ask searching questions about the conduct of the community and taking corrective action.

A third implication of the substitutionary role of penitential prayers relates to lament. Any theological application of lament relies on a prior penitential prayer that deals with impediments in the divine human relationship. For the Christian church that prayer relies on the efficacy of the cross and resurrection and is often standard in liturgies. However, theological application of lament to contemporary faith frequently overlooks the need for a prior confession. Hayes argues that prophetic lament led to penance, but in Christian practice penitential prayer can lead to lament.[43]

The case for a theological application of lament has been well made by Patrick Miller.[44] However, I have one point at which I question Miller's conclusions, that is his claim that lament is the expression of personal pain which does not belong in public worship. The majority of lament psalms may be individual laments but that does not remove them from community worship.[45] The fact that they feature in a book of prayers for

42. Boda, "Theological Commentary," 139–50

43. Hayes, "When None Repents."

44. Miller, "Heaven's Prisoners."

45. A point Miller acknowledges with reference to Gerstenberger, *Der Bitte Mensch*. Gestenberger argues that lament took place in a small group setting. Miller

temple use should warn against turning individual complaint into private worship. Further there are communal laments that Miller brackets out. I do not think this is necessary or defensible. Suffering, even at a largely individual level, has community implications as Job's friends illustrate. There are also times when a community needs to express its protest against excessive suffering.[46] These need not be restricted to the regular worshiping community. Contemporary Western society is becoming increasingly willing to recognize the impact of suffering on a community and that the church has a role in leading such events. Recent New Zealand examples are the community memorial services held for the Pike River mining disaster and the Christchurch earthquake in which the churches played a significant role.[47]

One further implication arises from the psychological perspective of the prayers noted earlier. Penitential prayers responded to the deep fears of the community following the trauma of the exile. They enabled the community to deal with their failures and confront their suffering by removing impediments to the covenantal relationship. Laments approach God with a sense that the suffering is not the result of sin, or that it is excessive if sin exists. Whether lament or penitential prayer is most appropriate may depend on the psychology of the community and its sense of relationship with God.

The exile was a watershed that brought huge changes to Israel's experience of God. One of the outcomes was that complaint prayers transitioned into penitential prayers. Yet that did not remove lament from human divine interaction nor remove questions of theodicy from that interaction. Both forms of prayer had a life in post-exilic faith practice and, I suggest, had complementary roles. That complementarity offers theological perspectives that can benefit contemporary faith practice.

---

argues that individual lament was primarily private and points to Hannah's prayer at Shiloh (1 Sam 1) as the paradigm while suggesting Jephthah's daughter bewailing her virginity with her companions is the exception (Judg 11). I wonder, in line with Gerstenberger, if the reverse is true and Jephthah's daughter reflects the more normal setting and Hannah's private and silent lament is the exception.

46. Broyles *Faith and Experience*. He notes that what prompts lament is not suffering but prolonged suffering that indicates Yhwh has not responded to the initial plea for help.

47. Sally Brown points to examples of American church leaders turning to lament to help their congregations make sense of the September 11 attacks ("When Lament Shapes a Sermon," 27–37).

8

The Doubtful Gain of Penitence

The Fine Line between Lament and Penitential Prayer

LENA-SOFIA TIEMEYER

INTRODUCTION

WHEN SHOULD WE LAMENT[1] and intercede and when should we turn to God in penitence or stand before God's awesomeness in stunned silence?

1. "Lament" can be understood simply as an expression of pain, sorrow, and grief. According to this definition, a person can lament but need not hold God responsible for his/her pain. My own definition of "lament" is narrower and includes an element of "complaint." It assumes that the person who is praying sees God as either directly or indirectly responsible for his/her situation. The book of Job illustrates the matter well. As readers, we know that God is ultimately responsible for Job's situation, even though the satan is carrying out the deeds against Job. A faith that upholds God's omnipotence will inevitably hold God responsible for suffering. Lament will therefore always contain a note of complaint, whether outspoken or not. See further the discussion in Harasta and Brock, *Evoking Lament*, 4–5 (introduction). There will also be an element of "rage" in lament. As stated by John Swinton (*Raging with Compassion*, 104–5), "lament suggests that a person who is lamenting has a genuine grievance. . . . Lament . . . is the cry of the innocent, the one who feels treated unfairly, who feels that God has somehow not lived up to the sufferer's covenant-inspired expectations." Lament expresses rage to God for the injustices that happen to us. From a different perspective, see also Levenson, *Creation and the Persistence of Evil*, xvii–xviii, who points out that the question of the suffering of the innocent is not an intellectual exercise but an attempt to goad God into delivering the suffering persons from their plight.

Is it possible to know which approach to take when we draw near to God in supplication? Does it depend on the quality of the sin, the size of the punishment, or on our own feelings of guilt or innocence? Moreover, are lament and intercession always open possibilities or are there times when these kinds of responses are inappropriate?

Any answer to these questions lies beyond the scope of an academic paper. The present paper is inspired by these questions yet its aims are more humble. It explores the interaction between lament and penitential prayer in the Hebrew Bible, with focus on whether one replaces the other historically and, by extension, whether one is therefore to be considered superior to the other. I shall explore the laments/ penitential prayers in Isa 40–66 and Neh 9 and seek to determine their *Sitz-in-der-Literatur*, i.e., the specific role that these texts play in their literary context. First, what role do Daughter Zion's expressions of lament in Isa 49 play within Isa 40–55, what is the function of the lament in Isa 63:7—64:11 and the penitential prayer in Isa 59:9–15a in Isa 56–66, and how do both sets of texts fit in the wider literary context of Isa 40–66? Secondly, what is the role of the penitential prayer in Neh 9 in its larger context of Ezra-Nehemiah, and how does its role compare with that of the laments in Isa 40–66?

The chapter falls into two parts. The first part surveys previous research on the historical development of and relationship between lament and penitential prayer. I shall argue that although there is a historical connection between the two genres, given that penitential prayer served as a polemic against lament at one point, there is no linear development from lament to penitential prayer. On the contrary, both types of literature existed in parallel and expressed theologies at variance with each other. The first part also looks briefly at some theological issues related to lament and penitential prayer. From a Christian perspective, what is a healthy balance between these two types of interaction with God and what are the dangers when we overemphasize one type over and against the other?

The second part constitutes an exegetical study of select texts in Isa 40–66 and Neh 9. I shall examine their function(s) and meaning(s) at the times of their composition and subsequent incorporation into their present literary contexts. Building upon this foundation, I shall look at their role in the canon of the church, and suggest that that role allows the church to incorporate both penitential prayer and lament alongside each other in its beliefs and liturgy.

My chapter belongs within the study of the Hebrew Bible. The textual evidence of the Hebrew Bible constitutes the focal point of the discussion and also its perspective. I shall therefore refrain from making explicit connections to the New Testament and I shall not propose overtly practical application of my research for contemporary Christian life. Yet it is my sincere wish that other scholars who are more qualified than I am in this respect will use my research for exactly those purposes. In other words, my task as a scholar of the Hebrew Bible is to analyze the evidence of this textual corpus as faithfully as I can, and to present the results to other scholars who can then use them as building blocks for the formation of a theology of lament and penitential prayer for the church.

PART I

1. *Lament or Penitential Prayer—Which One Is Preferable?*

In his seminal article "The Costly Loss of Lament," Brueggemann laments the fact that the modern church has lost the ability to lament. He writes that lament "redresses the redistribution of power." In lamenting, the petitioner is taken seriously and God's unmitigated supremacy is questioned.[2] However, when there is no lament, "a theological monopoly is re-enforced, docility and submissiveness are engendered."[3] Brueggeman suggests that the loss of lament has two main repercussions. First, we lose an expression of genuine covenant interaction and, as a result, the communication between God and the worshipper suffers. Secondly, theodicy, i.e., the capacity to raise legitimate questions of justice in the society, is stifled.[4]

In his response to Brueggemann, Boda ("The Priceless Gain of Penitence") questions whether the loss of lament necessarily results in psychological lack of authenticity and social immobility.[5] Instead, Boda maintains that the key aspects of lament have been preserved in penitential prayer. The church has therefore not really lost lament but gained a transformed form of communication with God that lacks the accusing tone of lament yet enables the speakers to express their grief.

2. Brueggemann, "Loss of Lament," 57–71 (59).

3. Ibid., 59.

4. Ibid., 60–64.

5. Boda, "Priceless Gain," 81–101.

Boda further argues that Brueggemann's conclusions are not born out by the life of the ancient Jewish community. Assuming a chronological development from the Judahite exilic Lamentations to the later Persian period penitential prayer, Boda argues that Ezra 9; Neh 1; 9; and Dan 9 all contain expressions of lament (expressions of distress, requests that God recognizes that distress, remembers his promises to his people, and changes his behaviour towards them), yet also admissions of sins (Ezra 9:6–7, 10, 13–15; Neh 1:6–8; 9:33–35, 37; Dan 9:5–11, 13–16, 18) and acknowledgements of God's awesomeness and righteousness.[6] The relationship between lament (exemplified by the book of Lamentations) and penitential prayer is a matter of proportion. While both types of texts plead for divine recognition of distress and identify God as responsible for the situation, and both acknowledge the people's sin and declare God's righteousness, penitential prayers devote *more* attention to God's mercy and the people's admission of guilt and *less* on his anger than the laments.[7] Boda concludes that, *contra* Brueggemann, the chronologically later penitential prayer combines confession of guilt and penitence with authentic expressions of pain and that it, in this manner, upholds the dialogue between God and Israel and continues to criticize social injustice.[8]

2. *The Chronological Relationship between Lament and Penitential Prayer*

Boda's view of penitential prayer as having developed out of lament is shared by many biblical scholars. Westermann postulated a three stage development. The first stage arose from natural situations in life and is preserved to us embedded in narrative (e.g., Exod 18:10; Judg 15:18; 2 Sam 15:31). The second stage was dominated by complaints against God and by pleas that God should not hide himself or remain silent (e.g., the lament psalms). The third stage shifted the focus from lament and complaint to confessions of sin (e.g., Neh 9; Dan 9).[9] At this last stage, the emphasis swung from what God had done to what the people had done. The people of Israel, rather than God, were held responsible for a calamity. As a result, the motif of the suffering human receded into the

6. Ibid., 82–85.

7. Ibid., 88–90.

8. Ibid., 98–100.

9. Westermann, *Praise and Lament*, 206.

background and lost its significance. As later Brueggemann, Westermann disapproved of this shift as it appeared to disallow complaint and instead fostered a theology that upheld God's righteousness no matter the cost.[10] In later Christian tradition, the emphasis on penitence resulted in a theology that focused exclusively on Jesus' salvific action on the cross for the sake of obtaining forgiveness for human sin. However, as Westermann stresses, forgiveness of sins ought not to *replace* healing (but should exist alongside it).[11] If this happens, the church is in danger of becoming more concerned with the guilt of sin than with the suffering of the world.

Westermann's and Boda's chronological approach assumes that specific historical events brought about the shift from lament to penitential prayer. Westermann suggests that the trauma of exile, in conjunction with the growing influence of the Deuteronomistic theology, triggered the shift. Israel came to be depicted as a people with a history of disobedience and the calamities that befell Israel came to be viewed as God's just punishment of his people.[12]

More recently, Boda suggests that both prophetic and priestly circles helped transforming the lament *Gattung*. The resulting penitential prayer, which gradually became the dominant expression of pain for those facing the repercussions of the destruction of Jerusalem and the ensuing exile, is therefore an amalgamation of both Deuteronomic/Deuteronomistic and Ezekiel/Priestly traditions and theology.[13] Boda further regards Jer 14:19–21, dated to the late pre-exilic Judah, as an early form of penitential prayer.[14]

Other scholars reject a diachronic development from lament to penitential prayer. Werline accepts Westermann's idea that penitential prayer

10. Ibid., 203: "By way of this kind of self-conscious piety which is forced to justify God's actions, what heretofore had been an occasion for lament now becomes an occasion for praising the righteous God. Thus, the polarity between lament and praise is abolished. Where complaint against God is disallowed, there can be no lament in the strict sense of the word. The lament is excluded from prayer. Instead of complaint against God there perforce arises the doctrine of the righteousness of God."

11. Ibid., 274–75.

12. Ibid., 171–72.

13. Boda, *Praying the Tradition*, 43–73. See also Boda, "Confession as Theological Expression," 21–50, where Boda explores the roots of penitential prayer in Deuteronomic, Priestly, and prophetic traditions. In particular, Boda detects strong influence from Lev 26 (Holiness Code) in the biblical penitential prayer.

14. *Boda*, "Complaint to Contrition," 196–97.

is indebted to Deuteronomic/Deuteronomistic ideas and embraces the possibility of Priestly influence on especially the prayer in Ezra 9. Yet, as Werline traces the development of penitential prayer back to pre-exilic material in Deuteronomy (from Deut 4; 28–30, via 1 Kgs 8:22–61; Jer 29:10–14; Isa 56–66, to the full-blown penitential prayers in Ezra 9; Neh 1:4–11; 9), he contests Westermann's (and later Boda's) proposition that penitential prayer is a chronologically later form of lament.[15]

Rom-Shiloni also challenges the view that penitential prayer is a later variety of lament. Instead she argues that penitential prayer originated as a polemic *against* lament and that both existed side-by-side throughout the Neo-Babylonian period. This co-existence of lament and penitential prayer testifies to a tension between more orthodox circles that adhered to the Deuteronomistic, prophetic, and priestly types of theology of sin and punishment, and less orthodox circles that expressed complaint and protest against God. The former circles maintained that God was upholding his part of the covenant and proclaimed that although Israel had violated the covenant, God nevertheless chose to cleave to them. In contrast, the latter circles declared that God (rather than the people) had broken his side of the covenant by abandoning them and handing them over to their enemies.[16]

In my estimate, Werline's and Rom-Shiloni's interpretations explain best the biblical evidence. As we shall see shortly, the lament in Isa 63:7—64:11 and the penitential prayer in Neh 5 can be dated roughly to the same time period and place (early post-monarchic Judah). I therefore suggest that lament and penitential prayer, although interconnected, reflect different types of theology and fill different functions at one given time.[17] This, in turn, shows that one cannot be substituted for the other and one did not supersede the other. The loss of one is not the gain of the other.

3. *The Problem with Penitential Prayer*

In his discussion of the Deuteronomic/Deuteronomistic roots of penitential prayer, Werline phrases aptly the central problem that this chapter

15. Werline, *Penitential Prayer*, 11–64 (esp. 62–64).

16. Rom-Shiloni, "Socio-Ideological Setting or Settings?," 51–68.

17. Don Moffat, this volume, makes the same point as he states that "lament and penitential prayer are related but different responses to suffering and crisis."

seeks to address: "There is no place in Deuteronomy for the language of the innocent sufferer." The laments reflect the belief that the lamenting persons are suffering *unjustly* for no fault of their own. The casuistic Deuteronomic theology makes lament impossible as it always "maintains a correlation between obedience and reward, between disobedience and retribution."[18] In our present, post-holocaust world, such a theology is often inappropriate as we must seek to uphold a balance between unjust suffering and rightful divine punishment. The correlation between sin and punishment has broken down as no sin can justify the killing of six million Jews.[19]

In his article "Priceless Gain," Boda states that "complaint against God for difficult circumstances is inappropriate when these circumstances are the result of sin."[20] This is correct, yet it is also my bone of contention. How can we, from a human perspective, determine when hardship is the result of sin and thus a correct punishment and when it is not?[21] The book of Job presents the ultimate example of the conundrum wherein Job upholds his innocence and refuses to confess any sins in the face of his friends' claim that he must have sinned. There has to be an alternative to penitential prayer for those persons who, judged from their own human perspective, suffer calamity despite not having trespassed any divine rule or where the disaster is not in proportion to their sins. It must be possible for an innocent victim to lament without being burdened with feelings of guilt that their present suffering is the result of sin. For instance, the parents whose child dies in cot-death must be free to lament the loss of their child without having to search their lives for a sin committed that can explain the death (*contra* 2 Sam 12:15).

18. Werline, *Penitential Prayer*, 25.

19. Balentine, "I was Ready," 7–8. See also Nasuti, *Sacred Songs*, 12–17 (mentioned by Balentine), who discusses the fact that a scholar's focus on a particular matter is intimately connected with his/her own historical situation and the focus of the surrounding world of scholarship.

20. Boda, "Priceless Gain," 94.

21. Boda addresses the issue of differentiating between the need to lament and the need to ask for forgiveness in ancient Israel. Boda argues that the textual evidence in Jer 7:16; 11:14, and 14:11 where Jeremiah is forbidden to intercede suggests that the prophet participated on several occasions where communal lament took place. Furthermore, as shown by Jer 21:2 and 37:3, Jeremiah's role on these occasions would have been to ask for and receive a divine oracle. He argues that the prophets, with their access to the divine council of God, were in a unique position to discern "between a moment when Lament was appropriate and one that demanded Penitential Prayer." See *Boda*, "From Complaint to Contrition," 186–97 (esp. 196).

From a Christian perspective, there is grace and forgiveness from God to receive for those who confess their sins (1 John 1:9). Yet this statement must be seen in the larger context of Christian theology of sin according to which sinfulness is an integral part of the human condition. Everyone is a sinner and thus deserving of punishment and in need of grace. This type of theology, although having its roots in the Hebrew Bible, is not the *only* theology of sin and punishment extant in the Hebrew Bible. Notably, both Job (Job 1:8) and Mordecai (Esth 10:3) are portrayed as good and righteous.

Moffat points out that by the second temple period, penitential prayer had become the appropriate response to suffering, whether deserved or not, and where righteous sufferers pray penitential prayers (e.g., Tob 3:2–6 and the Prayer of Azariah). Moreover, it was better adapted to the religious landscape that was to give birth to Judaism and Christianity.[22] Yet I hesitate to advocate this model of prayer to the modern church. It runs the risk of introducing an element of insincerity into prayer as penitential prayer becomes the expected format of prayer and it may cause people to include confessions of sins simply as a matter of *pro forma* without any deeper reflections. As cautioned by Bruggemann (above), honest communication between God and the worshipper will suffer. Moreover, it will inevitably induce a feeling of guilt into the mind of the suffering person. This, in turn, may make it difficult for that person to express his/her distress as there is a prevailing sense that only a person without guilt can lament. Rather, I agree with Bauer who differentiates between lament and guilt.

In cases of "actual sin," i.e., when a person has violated, rebelled against, or in any other way resisted God's will, there is healing in the acts of confession and penitence. Smith-Christopher argues that public admissions of wrongdoing such as Ezra 9:6 (using the three words "sin" [עונתינו], "shame" [בשתי] and "guilt" [ואשמתנו]); Neh 9:26; and Dan 9:5–7 (using the terms "sinned" [חטאנו], "done wrong" [עוינו], "acted wickedly" [הרשענו], "rebelled," [מרדנו] and "turned away" [סור]) constitute the central theme of penitential prayers. The statements that relate to the behavior of one's ancestors can serve as recognition of our constant failure to live in accordance with specific laws and values, and as "narrative repair," i.e., lessons in what not to do.[23]

22. See Moffat's essay in this volume.

23. Smith-Christopher, *Theology of Exile*, 117, 120. See also Lapsley, "Shame and Self-Knowledge," 143–73 (esp. 154–59, where Lapsley argues that shame can lead to self-knowledge which in turn will result in a renewed relationship with God).

Yet we should also never have to carry a burden that is not ours to carry. A too strong focus on penitential prayer may lead a person to confess sins that they have not committed and to take on a burden of guilt that can actually be harmful. Many situations of suffering may contain elements of guilt, stemming both from acts committed and acts left undone, and those who are guilty should repent rather than lament. However, not all painful situations can be traced back to one's own or someone else's guilt because not all situations are caused by culpable actions.[24]

Turning to the Hebrew Bible, the lament psalms convey a *smörgåsbord* of sufferers, ranging from those who suffer the punishment of their sins (e.g., Pss 25:7, 11; 41:5 [Eng. v. 4]; 51:1–5, 9; 79:9) to those who suffer because of no obvious fault of their own (Pss 7:4–6 [Eng. vv. 3–5]; 17:3–4; 26:3–6; 44:18–23; 59:4–5 [Eng. vv. 3–4]). Indeed, a given psalm can contain both approaches (see Ps 69:5, 7–12 where the sufferer is aware of his sins, yet also laments that he suffers because of his actions for God's glory). There are examples where, from a human perspective, the divine punishment fits the crime and others where, again from our human perspective, the divine punishment appears to be excessive. Therefore, in line with the textual evidence cited above, penitential prayer and lament should not be pitted against each other but each be given its due time and place. Although penitential prayer gained dominance in the post-exilic period, in part as a reaction to the type of theology expressed in the lament, the Hebrew Bible in its final form contains both types of literature which, in turn, gives the church today access to both.

PART II

The central section of my chapter looks at the interchange between lament and penitential prayer in Isa 40–66 as the means to illustrate their co-existence and their divergent functions. I shall argue that Isa 40–66 is a so-called "open text" that contains more than one voice regarding suffering and that the church today can draw upon that diversity in its search for an appropriate balance between lament and penitential prayer.

24. Bauer, "Absence of Lament," 25–43 (esp. 42–43).

4. Isaiah 40–55

A single text may allow for more than one opinion and more than one theology. Such plurality need not be a sign of multiple authorship but instead may reveal the author's or the editor's conscious strategy to offer more than one answer. Notably, several scholars have highlighted the multiple and often contradictory attitudes towards suffering within the book of Lamentations. Boase demonstrates that Lamentations contains many competing voices and themes. For instance, the material in Lam 1:8–9 depicts the destruction of Jerusalem as the just punishment for its sins, yet the portrayal of Jerusalem as a victim of assault in the same passage questions and subverts that viewpoint.[25] Likewise, Heim argues that the different voices in Lamentations reflect the various and conflicting opinions in the community responsible for its composition. In this manner, Lamentations is an "open text" that provides multiple answers to the complex questions related to the destruction of Jerusalem.[26]

I have argued elsewhere that Isa 40–55,[27] like Lamentations, is such an open text. It contains several voices (Jacob-Israel, Zion-Jerusalem, the Servant, etc.) that express distinct and at times also contradictory opinions. Yet, in contrast to Lamentations, Isa 40–55 contains a dominant voice—God's voice—that articulates a divinely sanctioned response to these voices. Besides God, Zion-Jerusalem and the Servant are the two dominant literary personae. They represent two divergent ways of relating to the destruction of Jerusalem or, expressed more generally, as two different models of response to suffering.[28]

Zion-Jerusalem is the clear representative of the voice of laments in Isa 49:14–15a, 21, and 24, and she embodies the theology of Lam 1–2, 4–5.[29] In Isa 49:14–15a, she exclaims that the Lord has forsaken her and forgotten her (עזבני ה׳ ואדני שכחני), and accuses God of unnatural behavior, akin to that of a woman who forgets her baby and who has no

25. Boase, *Fulfilment of Doom?*, 43–44, 204–38 (example taken from p. 211).

26. Heim, "Personification of Jerusalem," 169.

27. Although there is no evidence to suggest that Isa 40–55 ever existed as an independent composition, form critical and composition critical criteria favour treating Isa 40–55 as a literary unity. See, for example, Melugin, *Formation of Isaiah* 40–55, and Gitay, *Prophecy and Persuasion*.

28. Tiemeyer, *Comfort of Zion*, 212–320.

29. Cf. Tiemeyer, "Lamentations in Isaiah 40–55." See also Tiemeyer, "Isaiah 40–55."

compassion for her child (התשכח אשה עולה מרחם בן בטנה). In Isa 49:21, we partake of Zion-Jerusalem's thoughts at the time when her children will be arriving: מי ילד לי את אלה ואני שכולה וגלמודה (אתנחתא) גלה וסורה ואלה מי גדל הן אני נשארתי לבדי אלה איפה הם = "Who has borne me these? I was bereaved and barren / an exile and passing away[30] and these, who raised [them]? / Behold, I was left behind alone. These, of what kind are they?" Again, Zion-Jerusalem embodies the voice of lament. Finally, we hear the lamenting voice of Zion-Jerusalem anew in Isa 49:24. This verse expresses her doubts as to God's ability and willingness to save ("can booty can been taken from the mighty one, or can a captive can be delivered from an awe-inspiring one?") (היקח מגבור מלקוח ואם שבי צדיק ימלט).[31]

In comparison, the Servant personifies a more traditional theology, akin to but not identical with the theology of penitential prayer, and he has a parallel in Lam 3.[32] In Isa 49:4–5, the Servant wavers between lament and gratitude in a manner reminiscent of penitential prayer, although with the significant exception that he does not confess any sin. Verse 4a presents a person on the brink of despair, while the speaker in verses 4b and 5b expresses his confidence in God's salvation. The Servant's speech in Isa 50:4–11 continues on this confident note. The Servant articulates his firm belief in God's righteousness despite oppression. The Servant neither rebelled nor turned away when God "opened his ears"[33] (v. 5), nor did he raise any objections when people treated him badly (v. 6). Instead he trusted that God would see him right (vv. 7–8aa).

The Servant's attitude is similar to that of Job in that both characters reflect on those who act wrongly towards them and both confess their belief that God will put their situation right, yet neither holds himself

30. For the translation of וסורה, see the discussion by Goldingay and Payne, *Isaiah 40–55*, 191.

31. The *Niphal* of ימלט can have both an active and a passive sense. Here, assuming that verse 24b is parallel to verse 24a, I have chosen the passive sense. A passive sense is also assumed by the LXX (σωθήσεται = "be rescued"), although the whole of verse 24b in the LXX ("and if one should take [a man] captive unjustly, shall he be delivered?") seems to paraphrase the MT. A passive reading is adopted by, among others, Childs, *Isaiah*, 388, and Blenkinsopp, *Isaiah 40–55*, 313–14, including note a. As to the word צדיק, much favours adopting the reading of 1QIsa[a] (עריץ). In particular, both the V (*a robusto*) and the Peshitta (עשינא) seem to support the Hebrew consonantal text עריץ ("awe-inspiring"). In addition, verse 25 parallels the two concepts of גבור and עריץ. Cf. Tiemeyer, *Comfort of Zion*, 190.

32. Cf. Tiemeyer, "Lamentations in Isaiah 40–55."

33. The notion of God "opening the ear" of someone is probably a metaphor for God's revelatory speech. See further Goldingay and Payne, *Isaiah*, II, 210.

responsible for his situation. As we have seen, the Servant expresses a theology with only partial correlation between sin and punishment. Isaiah 42:1–9 contains no word that the weak ones (v. 3) are suffering because they have sinned. As for Isa 52:12—53:13, this passage, on the one hand, epitomizes a direct correlation between sin and punishment while, on the other hand, collapses this very type of theology. Those who are guilty are *not* suffering because the Servant is suffering in their place. An innocent person can be afflicted by God (Isa 53:4) although he is righteous (Isa 53:11ab). In this manner, both the Servant and Zion-Jerusalem, albeit in very different ways, challenge the idea that suffering stems from sin, and neither character confesses any sins.[34]

As for Isa 40–55 as a whole, Scheuer has recently shown that Isa 40–55 conveys a tension between God's invitation to return to him and his exhortations to repentance. In particular, Scheuer demonstrates that salvation *leads* to repentance (rather than being its *prerequisite*). In Isa 40–55, God offers his salvation freely with no preconditions attached to it. God's offer of salvation will then cause the people to turn to him in repentance. Thus, in contrast to the theology of Dtn/DtrH where salvation depends on repentance, Isa 40–55 envisions a sequence of sin-punishment-deliverance-repentance.[35]

5. *Isaiah 56–66*

As Isa 40–55, the subsequent material in Isa 56–66 expresses multiple theologies of sin and punishment. This is evidenced by the difference in outlook between the penitential prayer in Isa 59:9–15, the lament in Isa 63:7—64:11, and the responding material in Isa 65:1—66:17. In contrast to the situation in Isa 40–55, it is likely that the various textual blocks were composed at different times and by different authors; yet the group of people responsible for putting the final text together chose to place these seemingly contradictory texts side by side and thereby created a polyvalent final text.

From a text-historical perspective, the lament in Isa 63:7—64:11 probably stems from early post-monarchic Judah and thus constitutes the oldest material in Isa 56–66. A sixth-century dating is inferred partly from the references to the temple being trampled by enemies in Isa 63:18

34. Cf. Tiemeyer, *Comfort of Zion*, 318–23.

35. Scheuer, *Return of YHWH*.

and to the ruins of Jerusalem and a temple that has been destroyed by fire in Isa 64:9–10 (Eng. 64:10–11), and partly from its resemblance to other early post-monarchic Judahite texts (Lamentations, Neh 9).[36] As to the material in Isa 59:9–15 (part of the longer section of Isa 56:9—59:21),[37] its many structural and thematic similarities with the material in Isa 65:1—66:17 suggests common authorship. It is furthermore likely that that author/ group of authors composed Isa 65:1—66:17 as a response to the lament in Isa 63:7—64:11 (see further below).[38]

I have so far referred to Isa 63:7—64:11 as a lament, yet many scholars see it as a penitential prayer.[39] The hinge of the matter is Isa 64:4–6 (Eng. vv. 5–7). As I have shown in detail elsewhere, the expression פגעת את שש (v. 4aa) is best translated as "you have stricken the one who rejoices in doing what is right." It is further syntactically preferable to translate the statement הן אתה קצפת ונחטא (v. 4ba) as "you were angry and therefore (as a consequence) we sinned." In other words, God's anger (perfect) *precedes* the people's sinning (imperfect). As to the near incomprehensible expression בהם עולם ונושע (v. 4bb), I emend it to the orthographically similar בהעלמך ונפשע and translate it as "and when you hid, we erred." This reading agrees with Isa 63:17 that ascribes the cause of sin to God, with Isa 63:19a that complains against God, and with Isa 64:5 that states that the people's righteousness has become like an impure rag. Isa 64:4 is thus more of a declaration of innocence and less of a confession of sins.[40]

A broader look at all of Isa 63:7—64:11 confirms this impression. It rejects the notion that the people praying are responsible for their present suffering. Although it refers to sins in general (64:8) and to past sins

36. See my discussion and cited bibliography in Tiemeyer, *Priestly Rites and Prophetic Rage*, 57–60, and "Two Prophets," 187–89. See also Bautch, *Developments in Genre*, 62–63, who argues that Isa 63:7—64:11 was used as a communal lament by the people of Judah, probably constituting both indigenous Judahites and newly returned exiles. Cf. Boase's essay in this volume, who suggests that Isa 63:7—64:11 was composed in the early post-monarchic period.

37. See, e.g., Smith, *Rhetoric and Redaction*, 138; and Polan, *Justice towards Salvation*, 318–19. See my summary of their views in Tiemeyer, *Priestly Rites*, 45–48.

38. Tiemeyer, *Priestly Rites*, 48–65.

39. E.g., Werline, *Penitential Prayer*, 41–45. In particular, he regards Isa 63:4–7 as a confession of sins. See also Bautch, *Developments in Genre*, 61–63, who interprets Isa 63:7—64:11 as a proto-penitential composition/communal lament, and stresses its combination of complaints of God's perceived absence and confession of sins. Cf. his "Lament Regained," 83–99. See also Boda, *Severe Mercy*, 216–18 (esp. 218).

40. Tiemeyer, *Priestly Rites*, 102–8.

that have caused God to act against his people (63:10),[41] the greater part of the material contests any correlation between sin and suffering. Isa 64:8 (Eng. v. 9) is a case in point. The speakers are careful to distance themselves from the sin. Rather than saying that *they* have sinned, they plead with God not to remember iniquity forever (ואל לעד תזכר עון). The indefinite form[42] of עון suggests that the "iniquity" is that of the ancestors in Isa 63:10. The people praying in Isa 63:7—64:11 furthermore places the responsibility for their current suffering upon God (Isa 63:10b, 15–19; 64:4–6 [Eng. 64:5–7]). In particular, they maintain that God has contributed to their suffering as he allowed them to go astray and as he hardened their hearts (63:17). Really, the people sinned *because* God was angry (64:4 [5]).

6. Daughter Zion in Isaiah 40–55 and the Lament in Isaiah 56–66

So far, we have noted a certain affinity between the theology of Zion-Jerusalem in Isa 49 and the theology of the lament in Isa 63:7—64:11. We have also seen that that theology is different from the theology of the surrounding material. Put succinctly, what is the *Sitz-in-der-Literatur* of Zion-Jerusalem's lament and the lament in Isa 63:7—64:11 within Isa 40–66?

Beginning with the speech of Zion-Jerusalem, the authors/redactors responsible for Isa 40–55 neither fully endorse Zion-Jerusalem's view of the situation in Judah nor criticize it openly. Instead, they let Zion-Jerusalem's statements stand as they are so that the audience can identify themselves with her, yet they present the way of the Servant as an ultimately better way and seek to convince their audience to embrace his attitude. There is a strong awareness throughout all of Isa 40–55 that the audience has fared ill and must be treated with delicacy. The audience needs to be convinced *carefully* that they would benefit from giving up their critical attitude towards God.[43]

41. Cf. Boase, in this volume, who argues that this verse betrays a retributive theodicy, akin to the theology of Dtr/DtrH. Yet, those lamenting apply this theodicy only to past generations and not to their own situation (see further below).

42. *Contra* LXX which has a plural form and a 1pl. possessive suffix "our sins" (ἁμαρτιῶν ἡμῶν).

43. See further Tiemeyer, *Comfort of Zion*, 318–29.

By contrast, the authors/redactors of Isa 56–66 reject to a large extent the sentiments expressed in the lament in Isa 63:7—64:11. They bring the lament, presumably a text familiar to the people of Judah, into dialogue with the rest of the Isaianic textual corpus and furnish it with a purpose-written negative response (Isa 65:1—66:17). The textual relationship between the lament and Isa 65:1—66:17 can be deduced from the impressive number of shared lexical, stylistic and structural features.[44] The later authors of Isa 65:1—66:17 thus emphasize that they disagree with the sentiments voiced in the lament and that they consider the people lamenting to be sinners (65:7a). The people have failed to seek God even though he has sought them (65:1–2), they have humiliated him by acting in a manner not pleasing to him (65:3–4, 7; 66:3 17), and they have committed idolatry (65:11). Yet there are people in Judah, possibly including some of those lamenting, that have remained faithful and for whom God will care (65:8–10).

7. The Penitential Prayer in Isaiah 59:9–16a

It is likely that the authors responsible for Isa 65:1—66:17 also wrote Isa 56:9—59:21 (cf. above). As the lament in Isa 63:7—64:11, the material in Isa 56:9—59:21 articulates the problem of the current suffering in Judah, yet it determines its cause differently: the difficult situation in Judah must mean that its inhabitants have sinned and the solution is penitence and confession of sins. It spells out the types of sins that the people have committed (Isa 56:9—57:13; 58:1–14; 59:1–8) and it affirms that the people's sins have separated them from God (59:2). This kind of theology belongs firmly within the tradition of sin and punishment familiar from Dtr/DtrH. The promise of salvation in Isa 57:14–21 continues in the same vein as it claims that God became angry *because* of the people's sins and *therefore* punished them and hid himself. The people failed to take heed and continued to walk their own way (v. 17).

In many ways, the material in Isa 59:9–15a constitutes the counterpart of the lament in Isa 63:7—64:11. The first person speakers admit their many sins (v. 12) and confess to rebellion, deceit, extortion, backsliding and turning away from God, and all kinds of lies (v. 13).

44. See especially Steck, *Studien*, 221–24, Koenen, *Ethik und Eschatologie*, 159, 168, 183 (summaries), 252–56 (translation), and Smith, *Rhetoric*, 128, 132, 134, 136, 140, 142, 172.

Furthermore, the juxtaposition of verse 13 and verses 14–15a implies that these actions have caused the lack of justice in the land. Although Isa 59:9–15a contains elements of lament (vv. 11b, 14–15a),[45] its dominant impression is penitence.

The preceding material in Isa 59:1–8 likewise expresses sentiments at odds with the theology of Isa 63:7—64:11. In particular, the opening sentence in verse 1 which exclaims that God's arm is not too weak to save, as well as the ensuing statements which maintain that God is willing to save but that the sins of the people hinder him (v. 2) as they walk their own way (v. 8), explicitly contradicts the claims in the lament that God is responsible for the people's situation and that he is causing them to err from his way (e.g. 63:17).

As evidenced by the positive response in Isa 59:15b–20/21, the people's penitence recorded in Isa 59:9–15a received the approval of the final redactors of Isa 56–66. In contrast to the negative response in Isa 65:1—66:17 to the lament in Isa 63:7—64:11, here God expresses his feelings of dismay that he felt when he saw the lack of justice in the land, and how he therefore decided to act on behalf of those "who turn from transgression" (Isa 59:20ab). In this manner, the final authors/editors of Isa 56–66 emphasize that confession of sins and penitence will bring God's redemption while lament will not. Isa 56–66 is thus a significantly less "open text" than Isa 40–55. While Isa 40–55 presents the lament of Daughter Zion as a legitimate although not the ultimate way of responding to suffering, Isa 56–66 proclaims that for God's servants, the heirs of the Servant in Isa 40–55, confession and penitence are the only right way forward.

At the same time, the very fact that these authors/editors incorporated the lament in Isa 63:7—64:11 together with their own material provides later readers with access to the lament and thus gives them the option either to accept the sentiments voiced in the lament or to adopt the theology of sin and punishment expressed by Isa 65:1—66:17.[46] Probably contrary to the intent of the authors/editors of Isa 56–66, their decision to incorporate the lament in Isa 63:7—64:11 into the larger literary context of Isa 56–66 helped to create a polyphonic compilation of texts that allows for conflicting view points and theologies. In the same way as Isa 40–55 contains not only God's perspective but that of Zion-Jerusalem

45. Cf. Werline, *Penitential Prayer*, 39.

46. See further Tiemeyer, "Two Laments," 195–201.

and the Servant, as well as that of Jacob-Israel and yet others, so Isa 56–66 contains the perspectives of both the people who lament in 63:7—64:11 and those who see themselves as the Servant's heirs (e.g. Isa 65:13–15 and 66:2) and who advocate a theology according to which calamity is the result of sin and where penitence constitutes the only way forward.

8. Lament and Penitential Prayer in Isaiah 40–66: Reflections

Modern readers of the Hebrew Bible who are uncomfortable with the uncompromising Dtr/DtrH theology and who seek a balance between lament and confessions of sin can find solace in the multivalent text of Isa 40–66. As readers of the final text, we can identify with Zion-Jerusalem in Isa 40–55 and with the lamenters in Isa 63:7—64:11 if an honest estimation of our suffering enables us to say that it is not caused by our sins and that it has become worse as a result of God's silence and perceived absence. We can also bear in mind the way of the Servant in Isa 40–55 and ask whether we can adopt his approach to suffering. Can we, like Job, reject the notion that we have committed any specific sin that has caused our suffering, yet at the same time accept the suffering as something that is from God and that fills a purpose that is unrelated to our own situation and well-being? Finally, the divine oracles in Isa 59:1–8, 15b–20/21, and 65:1—66:17, as well as the penitential prayer in Isa 59:9–15a, remind us that our sins can have caused or contributed to our present suffering. Could it be that we have not looked for God while he has been there for us, along the lines of Isa 65:1–2, and could it be that we have humiliated God by our actions in the same way as the people are accused of doing in Isa 65:3–4? If so, then the correct response should be repentance and penitential prayer.

PART III

9. Nehemiah 9

The penitential prayer in Neh 9:5b–37 also has a bearing on the issue of lament versus penitence. In the final form of the text of Ezra-Nehemiah, Neh 9:5b–37 is a prayer, uttered by the Levites,[47] that follows Ezra's reading

47. I follow the reading of the MT which attests to no change of speaker (*contra*

of the law. From a historical-critical perspective, there are good reasons for distinguishing between Neh 9:5b–37 and its immediate literary context. In particular, Ezra's absence from Neh 9:5b–37, the disagreement between the content of Neh 9:5b–37 and the specific historical circumstances of the time of Nehemiah, and the contrast between Neh 9:5b–37 and the prayers of Ezra 9 and Neh 1, set Neh 9:5b–37 apart.[48] Furthermore, the ideology of Neh 9:5b–37 differs from the prevailing ideology of Ezra-Nehemiah. For instance, the critical attitude towards Judah's political overlords in Neh 9:32, 37 differs from the more positive outlook in the rest of Ezra-Nehemiah,[49] which, in turn, suggests that Neh 9:5b–37 was composed earlier than the surrounding Neh 7:72b—10:40. It is therefore probable that the authors/redactors responsible for Neh 7:72b—10:40 incorporated an already existing prayer into their composition.

An early post-monarchic dating and a Judahite setting of Neh 9:5b–37 can be inferred from its content. The exile, although alluded to in vv. 30–31, plays an insignificant role in the prayer.[50] The many literary and thematic connections to Haggai and Zech 1–8 suggest a dating around 520 BCE,[51] and the material in both Zech 7:1–7 and 8:18–23 testifies to the existence of penitential liturgies in early post-monarchic Judah.[52] In addition, several scholars have noted the marked affinity between Neh 9:5b–37 and Isa 63:7—64:11[53] and suggested that the two texts share the same geographical setting and date of composition. Williamson, for example, points out that the fact that we can argue convincingly and independently of one another in favor of an exilic Judahite setting of Neh 9:5b–37 and Isa 63:7—64:11; the similarities of the two texts strengthen the probability that they both stem from exilic Judah.[54]

LXX that assigns Ezra as the speaker). See further Duggan, *Covenant Renewal*, 161, and Werline, *Penitential Prayer*, 57.

48. Williamson, "Structure," 282–83, with supporting bibliography. See also Boda, *Praying the Tradition*, 10–11.

49. Clines, *Ezra, Nehemiah, Esther*, 192–93; Blenkinsopp, *Ezra-Nehemiah*, 301; Williamson, "Structure," 283, 289–90.

50. Welch, "Nehemiah IX," 135.

51. Boda, *Praying the Tradition*, 190–95.

52. Williamson, "Isaiah 63,7—64,11," 57–58.

53. E.g., Blenkinsopp, *Ezra-Nehemiah*, 302; Williamson, "Isaiah 63,7—64,11," 56–58.

54. Williamson, "Isaiah 63,7—64,11," 57–58.

The penitential prayer in Neh 9:5b–37 differs significantly from the lament in Isa 63:7—64:11 in terms of both content and emphasis. Neh 9:5b–37 stresses God's acts of mercy on behalf of Israel to a much larger extent than Isa 63:7—64:11 (Neh 9:6–31 *versus* Isa 63:7–14). In parallel, the present predicament of the people plays a smaller role in Neh 9:5b–37 than in Isa 63:7—64:11 (Neh 9:32, 36–37 *versus* Isa 63:15—64:12). In addition, Neh 9:5b–37 maintains that the people are responsible for their situation (Neh 9:33–35) and exonerates God (Neh 9:33), whereas Isa 63:7—64:11 claims that God's lack of care has caused the people's sin (Isa 63:17; 64:4).

On another level, Neh 9:5b–37 is comparable to Isa 63:7—64:11 in that both texts constitute originally independent compositions that have been incorporated at a later stage into another text and thus find themselves in a new and potentially incompatible *Sitz-in-der-Literatur*. Can we therefore say that Neh 7:72b—10:40 (or Ezra-Nehemiah) is an "open text" in the same way as Isa 40–66 is? In the specific case concerning the relationship between sin and punishment, the answer is no. Although the prayer in Neh 9:5b–37 and the surrounding Neh 9:1–5a, 38 stem from different authors, and although the prayer reflects a different historical situation and different attitudes towards Persia than the surrounding material (and in this one respect, Ezra-Nehemiah is actually an "open text"), Neh 9:5b–37 agrees with the surrounding material when it comes to the relationship between sin and punishment. Nehemiah's prayer in Neh 1 connects the miserable situation in Jerusalem (v. 3) with the people's sins (vv. 6–7), and it attaches promises of repentance to the plea for restoration (vv. 8–11). The final form of Ezra-Nehemiah further suggests that the sin of intermarriages (Ezra 9:10–15; Neh 9:2; 10:30) triggered the penitential prayer in Neh 9:5b–37. Along the same lines, Ezra 9:10–15 connects the miserable situation in Judah with the intermarriages and calls them "evil deeds" (מעשינו הרעים) and "great guilt" (אשמתנו הגדלה) (Ezra 9:13a).

From a broader perspective, the readers of the final text are steered towards accepting Nehemiah's estimation of the situation because neither the divorced wives nor Nehemiah's opponents (e.g., Noadiah, Sanballat, Tobiah) have a voice in Ezra-Nehemiah. The text of Nehemiah does not, in a fundamentally different manner than especially Isa 40–55 but also Isa 56–66, pick up the various sentiments among its audience and present them as a *smörgåsbord* of choice. And we should not expect it to do so either. In a sense, the texts of Job, Isa 40-66, and Lamentations are unique among the biblical writings in that they present more than one attitude to sin and punishment within one and the same text. In the book of Job, the readers are free to make Eliphaz's attitude their own, in the same manner as they can choose Job's attitude or that of Lady Wisdom. Of course, the overall structure of the book of Job favours the approach of Job. Likewise, although the readers of Isa 40–55 and, to a significantly lesser extent, the readers of Isa 56–66, have different stand-points to choose from, the authors/redactors of the texts make their own dispositions clear. The readers of Nehemiah, however, have but one option if they wish to read the text with the grain.

CONCLUSION

This study has shown that lament and penitential prayer are two distinct yet related forms of communication with God. Both types of communication are present, often alongside one another, in the Hebrew Bible. It has further demonstrated that penitential prayer is not an improvement of lament. The loss of lament in contemporary Christian settings is a serious matter and penitential prayer cannot fill that gap. Penitential prayer is also not inferior to lament. Lament and penitential prayer are rather two different types of communication with God, aimed at two different situations, and one cannot replace the other. There is a time and place for penitential prayer, yet it is important that we hold on to lament as a form of communication with God where we are not forced, by the very genre, to take the blame for our misfortunes.

PART TWO

Reflections

9

Wrestling with Lamentations in Christian Worship

Robin A. Parry

INTRODUCTION

The book of Lamentations was birthed in order to bring a deep and profound grief before the throne of Yhwh in the context of communal worship. It found ongoing relevance for the people of God in the worship of Jewish and Christian communities over the centuries and, if it is to function as *Holy Scripture* today, it must do so by finding a place in the ongoing worshipping life of synagogue and church. This chapter offers some reflections on *Christian* theological interpretation of Lamentations in doxological contexts.

LAMENTATIONS IN LITURGICAL CONTEXT

Lamentations in the Worship of Ancient Israel

Biblical scholars have devoted considerable attention to the question of the original life setting of the poems that make up Lamentations. While there is much disagreement on such issues, the almost unanimous view of biblical scholars is that the poetry of Lamentations was composed as a liturgical response to the Babylonian destruction of Jerusalem in 587 and its aftermath.[1] The poems, in other words, were written for use in public worship. It may well be that they were used in services held on the ruined temple site, although we cannot be certain of this.

The evidence for the use of Lamentations in public worship is mainly internal. Both the form and content of the poems are strongly suggestive of a liturgical function for the book (or, at least, its component parts). The poems of Lamentations have strong formal similarities to numerous Psalms and also some similarities to ancient Near Eastern city laments both of which strongly suggest a public use for the poetry.[2] In terms of content we could note that the communal prayers in the book, for instance, seem to have little use outside of a communal worship setting. The fact that later Jewish tradition came to employ Lamentations for liturgical use on the 9th of Av only reinforces these impressions.

There are numerous issues debated amongst scholars regarding the formal classification of the different poems. Chapter 5 is the most straightforward—the majority of scholars see it as more or less a communal lament. It contains a complaint in the face of disaster, a request that God rescue his suffering people, and a self-reproach for the arising of the situation. Middlemas, while seeing no hope communicated through the *content* of the poem (I take a more positive approach towards the content), does see hope embodied in the poetic *form* because communal lament was motivated by the hope that God might act to redeem.[3]

Chapter 3 is the least straightforward poem to analyze, being a unique combination of elements from a range of literary genres unlike any other in the Old Testament. Consequently suggestions regarding its prehistory prior to inclusion in the book or of its specific liturgical function are heavily speculative.

Chapters 1, 2, and 4 combine forms. To take chapter 1 as an example; since the work of Jahnow in 1923[4] and Gunkel in 1929[5] most commentators recognize elements from *the funeral dirge* in the poem.

1. Even if, with a few scholars, one questions the traditional dating (e.g., Provan, "Reading Texts") that does not affect one's conclusions regarding the liturgical function of the book.

2. On the debate about links between Lamentations and ANE city laments see Kramer, *Lamentation*; Michalowski, *Lamentation*; Dobbs-Allsopp, *Weep, O Daughter of Zion*.

3. Middlemas, *Troubles*, 222, 226.

4. Jahnow, *Das Hebräische*.

5. Gunkel, "Klagelieder Jeremiae."

These include the mournful cry "Alas!" (אֵיכָה, 1:1), the description of misery that follows it (2a, 4c), and the presence of the reversal motif (1:1, 6). Clearly the dirge form has been modified because certain elements, such as the announcement that someone has died, are missing while alien elements, such as the plea to Yhwh and the confession of guilt, are present. Westermann, on the other hand, argues that Lam 1, especially the second section, is primarily a *communal lament*.[6] He sees the following major elements from the communal lament in the poem: (a) the community's direct complaint (1:9c, 11c, 20a), (b) the accusation against God (1:12c–15), (c) the complaint about enemies (1:5a, 9c, 21b). He also thinks that the following minor elements are drawn from the communal lament form: (d) the acknowledgement of guilt (1:14a, 18a, 22b), (e) the plea for Yhwh to take heed (1:9c, 11c, 20a), (f) the plea for reprisal on the enemies (1:21–22) and, (g) the motif of God's justification (1:18) set over against the accusation against God (1:12c–15). However, there are also elements from the communal lament form, such as the expression of trust, that are missing in Lam 1. Also our poem does not always follow the expected order of elements in the communal lament. Westermann sees this as resulting from the pressure of the acrostic form but even if this were the case the form is still disrupted. Whether we see Lam 1 as a dirge modified by elements from the communal lament or vice versa we must concede that it is not close to a "pure" form. This poem includes some, but not all, elements from both forms and blends them in a unique way. We need to adequately respect the *uniqueness* of the poem as well as what it shares with other poems.[7]

For our purposes, however, we do not need to settle all the controverted questions debated by modern biblical scholars, nor can we afford to spend all our time in their august company, because the context within

6. Westermann, *Lamentations*, 114–19. Eissfeldt, while seeing a dirge in 1:1–11 and 17, maintains that 9c, 11c, and 12–16 are in the form of an *individual lament* (Eissfeldt, *The Old Testament*, 501–5. See also Re'emi, "The Theology of Hope," 79).

7. Renkema, *Lamentations*, 91–93. Tod Linafelt proposes that it is not a coincidence that the elements of the dirge form cluster in the narrator's speech while elements of the lament cluster in Lady Zion's speech. The narrator's speech is dominated by the overtones of death even though Zion is not dead. Zion, however, is a survivor and when she speaks it is a lament straining towards life, and not a dirge looking back to death, that she employs. Thus the very form of her speech indicates a resistance to her fate not found in the narrator's speech, the form of which suggests a mournful resignation (Linafelt, *Surviving*, 35–43).

which we need to read Lamentations is far wider than that with which biblical scholars are normally concerned.

All sacred texts are inherited by worshippers within a living tradition of reception that informs the ongoing use of the text though a process of sedimentations and innovation.[8] The poems of our book were created for worship and have been used within worship throughout Jewish and Christian history and this should inform their ongoing reception within both synagogue and church. If these poems are to *function* as Scripture for believers then they can only do so within *doxological* contexts.

Now academic biblical scholarship plays a constructive role in the hermeneutical enterprise by enabling a relative "distancing of horizons" between a text and its modern interpreter. This allows texts to stand over against us and surprise us and in that way it helps us avoid domesticating them. As such it can serve to limit the range of legitimate meanings that a text can have. But if we leave biblical texts in the hands of scholars without returning them to their natural habitat those texts have ceased to function as *Scripture*.

Lamentations in the Worship of the Synagogue

Lamentations has long occupied an important place in the Jewish liturgical calendar. It strikes me that there are at least five things of critical importance that the churches can learn from the Jewish tradition here. First, the text of Lamentations is used as a means for reflecting on other catastrophes that have touched the Jewish people. In this way the text is allowed to be read in the presence of horrors not considered by its author(s), thereby opening up new horizons of meaning and ways in which the text finds ongoing significance within a community.

Second, while the Jewish tradition allows the text to interpret, and be interpreted by, catastrophes other than that which occasioned its creation, the original historical referent is not eclipsed in the process. That is to say that the Jewish tradition has always used Lamentations to remind the community of the original Babylonian destruction of Jerusalem. This event may serve as a model for other, later horrors thereby allowing the words of the text to encompass that which its authors did not see, but the text is emphatically *not* dehistoricized. Its embeddedness in the ongoing

8. The metaphor is that of Paul Ricoeur. See Ricoeur, *Time and Narrative*, 68–70. See also Parris, *Reception Theory*.

story of the people of God is affirmed. In fact, it is precisely this affirmation that guides the creative extension of the textual significance.

Third, it is clear from the above that the Jewish practice of reading Lamentations alongside other, later events is not ad hoc but hermeneutically controlled. Most obviously the destruction of Herod's temple finds a parallel in the destruction of Solomon's. But, more than that, the community suffering in Lamentations are the ancestors of the Jewish people and so it is natural to make links between the plight of those in the texts and later Jewish sufferings. Now Lamentations can speak to sufferings beyond those of Jewish communities—indeed it can only function as *Christian* Scripture if this is the case; but such applications of Lamentations need to have hermeneutical controls. And, more specifically, we need to be able to provide a biblical-theological rationale for such extensions in application.

Fourth, the use of Lamentations on 9th of Av must be understood as located within a broader liturgical context spanning from the 17th of Tammuz to Rosh Hashanah. Its community-shaping role must be located within that wider liturgical framework. Elsie Stern helpfully shows how this works with the Sabbaths before 9th of Av (focusing on Israel's sin), Tisha b'Av itself (with its reading of Lamentations attending to the terrible consequences of that sin), and the Sabbaths that follow charting "a process of reconciliation and consolation" in which God comforts Israel and restores her to himself.[9] This tradition allows liturgical space for the sorrow and despair of Lamentations to be expressed without being crushed by the premature arrival of "good news." Yet, at the same time, it does not allow Lamentations the last word. In this way lament and rejoicing and held in balance and in place.

Fifth, the Jewish tradition has offered not simply liturgical room for the text of Lamentations within the ongoing life in the community but has also offered guides to its interpretations. In this book we have explored how *Targum Lamentations*, *Lamentations Rabbah*, and Rashi's commentary all served this function within the context of private and/or public Jewish devotion. These guides serve different functions. The Targum, for instance, is concerned in part to vindicate God's justice and to guard against what its authors may perceive as impious "readings" of Lamentations. *Lamentations Rabbah* importantly aimed to situated the text within the *ongoing* covenant relationship between God and Israel

9. Stern, "Lamentations in Jewish Liturgy."

(as well as vindicating God). Rashi, is concerned to explain problematic words in order to help people understand better the literal meaning of the book. These interpretative samplings have ongoing importance for Jewish reception of the text, though not in the sense that a reading that departed from them ceases to be Jewish. Some contemporary Jewish hearings of the scroll, out of respect for the content of the text itself, have objected that the classical interpretative tradition, in its eagerness to vindicate God, has domesticated Lamentations by stifling the book's more critical edge. They argue that we should be less keen to fit Lamentations into neat theological categories.[10] But Jewish interpretation was never univocal. The midrashic tradition was always multi-vocal, dialogical, and incomplete. It was never about imparting the single, correct Jewish interpretation.

Christians have no influential reception traditions for interpreting Lamentations because the book has not featured as a major text in the way that it has for Judaism (a situation that is not going to change, for the Gentile section of the *ekklesia* at any rate). If Christians are to grant Lamentations a place in public worship, however, then we would be well advised to mine our own historical traditions to uncover the oft-forgotten insights of past readers. Some of the chapters in this volume begin the task of doing precisely that. On top of that, Christians would be well advised to listen closely to the historic Jewish interpretations. Gentile believers in Jesus need to appreciate afresh that this is a book, in the first instance, addressing the sufferings of *Israel*. Gentile Christians thus hear it over the shoulder of Israel, through union with Yeshua the Messiah.

Lamentations "Outside In"—In the Worship of the Church

So Gentile Christ-believers need to hear the text as a word addressed, in the first instance, *by* the people of Israel to Yhwh, and written down *for* the people of Israel. Christians instinctively read the texts as *insiders*—we hear our own voices in the anguished words of those in pain. This is right but I want to propose that there is a place for a different, far more unsettling reading stance vis-à-vis the text.

The book speaks of the brutal violence of the nations against Israel and it is sobering for Gentile Christians to read the text not from the position of suffering-Israel, but *in the role of the oppressive nations*. Read

10 See Braitermann, "Lamentations in Modern Jewish Thought."

in this way the book serves to invite the communities that have persecuted Israel to listen to the voices of their victims. Even a glancing familiarity with the shocking treatment of Jews by Christians through the ages goes a long way towards indicating the potential power of such a reading strategy.

But, someone may protest, surely this is not to read Lamentations as *Christian Scripture* for it puts Christians on the outside looking in (in contrast to Paul's indication that Israel's Scriptures were written for the church; cf. 1 Cor 9:10). So long as this is not the only stance that Christian readers take to the text I must beg to differ.

In this dangerous, almost prophetic, mode the word of God comes as a harsh word of rebuke, a shocking exposure of an oft-forgotten crime, a call to the painful task of listening to one's victims, and an invitation to repentance. In this way, the text of Lamentations fleshes out part of the function of Scripture as a prescient "rebuke" to believers (2 Tim 3:17). Christian oppression of Jewish people may have been at its worst in times past but it is certainly not a thing of the past. Christians live with the ever-present temptation to think that since the Messiah came God has abandoned the Jewish people in favor of the church.[11] This, to my mind, represents a fundamentally unbiblical ecclesiology but it has been the theology at the root of a lot of anti-Semitic attitudes and actions over the centuries. Hearing Lamentations as a text *by Jews and for Jews* in which Gentile Christ-believers have often shamefully played out the role of the destructive nations would actually be one very constructive, chastening reading strategy.

The text of Lamentations strikes a very different sound in the context of the church when heard in such ways. Consider the different ways in which the nations are related to Israel in the book:

- Some of the nations are those who were supposed allies, bound by treaties to support Israel if she was attacked. Yet, when the moment of truth arrived, they abandoned her to her enemies without a word of protest (1:2, 7; 4:17).
- The attacking nation uses lethal violence against Jerusalem and her people (1:15; 2:4, 21; 4:1–10).
- They enrich themselves on her wealth, stealing goods and property, and desecrating places and items of religious value (1:10; 2:6–7).

11. See Soulen, *The God of Israel and Christian Theology*.

- They expel her people (1:3, 5, 18).
- They mock Jerusalem's suffering and rejoice in her downfall at their hands (1:7, 21; 2:15–17).
- They fail to offer comfort to the suffering city (1:2, 9, 16, 17, 21).

It does not take much knowledge of Jewish-Christian relations throughout history to see how Lamentations might serve to expose past Christian acts for what they are.[12] As such, Christians would be wise to pay careful attention to the traditional Jewish reading of the text on the 9th of Av as a prism for understanding a wide range of Israel's sufferings. We need to hear that and acknowledge the legitimacy of that interpretation—*a legitimacy retained within a Christian theological frame of reference.*[13] If we who are Christians are not prepared to face our history and to allow Scripture to expose our infidelity then what claims do we have to honor and tremble before God's word? I think that it would be perfectly appropriate for such unnerving use of the text to take place in the context of public Christian worship.

However, the Christian conviction is that while this text is truly Israel's Scripture, Gentiles—through union with Israel's Messiah—can stand alongside an eschatologically renewed Israel as the new covenant people of Yhwh (cf. Eph 2:11–22). As such Lamentations is part of Christian Scriptures too and can thus be read by Gentiles, as by Jews, from the inside out.

Lamentations "Inside Out"—In the Worship of the Church

The use of Lamentations in the Christian churches has been a far more ambiguous affair. It was not a text that generated a lot of comment in

12. See Cohn-Sherbok, *The Crucified Jew*; Keith, *Hated Without a Cause?*

13. The recent revival of a Messianic Jewish movement in the zone between Christianity and Judaism serves as a challenge to the way in which both faiths have defined themselves over against each other (see Rudolph, "Messianic Jews and Christian Theology"). This challenge seems to require that Christians rethink their ecclesiologies (on which see Kinzer, *Postmissionary Messianic Judaism*) and, if they do so, creates the theological space for the unconventional of use of Lamentations that I am proposing here.

the New Testament,[14] nor in the patristic period,[15] although, as we shall see, both can provide fruitful resources for Christian recovery of Lamentations.

The most conspicuous use of Lamentations in Christian worship was in the Western church from the Middle Ages onwards in the Divine Office of Matins on Maundy Thursday, Good Friday, and Holy Saturday (otherwise known as Tenebrae).[16] Matins took place before dawn[17] and one can imagine the effect, in the days before electric lighting, of extinguishing fourteen of the fifteen candles illuminating the building one by one as the sacred texts were read out.[18] The Office was treated, for these three days, as a kind of funeral service.

The choice, number, and order of the readings from Lamentations varied from region to region (as did the number of candles to be extinguished) until the Council of Trent (1545–63). Trent standardized the readings and laid down rules for the musical and poetic structure of the Lamentations, though not so much as to remove all local discretion.

It is very interesting to observe the way that Lamentations was used in communal Christian worship. They were used in the fist nocturne of each day as follows:

14. Arguably Lam 4:13 is alluded to in Matt 23:35, and Lam 2:15 in Matt 27:39. There are also some other less certain allusions.

15. See Thomas, "Lamentations in the Patristic Period."

16. Tenebrae is Latin for "shadows." The number three looms large in Tenebrae: three services, with three nocturnes each, each containing three psalms (and their antiphons) and three readings (each followed by its response—extracts from the Bible or Augustine). The associations with Christ's three days and three nights in the tomb as well as with the Trinity are obvious.

17. The service was brought forward to the early evening of the previous day (i.e., Wednesday, Thursday, and Friday) from possibly as early as the thirteenth century, because it was more convenient.

18. There were fifteen candles. One candle was extinguished after each Psalm reading (nine in all) leaving six alight. Tenebrae was immediately followed by Lauds during which a further five candles were extinguished after readings leaving one alight. The extinguishing of the candles might date back to the fifth century.

Thursday (Wednesday)						
Nocturne 1	Ps 68	Ps 69	Ps 70	**Lam 1:1–5**	**Lam 1:6–9**	**Lam 1:10–14**
Nocturne 2	Ps 71	Ps 72	Ps 73	Augustine on Ps 54:1	Augustine on Ps 54:1	Augustine on Ps 54:1
Nocturne 3	Ps 74	Ps 75	Ps 76	1 Cor 11:17–22	1 Cor 11:23–26	1 Cor 11:27–34

Friday (Thursday)						
Nocturne 1 Matins	Ps 2	Ps 21	Ps 26	**Lam 2:8–11**	**Lam 2:12–15**	**Lam 3:1–9**
Nocturne 2 Lauds	Ps 37	Ps 39	Ps 53	Augustine on Ps 63:2	Augustine on Ps 63:2	Augustine on Ps 63:2
Nocturne 3	Ps 58	Ps 87	Ps 93	Heb 4:11–15	Heb 4:16–5:3	Heb 5:4–10

Saturday (Friday)						
Nocturne 1 Matins	Ps 4	Ps 14	Ps 15	**Lam 3:22–30**	**Lam 4:1–6**	**Lam 5:1–11**
Nocturne 2 Lauds	Ps 23	Ps 26	Ps 29	Augustine on Ps 63:7	Augustine on Ps 63:7	Augustine on Ps 63:7
Nocturne 3	Ps 53	Ps 75	Ps 87	Heb 9:11–14	Heb 9:15–18	Heb 9:19–22

So it was that texts from all five chapters of Lamentations were brought, in the context of Christian worship, into association with the darkness of Gethsemane, Golgotha, and the tomb of Christ.

The setting of the lessons from Lamentations to music was practiced from at least the twelfth century but it was the Renaissance that saw a veritable explosion of such musical settings for use in Tenebrae. Schopf's chapter very helpfully illuminates the work of Tomas Luis de Victoria but it could just as easily have considered the haunting settings of Thomas

Tallis, Palestrina, Robert White, William Byrd, or a host of others.[19] These very carefully crafted polyphonic compositions were intended to create a solemn, lamenting frame of mind. Singers were careful to avoid any vocal ornamentation that might make the tone more joyful. They functioned as interpretations of the biblical text which, in turn, shaped the way in which congregations would hear it afresh (at least, those few that could understand Latin).

It strikes me that two of the features of Jewish reception to which I earlier drew attention are analogous to features that can be found in this particular Christian doxological tradition. First, the text of Lamentations is allowed to be a filter through which other catastrophes—in this case the death of the Messiah—are interpreted. And those other events, in turn, affect the way in which Lamentations in interpreted. Second, Tenebrae, as the 9th of Av, is overtly located in a wider liturgical context that culminates in redemption. On Easter Sunday the remaining lit candle is brought out and the building is once again illuminated. So Lamentations finds its home in a luminal liturgical zone that both gives it space to be itself and yet will not allow it to be the last word.

The planting of these Lamentations readings in the midst of a forest of readings from the book of Psalms also plays a role in influencing the way in which they are heard. The rationale behind the selection is sometimes clear enough, although it is not always perspicuous and the effect that it might have on the Latin-speakers present is, of course, underdetermined by the texts themselves. Once such a range of texts are set alongside each others it is not possible to tightly control the interpretative resonances that might be created. The following reflections are simply my own response to the way in which the selected Psalm readings affected my engagement with the Lamentations passages. Some of the resonances may not have been in the minds of those who selected the texts, but nonetheless they cohere within the liturgical context in which they exist.

One theme that is prominent in a number of the selected Psalms is that of the righteous individual who is suffering at the hands of his enemies and cries out to God for salvation (in Tenebrae order: Pss 69, 70, 71, 73?, 26). In the Christian tradition, and clearly in this liturgical context, such Psalms were often read as Christ's prayers to the Father as well as models for the prayer of the faithful (the final reading from Hebrews

19. Not to mention the musical settings for Lamentations that are not linked to Tenebrae (e.g., Leonard Bernstein's Jeremiah Symphony).

on day 2 reinforces this interpretation). The reading from Augustine for the third day speaks of the importance of coming to God when we are in the "desert," driven by thirst, so that God can appear to us. This idea seems to be one of the keys behind the selection of Psalms. That this is so is evident also from our second theme.

A second recurring theme is the hope that God will indeed save the suffering one who seeks him, and will punish his enemies (in Tenebrae order: Pss 71, 73, 75, 37, 4, 23. cf., Tenebrae Psalms which promise blessing and salvation for those who walk in God's ways: Pss 37, 15, 26, 75). In the context of this service it is the resurrection of Christ that serves as his salvation. This would perhaps have been seen in the words from Psalm 71:20, "You [i.e., God] who have made me [i.e., Jesus] see many troubles and calamities will revive me again; from the depths of the earth you will bring me up again." Related to this is the theme that God will cause his Davidic king to triumph (in Tenebrae order: Pss 72, 2, 21).

The third theme concerns the grounds for such hope—that in *all* things God is in control (in Tenebrae order: Pss 68, 93, 29). The reading from Augustine on day 1 (commenting on Ps 54:1) brings this out. Augustine reads King David as a type of his descendant, King Jesus. The Ziphites betrayed David to Saul but it was not in Saul's power to capture him. Similarly Christ's enemies betray and attack him but to destroy him is not in their power. Their attempt merely exposes their wickedness. This is the theological context within which Christ's death is situated.

The fourth Psalmic theme is one more obviously related to Lamentations. It concerns the suffering of *Zion* at the hands of its enemies, the prayer for salvation, and the promise that deliverance will come (in Tenebrae order: Pss 74, 76, 53, 87?, 14, 53, 87).

What are the theological connections that might be made here and how might they set up ways of interpreting Lamentations? Clearly this is Holy Week and the narrative of Jesus is central as the interpretative key. I suggest that it is the representative role of the Davidic king that brings all of the above themes together. The king represents his people and so his story of suffering, supplication, and salvation serves as a participation in and the pattern for the suffering, supplication, and salvation of Zion.[20]

Psalm 69, the second Psalm reading in Tenebrae, serves as a hermeneutical doorway through which the rest of the readings are approached. It is a Psalm of David, the righteous Messiah. He cries out to the God of

20. On the paradigmatic role of Jesus as Zion/man in Lamentations as well as Zion/church see Thomas *"Until He Looks Down and Sees."*

Israel from the midst of his desperate situation and looks with hope to Yhwh to punish his enemies and redeem him, but not to redeem *only him*. The Psalm ends with the words, "For God will save Zion and build up the cities of Judah." The redemption of the king of Israel has implications for the suffering community of Zion. In this way the subsequent Psalms—which address the themes of the lament of the righteous individual, the vindication of the Davidic king, and the suffering and salvation of Israel—are intimately linked. And in Christian context this link is understood to be realized in Jesus.

In is within this biblical-theological framework that the Lamentations texts in Tenebrae are to be understood. Psalm 69 serves as a doorway yet again. There David says, "I looked for pity, but there was none, and for comforters, but I found none" (Ps 69:20). In the very same nocturne we get our first three Lamentations texts in which we read that Zion, like David, had none to comfort her in her suffering (Lam 1:2, 9). The difference is that Zion, unlike David, is not a *righteous* sufferer but an *unrighteous* one (Lam 1:5, 8, 14).

It is more than likely, given the replacement theology operative in most of Christian history, that Zion was seen as a type of the church. So the worshippers are invited to see themselves as Zion, the city of God, beloved of the Lord yet sinful, afflicted, looking for a coming deliverance akin to that experienced by her Messiah, Jesus.[21] Each Lamentations reading is followed by an exhortation based on Hos 14:1, *Jerusalem convertere ad Dominum Deum tuum* (Jerusalem, return to the Lord your God). Thus the readings serve to call the congregants to repentance.

THE CANONICAL FORM AND CANONICAL CONTEXT OF LAMENTATIONS

These Jewish and Christian liturgical practices are a faithful response to the canonical status of the book of Lamentations. The text is preserved in both Jewish and Christian Bibles in such a way that it demands to be heard *both* in its final form *and* in its canonical context. Lamentations ends without resolution. By the end of the book God has neither spoken the longed for word of comfort nor acted to redeem. The book was

21. In this connection note the use of Lamentations in the current Church of England liturgy for Maundy Thursday: (http://www.cofe.anglican.org/worship/downloads/pdf/tspashw.pdf, 303).

canonized in this open and "incomplete" form, and, as such, any hearing of the text *as Scripture* demands that this fact is respected. Jewish and Christian Bibles give the text space to be itself and do not seek to tag on a happy ending in order to prematurely close down the pain or to tame the grief.

But the Jewish and Christian Bibles also locate Lamentations in a wider canonical context and as such they will not allow the book only to be heard apart from that wider story. Lena-Sofia Tiemeyer has very helpfully explored the ways in which parts of the book of Isaiah explicitly respond to the book of Lamentations.[22] The Jewish interpretative tradition has long recognized this fact and the Jewish liturgy reflects it. To read the "no comfort" of Lamentations as part of the Bible, is to read it alongside the "comfort, comfort my people" of Isaiah. The "no comfort" of Lamentations is part of the story. The canonical context calls on the worshipping community to refuse it the last word, but at the same time the canonical form warns the community against prematurely collapsing the "no comfort" into the "comfort."

The balance, inherent in the canonical status of Lamentations, of allowing space for mourning and darkness (thereby acknowledging the final form) but locating that darkness in a wider, redemptive narrative (thereby acknowledging the canonical context) is mirrored in the way that Jews and, to a lesser extent, Christians have used Lamentations in their worship. The 9th of Av is dark in tone but is followed by the word of salvation. It uses canonically inspired liturgical *time* to hold the sorrow of Lamentations away from the joy of subsequent deliverance and yet at the same time refuses to allow them to be separated. It allows a time for mourning and a time for joy and it does so in such a way to resist the bleeding back of coming joy into the pain. Christian liturgical use of Lamentations goes some way towards this. Tenebrae certainly places the readings in a wider liturgical context of darkness followed by light, death followed by resurrection. It also keeps a temporal gap between the growing darkness and the return of the light. Furthermore, the musical settings of Lamentations have been consistently mournful and somber. Yet the selection of Psalms read during Tenebrae very clearly and confidently anticipate the happy ending—more clearly and confidently than Lamentations itself. To some extent, therefore, this does dampen one aspect of the canonical *form* of the text.

22. Tiemeyer, "Lamentations in Isaiah 40–55." See too Parry, *Lamentations*, 162–68.

HEARING LAMENTATIONS AS CHRISTIAN SCRIPTURE

So the use of the text of Lamentations in the worship of Jews and some Christians provides helpful pointers for contemporary Christian use. In this section I wish to explore a little further the insightful association made in the Western church between Lamentations and the sorrow, death, and burial of Jesus. While the Tenebrae service offers no commentary at all on the readings of Lamentations, the very fact that the texts were associated with certain Psalms and particular events in the life of Jesus is deeply suggestive. I want to suggest that perceiving the sufferings of the Messiah in the sufferings of Lamentations is not arbitrary but is informed by the deep canonical logic of the Christian Bible.

Lamentations and the Rule of Faith

While, as Ricoeur says, texts mean all that they can mean,[23] not all such interpretations would count as legitimate *Christian* interpretations. Christian communities have long read their Scriptures in the light of "the rule of faith." The rule of faith, a term first used by Irenaeus, was simply a narrative summary of the apostolic faith of the church. It did not exist in a single, fixed form but all the diverse versions we have express a common core: the story of the creator God revealed in Christ. It speaks of God the Father who sent his Son as a man in order to redeem the world. Jesus—God the Son made flesh—was crucified, buried, was raised and ascended to the right hand of the Father from where he sent the Spirit and from where he will one day return.[24] What might it mean to appreciate Lamentations in the light of the story of God-in-Christ?

23. Ricoeur, *Time and Narrative.*

24. The rule of faith was a somewhat elastic distillation of the theological tradition passed down in the churches established by the apostles. We find versions of it in Irenaeus, Tertullian, Hippolytus, Origen, Cyprian, Novatian, Dionysius of Alexandria, and the *Didascalia apostolorum*. It served to represent the heart of that tradition and probably developed for catechetical purposes. The later creeds evolved from it and effectively standardized its form. The rule served both as a summary of key aspects of the theology of the sacred texts (which later became the NT) and as a normative guide for interpreting those texts in *Christian* ways. For Irenaeus, it was living by the rule of faith (not merely having the right Scriptures) that separated Christians from heretics. Both the proto-orthodox and the Gnostics read the same sacred texts but they interpreted them in very different ways. Irenaeus' point is that *Christians read according to the rule of faith.*

Lamentations and Christ

I understand the Bible to suggest that Jesus, the Messiah of Israel, stood before God as the representative of the whole people of Israel. He was, one might say, one-man-Israel.[25] I must emphasize that Jesus does not thereby *replace* the Jewish people (the Jewish people are irreplaceable in God's purposes), but rather *represents* them and, in his person, embodies their story with the purpose of redeeming them. This idea seems implicit, as we have seen, in the readings used during Tenebrae.

Suppose that one reads Lamentations with this theological belief. How might we connect Jesus' story to this poetry? I have developed the following brief suggestions at more length elsewhere.[26] Here I simply indicate links that provide a basis for further reflection.

Christ and Lady Zion (Lam 1 and 2). If Jesus takes the covenant curses experienced by Israel to their climax then we can draw connections between Jesus' suffering and Judah's exilic suffering personified in the person of Lady Zion in Lam 1–2. *Like* Jerusalem, tears were upon his cheeks as he prayed alone in the garden. *Like* Jerusalem, he knew betrayal by his "friends" who left him to suffer alone. *Like* Jerusalem, Jesus was beaten, stripped naked, publicly humiliated, and afflicted. *Like* Jerusalem, he was reduced from a high and noble status to dust. *Like* Jerusalem, he bore the divine curse for covenant disobedience. *Like* Jerusalem, he was violently attacked by a pagan occupying force. *Like* Jerusalem, he felt abandoned by Yhwh in the face of these pagan military oppressors. *Like* Jerusalem, he was mocked and despised by those who looked on at his destruction.

Christ and the destroyed temple (Lam 2). In the New Testament, Jesus was seen as embodying the Jerusalem temple in his body. His death and resurrection were seen in terms of the destruction and rebuilding of the temple (cf. John 2:19–22). As such the destruction of the temple spoken of in Lamentations can be seen in the light of Christ. Given the cosmic symbolism of the temple (it symbolized the created order) the destruction of the temple represents cosmic, ecological devastation. Bringing such themes into contemplation of the temple and the death of Christ has considerable potential.

25. I borrowed this phrase from Mark Kinzer's book, *Postmissionary Messianic Judaism*. The biblical-theological case for this claim is spelled out in Parry, *Lamentations*.

26. Parry, *Lamentations*, 168–73, 180–93.

Christ and the valiant man (Lam 3). The story solitary of the sufferer in Lam 3 seems to me to be structurally similar to the story of Jesus. This can be brought out in the following chart.

Valiant Man	Embodies the suffering of Jerusalem	In the pit (metaphorical death)	Redeemed from the pit	His redemption is a sign of hope for the Israel	His enemies still plot against him	Final defeat of his enemies is future
Christ	Embodies the suffering of Jerusalem (and humanity)	In the grave (real death)	Raised from the dead	His redemption is a sign of hope for Israel (and the world)	His enemies still fight against him	Final defeat of his enemies is future

Christ and the righteous victims (Lam 4:13). Matthew 23:35 alludes to Lam 4:13. In essence the Lamentations text sets out a general principle about divine judgment on those leaders who shed innocent blood. Matthew sees Jesus as the righteous victim *par excellence* whose innocent blood is shed by wicked leaders in Jerusalem. Therefore judgment will come upon them too.

Christ and the captured Messiah (Lam 4:20). Christians have long seen Lam 4:20 in the light of Christ. The text reads

> [The] breath of our nostrils, Yhwh's anointed,
> was captured in their pits:
> [He of] whom we said, "In his shade,
> we will live amongst the nations."

Lamentations is almost certainly referring to the capture of Zedekiah by the Babylonians. However, Christians have often seen a prefigurement of the death of Jesus at the hands of a pagan empire in these words. What is suggestive about the Christian interpretation is that this verse immediately precedes the most positive verses in the whole book (4:21–22). Lamentations 4:21–22 is akin to a prophetic oracle of salvation for Israel and judgment on its enemies. The promise comes from left of field and there is no obvious explanation for why it should occur here. But on a Christian reading, the very moment of despair—the defeat of

Israel's king by the pagans—becomes the very basis for salvation. So the flow of chapter 4 appears in a new light.

Lamentations and the Spirit

What of the Spirit of Yhwh? How does the Spirit stand in relation to the pain of Lamentations? The first thing that we must say is that Lamentations says absolutely nothing about the Spirit and so, at one level, it has nothing to contribute to our pneumatology. Any study on the theology of God's Spirit in Lamentations will rightly be composed of blank pages. But suppose that our Christian reader is coming to the text with a pneumatology that already has some grasp of the relationship of the Spirit and the grief of the world—how might that affect their theological engagement with the text of Lamentations? I shall offer a few thoughts on this possibility.[27]

Romans 8:18–30 helps us to get some insight into the Spirit and a certain mode of lament. Paul draws a parallel between Jesus' suffering, the suffering of Christians, and the suffering of the whole created order (8:17–25). Indeed, Paul's underlying theology is one that sees an intimate relationship between humanity, Israel, Christ, and the church. Israel represents all humanity before God (it is a microcosm of humanity). Jesus, as the Messiah of Israel, represents the whole people of Israel (he is Israel writ small).[28]

First of all, notice that the story of Christ, the church, and creation run in parallel: suffering then glory; death then life. Jesus was crucified, died, was buried, and *then* was raised from the dead by God through the Spirit (Rom 8:11). Paul is saying that the story of believers will be like Christ's. Currently we are in our mortal bodies and we suffer with Jesus. We shall die. But then we shall be raised by God (through the same Spirit he raised Christ by). Paul speaks of this future as one in which the very glory of God himself is revealed in us. It is a resurrection to immortality, it is our adoption as sons—that is, children and heirs of God.

27. The following section draws heavily on my article "The Trinity and Lament."

28. This theological theme of Christ as Israel is integrated well into the systematic theological work of Thomas F. Torrance and the biblical exposition of N. T. Wright. In Rom 8, Paul's focus in on Christ, church and creation. I only mention humanity as a whole and Israel in particular because it helps us begin to imagine how Paul's teaching might begin to have wider implications than those he brings out in this context.

In the same way, the story of the whole created order is one of frustration and slavery to death and decay followed by liberation and participating in the freedom of the children of God.[29] In other words, when God resurrects his people he will then resurrect the whole creation. And Paul pictures both the creation and the church—and, by implication, Jesus himself when he was on the cross—as currently "groaning." We'll come back to that.

So the story of the church and of creation is darkness now but light to come—a story *already* played out in the life of Jesus. Thus Paul can write that "our present sufferings are not worth comparing with the glory that will be revealed in us" (8:18). And Paul knew some serious sufferings and times of real despair (2 Cor 1:8–9; 11). But we need to see that for Paul this eager expectation of God's new day existed alongside the present experience of grief and sorrow. This is where the groaning comes in. Dunn notes that the groaning of Christ-believers is intended "to emphasize believers' involvement in the eschatological travail of creation. . . . The point needs to be emphasized that the Spirit does not free from such tension, but actually creates or at least heightens that tension and brings it to more anguished expression."[30] The groaning is three things at once.

First, it is an expression of sorrow, pain, and frustration at the current state of affairs. In this respect it is something like a lament. It is like moan from the depths of our being—a painful awareness that all is not as it should be.

Second, it is simultaneously a groan of expectation for a better future. Paul describes it as "groaning as in the pains of childbirth"—notice how that image blends pain with an expectation of, and longing for, new life. He speaks of us "groaning eagerly as we wait eagerly for our adoption as sons" (cf. 2 Cor 5:2–4).

The idea of lament as an expression of grief and expectation is well put by Nicholas Wolterstorff in his comments on Matt 5:4, "Blessed are those who mourn, for they will be comforted." The mourners, he writes, "are aching visionaries."[31] Aching visionaries who simply refuse to accept the current state of affairs. Here we also glimpse something of the way in which the Spirit moves the people of God into action, even rage, *against* injustice and *for* love in his gathering up of the people of God into the

29. For contemporary theological reflections on this theme in the light of Darwinism and ecological concerns see Southgate, *The Groaning of Creation*.

30. Dunn, *Romans* 1–8, 417.

31. Wolterstorff, *Lament for a Son*, 85–86.

responsive and creative action of lament. It is what John Swinton refers to as "raging with compassion."[32]

Third, it is intercession. Old Testament laments often serve as expressions of sorrow *and also* as prayers for salvation. In the same way, this deep primal moaning that Paul speaks of is also an expression of grief and simultaneously a prayer to God for new creation. It is at this point that Paul introduces the Holy Spirit. The Spirit himself groans. In *sorrow* for the present darkness? Yes. In *hope* for a better future? Yes. But most critically, in *intercession* for that new future. The Holy Spirit is praying for the church. The Holy Spirit knows the Father's will and purposes fully. We do not. So when the Spirit prays for us he is praying in perfect accord with God's cosmic purposes—his ultimate purposes for the whole created order.

I would like to reflect on the sufferings of Lam 1 pneumatologically. In the light of Rom 8, I suggest that the Spirit of God participates in Jerusalem's sorrows. The Spirit groans with all those who groan as they yearn for liberation.[33] Jerusalem groans at her humiliation and turns away her face from onlookers (1:8c), just as her priests groan at the cessation of temple festivals (1:4b) and her people groan as they search for food (1:11a). This groaning in Lam 1 looks back (mourning what is lost), looks around (expressing despair at the current situation), and looks forward (yearning for a reversal of the calamity). So also the Spirit, participating in the groaning of creation, groans as he looks back and looks around seeing a shattered world but he also groans like a woman in childbirth looking forward, bringing to birth a new creation (Isa 13:8; 21:3; 26:17–18; 66:7–8; Jer 4:31; 22:23; Hos 13:13; Mic 4:9–10). The Spirit's groaning, while a participation in creation's groaning, also transforms it. It is a hope-infused groaning which looks to the future with confidence. The Spirit can enable our groaning to become a participation in his groaning and in Christ's groaning.[34] That is to say, Spirit-transformed groaning is still an expression of pain at the current situation but it is not an expression of hopelessness. Indeed it is the foundation of the efficacy of our own intercessions

32. Swinton, *Raging with Compassion*. My thanks to Jason Goroncy for this observation on the active role of Spirit-inspired lament against injustice.

33. Liberation understood in various ways, e.g., liberation from oppression, injustice, or even deserved afflictions and sin.

34. We groan *because* we have the firstfruits of the Spirit (Rom 8:23, taking *echontes* as causal).

> We wait: but, because we wait upon God, our waiting is not in vain. We look out: but, because we have first been observed, we do not look out into the void. We speak: but, because there emerges in our speech that which cannot be uttered, we do not idly prattle. And so also we pray: but, because the Spirit makes intercession for us with groanings which—since his groanings must be songs of praise[35]—are beyond our competence, our prayers and groanings are distinct from that groaning which is weakness—and nothing else. The justification of prayer is not that we have attained some higher eminence on the ladder of prayer; for all ladders of prayer are erected within the sphere of the "No-God" of this world. The justification of our prayer and the reality of our communion with God are grounded upon the truth that Another, the Eternal, the Second Man from Heaven (I Cor XV.47), stands before God pre-eminent in power and—in our place.[36]

So the Spirit is groaning with and for us as he seeks to bring us through to resurrection. The Spirit is praying creation into glory. And here is the amazing thing—the Spirit does not simply pray for us: he prays for us *through us*. He makes our own groanings a vehicle for his groanings.[37] And that is good because so often we do not know what we should pray for or how we should pray for it. But the Spirit does and he helps us in our weakness. This opens up new ways of appreciating the significance and possibilities of lament in general and Lamentations in particular Christian worship. The prayerful use of this ancient text can become a vehicle for the Spirit of God to groan with us and with creation.[38]

35. I would wish to add that such "praise" must not be understood to exclude lament.

36. Barth, *Romans*, 317.

37. New Testament scholars disagree about whether the Spirit's groanings are "groans not formulated in words" (so, e.g., Dunn, *Romans* 1–8, 478) or glossolalia (so Fee, *God's Empowering Presence*, 580–85). I see no reason why the Spirit's activity of "groaning" might not manifest in various forms, including glossolalia but not restricted to it (see Parry, *Lamentations*, 190–91, 205–6). This opens up the possibility to develop an unusual approach to speaking in tongues (see Macchia, "Sighs too Deep")

38. Heath Thomas suggests, in the light of my reading of Rom 8, that perhaps one way in which the Spirit leads the church into all truth (John 16:13)—not simply assent to rational truths, but the truth of the reality of God-in-Christ—is through such prayer, which leads one more deeply into the realm of Jesus' victory now/not yet.

LAMENTATIONS AND THE NARRATIVE DIMENSION OF CHRISTIAN WORSHIP

Traditional Christian worship has always had a narrative shape to it. The Christian Year itself was woven around the story of Jesus so that year by year the faithful would worship their way through the plot and hopefully develop a narrative shape and roundedness to their spirituality. It was in this story-shaped liturgical world that Lamentations found a home and made its contribution. As we have seen there is a good theo-logic behind this traditional use.

Now it is easy to idealize such modes of worship and to forget how they can degenerate into an empty ritual (a danger Israel's prophets were alert to: cf. Isa 1:11–17) or a form of musical entertainment.[39] Nevertheless, the context from which I write is very different and the dangers that many churches I know face are not *this* danger. I belong for very many years to an evangelical, charismatic, free church strand of the Christian tradition. In such contexts the last forty years have witnessed major changes in the way in which we worship, some of which are good and some of which are bad. One of the bad changes has been the rapid and widespread move towards worship-as-singing-one-song-after-another-without-much-thought-given-to-the-theological-shape-of-the-whole. A new ministry of worship leader has arisen in place of the priest or pastor leading the congregational worship. Now, in my view, this is not, in and of itself, a problem. The problem is rather that these worship leaders are rarely trained in leading worship in a theologically informed way. Their ability is in playing an instrument (normally a guitar) and singing, and worship is often understood too narrowly as an immanent encounter

39. Historically the musical settings for Lamentations degenerated in some places into a form of entertainment rather than a means of spiritual formation. Catherine Cessac writes, "During the reign of Louis XIV, great crowds gathered for the *Tenebrae* lessons, which were celebrated in the capital's convents and churches. It is true that the lessons of Lambert, Charpentier, Couperin and Lalande offer a much more attractive style of music than the more generally practiced plainsong. The convent services were therefore gradually transformed into veritable society concerts. In his *Comparaison de la Musique française et italienne* published in 1705, Le Cerf de La Viéville could not hide his offence: 'They hire actresses who, behind the curtain that they lift up from time to time to smile at their friends in the audience, sing a lesson on Good Friday or a solo motet on Easter Sunday. One could hear them at a convent, where it was remarked: to their honour, the price you would have paid at the Opera is what you pay for the pew in the church.'" http://www.goldbergweb.com/en/magazine/essays/2004/02/20216_print.php.

with God mediated through song. So the focus becomes one of encountering-God-now-as-I-sing with little sense of past or future. Where we have come *from* and were we are *going* are secondary—feeling God's presence *now* is the goal.

One result of this is that worship in such settings is usually detached from the rhythms of the traditional Christian Year. Last week is forgotten and next week is not on the horizon—all that counts is the present moment. But this means that you can take any worship encounter and swap it for any other in the year without significant loss because each becomes a stand-alone event. A consequence of that is that it is easy to lose any sense of the grand narrative of Scripture within which the community lives and moves and has its being. This narrative, which we should inhabit in our worship, tends to be pushed to the margins. A second result of the changes in contemporary evangelical worship culture is that the terrain covered in liturgically structured worship—confession of sin, adoration, intercession, supplication, listening to the word, receiving the Eucharist, etc.—is greatly reduced. One will often find only praise, thanksgiving, perhaps space for prophetic words, and a sermon. The Eucharist is too often missing, intercession is very often absent, confession is exceptionally rare, and lament is almost non-existent. Any sense of a shape or directionality to worship is often minimalist at best. In such a context it is hard to find a place for the book of Lamentations because, as we have seen, it really needs a way of being narratively located (both within a liturgical narrative and a biblical-theological narrative). So within the free church tradition there is a great need to recover the narrative shape both of individual worship gatherings and of "seasons" of gatherings. Apart from that Lamentations, along with the practice of lament more generally, will struggle to find a foothold.

But there are a few bricks of hope within this kind of Christianity from which it might be possible to build some new homes for Lamentations, albeit modest ones. For even within these Christian traditions fragments of the Christian Year still hold their ground against the assaults of "spontaneity." Those fragments are the fundamental, gospel-shaped "moments" of Christmas, Good Friday, and Easter Sunday. And, as we have seen, it is Passion Week that has been the natural home for Lamentations within the Christian tradition. The fact that this liturgical space has not yet been abandoned by those of us who have forsaken so much else within the liturgical history of Christianity is a basis for hope. Of course, more traditional Christians will find things that much less awkward in attempts to recover a use of Lamentations.

The discussion above proposing that we recover the traditional link between Passion Week and Lamentations suggests a pre-planned use of the text within worship. Now some will have a natural concern about this. The problem is that the chances are that on any particular Good Friday service in which worshippers were invited to participate in some way in the laments of the book many, indeed most of those present, may very well not *feel* like lamenting. The text will simply not reflect where many people are at—indeed, at the level of detail, it will not reflect where *any* of the worshippers are at. Within the worship culture of many modern evangelical churches this is enough to preclude its use. After all, who wants to have disengaged congregants speaking words that they do not mean? Is such worship not inauthentic at best?

What are we to say about this concern? Well, one is tempted to reply that this problem is simply the reverse of the "problem" that one finds week after week in such churches already. Modern evangelical worship is uncompromisingly happy and those present engage weekly in declaring how thankful and joyful they feel about God. If the concern is not to have people sing songs that do not reflect where they are at then what are we to say about the culture of unremitting joy? Is this inauthentic? It certainly can be. The songs that Christians sing, however, are not always used in a declarative mode (I *am currently* rejoicing in God) but are often appropriated in aspirational mode (I *desire* to rejoice in God). The singing of the song can cultivate Christian desires and aspirations. In a very similar way one can use laments as part of a process of aspirational spiritual formation even if one is not currently sad.

Now the most obvious objection to this proposal is that while we might understandably aspire to rejoice in the Lord who on earth would want to encourage people to lament? Is an aspiration to *misery* a Christian aspiration? To deal with this objection I will need to outline some of the reason why we do need to learn to engage with lament literature in worship.

A TIME TO WEEP?

Is there "a time to weep" (cf. Rom 12:15) in Christian worship or have we moved into an era of unrelenting rejoicing since the resurrection? I have dealt with the issue of the general place of lament in Christian worship at length elsewhere,[40] but I would like to speak about the role that Lamentations in particular can play in spiritual formation, if used well within public worship. In opening that discussion it will be helpful to consider Stanley Hauerwas' exploration of the importance of engaging in Christian practices as a way of learning the habits essential to become a skilled practitioner in a trade. Hauerwas considers the way in which one learns to become as master bricklayer or a master stonemason.[41] To become such one must learn from the acquired wisdom of those who have practiced the trade before by inhabiting the history and traditions of the trade and by being apprenticed to a master. Part of this learning is learning the language of the trade and one must practice, practice, practice, and practice again the basic skills until they become second nature. Only then is one able to innovate with any skill. This is not cerebral learning but an engaged *learning by doing*. Now Hauerwas insists that a life of Christian virtue is acquired in the same way. Not by the impartation of information but by a participation of the prayerful and worshipful life of a Christian community. We learn to pray, "Our Father, in heaven," we partake in the Eucharist, we hear the Scriptures, and we intercede for others. We are inducted into the language of the Christian life through engaging in the prayers of the community even before we understand exactly what they mean and we practice, practice, practice, and practice again until the language and habits are part of the warp and weft of who we are. Engaging in the stories of the community in communal worship and Christian practice shapes us into a certain kind of people—people of Christian character. Clearly on this understanding of being formed into a Christian disciple there is an important place for engaging communally in practices that we might not fully understand and which might not express how we currently feel. But the ongoing participation in such practices is essential for rounded spiritual formation. So liturgical engagement with Lamentations can, in principle, play a role in the training of Christian emotions—not simply expressing how we currently feel but training us to see and to feel in certain kinds of ways.

Take Lam 1 and 2. The poetry presents the wretched figure of Lady Zion in her broken state—beaten, raped, and deprived of her beloved children. The narrator presents her tragic plight to the audience and

40. See Parry, *Lamentations*, 206–21.

41. See Hauerwas, "How we Lay Bricks"; and Hauerwas, "Carving Stone." See also Smith, *Desiring the Kingdom*.

we also hear her own impassioned voice. The poetry is unrelenting and refuses to allow the audience to glance away for relief but forces them to keep looking. The constant focus on the theme of Zion's lack of a comforter serves to invite the readers themselves to take on such a role—to weep with those who weep. To inhabit this poetry is to learn to become sensitized to pain, to pay attention to the suffering of others, to eschew the option to walk by on the other side. And as we proceed into chapter 2 we see that the narrator himself moves from his sympathetic but somewhat distant engagement with Zion's grief to a deep, gut wrenching sorrow. Readers are invited to make the same journey. To engage such literature in worship can play a role in the emotional formation of a community of disciples.

What public use of Lamentations and other laments will also do is to provide a language of lament. If the only prayer language into which believers are inducted through communal worship is that of thanksgiving, praise, and adoration then we are depriving believers of a language for dealing with the dark periods of life. We are also communicating the message that to speak to God with words of complaint and lament is somehow inappropriate, irreverent, and unfaithful (in spite of the fact that Jesus himself took the words of a complaint Psalm upon his lips while on the cross). In this way we are in danger of failing to train disciples to walk with God through the valley of the shadow of death. It is important that the Christian community acknowledges and affirms the legitimacy of articulating honestly both the awkward and the uncomfortable—the fact that "things are not as they should be." Learning how to speak to and of God in such situations is important and it can only be done through inhabiting the narratives and worship practices reflected in the biblical story and in the Jewish and Christian traditions.

Beyond the potential for fruitful use of Lamentations at Easter through a retrieval of aspects of the Tenebrae tradition, I would also suggest that this very habit-forming practice will enable the more spontaneous use of the text as a communal response to actual crises within the life of the community—the local community or a wider community. So, for instance, a community that has indwelled a book like Lamentations in habit-forming ways can make use of the text in a spontaneous and heartfelt manner in response to an event such as 9/11—an event that other believers might find themselves conflicted to know how to respond to.

CHRISTIAN USE OF LAMENTATIONS IN WORSHIP: A FEW IDEAS

The link between the death and burial of Christ and the "death" and "burial" of Judah in Lamentations will be the theological foundation upon which specifically Christian usage can creatively and innovatively build, but that building might be done in various ways. One way is that the connection between Christ and Jerusalem draws the attention of Christians to the very earthy, social, and political aspects of Christ's death. It is easy for believers to see the death of Jesus is purely "spiritual" terms and not to perceive its socio-political dimensions. But even a moment's thought would remind us that Jesus was "crucified *under Pontius Pilate*"; that he died the death of a political enemy of the Rome; that he was an innocent victim of lethal imperial violence—publicly humiliated and executed. His fate embodied Jerusalem's fate which also was not simply "spiritual" but actually a complete and utter social and political collapse along with all the human suffering that accompanies such things.[42]

Lamentations thrusts such suffering in our face and helps us see the cross afresh. And by opening our eyes to the way in which the cross engages real embodied human suffering it opens up new ways of seeing the social and political suffering of various communities today. For instance, when considering the situation of the persecuted church in various places today. If we view certain current events through binoculars that contain the lenses of both Lamentations and Golgotha then we may be equipped to see those events in fresh ways and to appreciate where God-in-Christ stands in relation to them and, further, how we should stand in relation to them. This is not about the application of simple hermeneutical rules whose outcome is easy to predict but about the learning of new ways of understanding, emotionally perceiving, and responding to the world.

There are many ways in which the text of Lamentations might find a space within worship. Most obviously in set readings, in sermons, or in music. The Tenebrae tradition offers a model for the use of set readings. I am not suggesting that communities take it off the peg, but I do think that there is scope for a range of various modified versions of Tenebrae. My own feeling is that some explanatory comments would be helpful to enable worshippers understand how the texts are being used. Similarly

42. On reading Lamentations politically, see Parry, "Lamentations and the Poetic Politics of Prayer."

with music. There is a rich treasure trove of Christian music based on Lamentations but most of it is very old and only able to be performed by a trained choir. It still has a place but there is a need for new songs that reflect the neglected text of Lamentations. One can also envisage intercessory prayers that weave texts from Lamentations with prayers for contemporary events. One can even imagine a creative use of Lamentations in the celebration of the Eucharist once the link between the cross and the exile is appreciated. This would need to be done with skill but there is no reason why it could not be done in such a way as to refresh the theological imagination and open us up in new ways to God and his world.

Lamentations can be read from inside-out as worshippers are asked to identify with Zion in her grief. It can also read from outside-in as worshippers are asked to identify with the narrator observing Zion, or those on the road passing by, or even as the oppressing nations who cause the pain. As such it has the potential to teach us to express our pain before God, to call us to comfort others (Rom 12:15; 2 Cor 1), or as a sharp exposé of our communal sin by causing affliction to others, bringing conviction of sin and offering a call to confession and repentance. Using this book well in worship is not about becoming self-obsessed, miserable people but about becoming people who can respond to the pain of others in more appropriate ways (an outward-looking and missional practice if ever there was one) and who can respond to our own pain (either individual or communal) more honestly and faithfully.

10

Liturgy and Lament

Colin Buchanan

[Personal: I am an Anglican liturgist from England, and I notified Tim Meadowcroft of Laidlaw that I would be in Auckland in February 2011, simply hoping to meet for a cup of coffee. However, he brought me into the theological seminar on "Lament," to contribute from my own discipline. I was well aware of the earlier earthquake in Christchurch (I had just been there on my travels), as well as of the more tragic mining disaster on the West Coast; and the raw memories of these events were sobering factors in my preparation and presentation. What none of us could well have anticipated when we met was that, less than eleven days after the seminar finished, the much more destructive second earthquake (and its aftermath) would strike Christchurch, inviting much closer identification of this latterday New Zealand city with the sorrowful city of Jeremiah's Book of Lamentations; and my main discussion below, while edited for publication, remains in tone and substance as it was delivered on 11 February 2011. But on return to England I was first of all struck by a lament on the Christchurch cathedral website, and was then asked by a member of the seminar if I would myself write a lament which could be forwarded to friends in Christchurch. This I did, though conscious of my own distance from the tragedy. So I have added as an appendix both these laments, which were born not out of academic research or seminar discussion, but out of the fallen buildings and broken lives in the wake of the actual second Christchurch earthquake.]

I am grateful and honored to be invited to take part in this seminar. I come in by a side wind, and, as happens with those carried by the wind, with less roots than those who have majored on Job, the Psalms, or Lamentations. Yet, I have found myself asked to contribute to your topic from the standpoint of my own discipline—Christian liturgy, and, in my particular case, Anglican liturgy. I reflect that I have never been asked for a presentation on this topic before, and it is possible that that is in part due to a lack of clear precedent in the New Testament, and a comparable lack of a charted liturgical discipline running through Christian history. To that extent I am an innocent exploring relatively unexplored ground, and I am still asking questions as much as answering them. To that extent, those who ask me questions will bear in mind that I am likely to reply with my own questions, rather than definitive answers. I must not, with this theme, be light-hearted, but I fear lest I be found light-weighted.

I also have a fear lest my presentation fail to connect organically with the topics presented in other papers. Christian liturgy should so connect with biblical data, and I therefore hope that those present will assist the drawing together of the biblical material with the situations to which I shall refer and assist the quest for the appropriate liturgical expression of the actually lament-able.

I have three other scene-setting points to make, before I come to two defining points of principle, and four life examples.

Firstly, then, in preparing liturgy—i.e., in preparing a form of congregational worship—we are endeavoring, by use of formal ritual so to enable people to express themselves to God and about God, as to move their Christian discipleship on from (a) to (b). With a congregation there normally has to be an element of "one size fits all," and almost by definition it has to "fit all." Let me illustrate this. When I was first ordained—fifty years ago this year—in those days we would frequently receive a word shortly before a Sunday service that "there is a funeral party here." There was a tradition, a convention—long since faded—that the mourners at a funeral would come to church the Sunday after, even if churchgoing was rare or non-existent in their lives the rest of the time. If this happened with new mourners week after week—and it could—there was no way we could adjust the service to meet them where they were. The most we could do, if we were alert, was to have a low-key word of welcome in the notices and a specific word of thanks for the departed and petition for those in mourning within the prayers. We could hardly abandon all expressions of praise or joy, simply because we had mourners present. Corporate liturgy, all being established for the mainstream of those who are coming, may well not fit various minority categories of those actually present. The exception, of course, is when we design and implement a service for specific persons and purposes, as, to take a good example, a wedding service might be. Then everyone present is expecting it to have a specific focus, a designed theme, a character which fulfils exactly what they are expecting. Thus, much discussion of liturgy and lament must inevitably be about the purpose-made liturgy—and, indeed, the case for that, however rare the need for it may be, arises in part from the self-evident inappropriateness of joyful worship for those present who are suffering in some way; and, when a communal tragedy has ravaged a community, then that proportion becomes a vast majority and the joyful agenda will simply not do. The question is whether a specific purpose-made rite can both meet believers at their point of tragedy and also enable them in some degree to draw a line across and "move on." The question involves the content of such liturgy, but you will sense it also involves the timing of it.

My second scene-setting point picks up the phrase I used earlier about enabling people to "express themselves to God and about God." Liturgy involves addressing God in the presence of each other, and each other in the presence of God—you can trace this in 1 Cor 14 or in Col 3:16–17. This is interestingly illustrated in the grammar of hymns:

(a) Hymns may address God direct, and gather each other into it—"O God our help in ages past"

(b) Hymns may address each other on behalf of God—"Come let us join our cheerful songs"

(c) Hymns may simply set out gospel assertions without grammatically addressing anybody—"Once in royal David's city" or "Low in the grave he lay . . . up from the grave he arose"

(d) Hymns may even take the form of an inward-looking sigh—"Oh, for a heart to praise my God," and, drawing upon the psalms, may run near to lament—

"Where is the blessedness I knew
when first I saw the Lord
where is that soul-refreshing view
of Jesus and his word?"

I should add that, for various reasons, I do not want to classify this as lament. I simply illustrate the inward-looking grammatical form.

And I mention these simply as scene-setting—hymnody illustrates the multi-directional dynamic of liturgy, and very strongly also embodies my previous point that, when a hymn is announced, it is largely on a "one size fits all" prospectus that it does so. I say "largely" because there is also an element of the dynamic in liturgy—as it processes the word of God for those participating it should not simply reflect or embody their present state of belief, interest, conscience, or resolve—it should actually be moving them on in these disciplines, and to that extent may (like the particular function of preaching) present an element of discomfort to the comfortable, just as it may present comfort to the discomforted. So in congregational terms, if we have reason to think some people are ready to lament, we may also reckon that others, who knowingly or unknowingly have thought it right to be present, may yet be appropriately moved into lament by the provision we make for them.

I have a third scene-setter—a recent Grove Booklet called *Sowing in Tears.*[1] I have drawn upon it in my own thinking; and, because Grove Books is a press I originally founded, I am generally keen to promote its products. A two-page appendix at the back of the booklet is reproduced in this chapter—and this provides one liturgical way into lament, as suggested by an actual practitioner of such liturgy. Overall the booklet discusses liturgical issues which are integral to forming a liturgy of lament—as, for instance, the place and role of confession of sin (that is, sin for which those present *are* answerable), and the ways in which it may be appropriate, having given vent to lament, to move on to hope and promise and perhaps eschatology.

I said I had two points of principle to lay down before looking at how a liturgy might express and foster lament. These are:

First, I reckon to use "lament" very specifically in relation to matters for which we have no responsibility, over which we have no control. If we had firsthand responsibility for what has gone wrong, we should be engaged not in lamenting, but in repenting. Furthermore, if we had direct control of what has gone wrong, we should be engaged not in lamenting, but in resolving and in addressing the situation. We may of course be lamenting natural action—as, e.g., earthquakes. We may be lamenting results of human sin. That which gives rise to lament may be connected

1. Bradbury, *Sowing in Tears.*

with us simply by our solidarity in the human race—or it may be because events stand near to us personally and bid a response from us for that reason. On the Sunday in 1991 which was the next day after I had been instituted as vicar of a parish, on that Sunday evening, when I went to church for what was intended to be a fairly joyful send-off for me in this charismatic parish, I found folk praying in the vestry in sorrow. Why? Well, a young couple with one young first child had lost that child in a cot-death two or three hours earlier. At 6.10pm we cancelled the whole programme for the 6.30 service and wrote it again with sobriety rather than joy, and with an element of lament touched by Christian hope. The point here was that the whole congregation knew the couple and had been delighted for them when that first child came, so the whole congregation could and would now want to be led in something near lament (though also with an element of support of the couple). I am sorry I did not keep a record of what we did. The inauguration of my ministry was properly set aside by the need for lament.

Secondly, lament with which Christians are concerned is not merely wringing hands and wishing things were otherwise. It is an exercise, an expression, done within the boundaries of faith. It may involve the fairly colorful features on which the Grove Booklet touches of crying out against God, of anger against God, of puzzlement—*aporia*—in the presence of God, but all such expressions are done with the knowledge that God, however inscrutable, however allowing wickedness to flourish, is nevertheless *there*, and in liturgy he is being specifically addressed. The lamenting factor may well mean we are saying under our breath "Come on, God, this is the time for a bit of *theodice*; please do get on with it"—but still it is said to a God who is *there*. If liturgy is addressing God in the presence of others, then corporate lament is corporate wailing to God. The faith which contextualizes the wailing may be shaken or wounded, but it also directs the wailing against or to God, and forbids it to be a mere wail.

I come now to actual samples. I begin with that sample outline from the back of Paul Bradbury's booklet. You will see in the introductory paragraph he envisages as one mode of operating a kind of targeted use to handle the lament of one person, with the pastor meeting with that one person on a one-to-one basis, to put into the open between them that which is causing lament, and then to lament together. But Bradbury is also interested in congregational lament, and in a congregational liturgy with robust interchange about the topic over which they are lamenting.

So he gives space for individual lament to be expressed within his outline, and the presumption must be that, at a service advertised as one of lament, the main part of the congregation are present specifically to give vent to their lament.

I suggest that his outline also raises questions about when and how to turn from lament to thanksgiving or hope. The basis of his thesis is that, in most liturgical situations we can be swept nowadays into instant supposed or proffered wonder, love, and praise from the outset, and that those in grief or sobering reflection cannot well go with it. But because his context is Christian, he does not wish his congregation to go away solely in sorrow or anger or empty depression, but with true Christian hope. His plea—rightly—is for authenticity; but the judging when authentic lament can be led into confident hope or quiet joy must remain a very sensitive decision.

What he does not mention here are specific topics for lament, some of which I shall be raising myself. He does add, in another appendix over the page, a suggested table of Psalms for a range of topics, and his list there may be bringing us near to actual examples.

I begin with the mine explosion in the South Island. I know the clergy were deeply involved with the local community. Was that a case for corporate lament? And how far did the actual ministering on the ground go towards lament? Perhaps the Queensland floods, devastating whole communities, qualify—though I recognize the problem of finding a right moment when the damaging has stopped, the people want to pause and wail before God, and someone is in position to set it up. But in principle it seemed to call for lament. The tsunami in the Indian Ocean five years ago had a clear finish, and a scale of damage and death almost beyond measuring. And as with these previous instances, there could well be lament by people who had themselves not suffered, but were identifying with the cry of those who had.

Suppose we go back in time. Are we in position to lament matters in the past, especially perhaps those with effects running on into the present? If you visit the battle-fields of Flanders, where thousands died pointlessly between breakfast and lunch-time, or stand on Gallipoli with its similar slaughter, should there be lament? Go back further, and does the Treaty of Waitangi still elicit not only thanks but also lament?

And go back further still, as in Britain in 2007 we were "celebrating" the second centenary of the abolition of the slave trade. But should there not rather have been lament?

With the contemporary cases, we stand near to them in time (which is why they impact us so deeply), though largely distant from them in terms of responsibility or relationship. Waitangi and the slave trade are distant in time, but much nearer in terms of corporate responsibility. I cannot say more regarding Waitangi for the moment. There have been issues in Britain about whether some parliamentary or political retrospective once-and-for-all apology for the slave trade was needed, though I suspect that, the more distant in time we get, the less authentic such an apology may seem. But was there not a case for lament?

In my own experience I came across a moving and memorable example of apology and lament almost coming together. The occasion was the Lambeth Conference of 1998, and I was responsible for putting together the worship texts, arranged to give each part of the worldwide Anglican Communion one morning or evening service for which they were responsible. As in 1988, we gave the Japanese bishops the communion service on the morning of the Feast of the Transfiguration, which, being 6 August, is also the anniversary of the dropping of the first atomic bomb on Hiroshima. They included what I want to call lament in the prayers at the heart of a service otherwise commemorating Jesus' transfiguration on the mountain. Before the prayer, however, they had a guest preacher—the only time I have known a church from somewhere on the earth's surface with responsibility for a service for the Lambeth Conference then ask someone of another nationality, from another part of the Communion, to preach. In fact they brought in Bishop Leonard Wilson's ordained daughter, Susan Cole-King—Wilson having been Bishop of Singapore at the outset of the Pacific war, and having been captured and in some degree tortured by the Japanese when they occupied Singapore. So Susan as preacher was highly symbolic. Then came the prayers. The people who died at Hiroshima were certainly mentioned, but the weight of what those bishops were saying to God in the presence of us all was that much of Asia, much of the Pacific, had suffered terribly at the hands of the Japanese and through the imperialism, arrogance, and sheer cruelty of the Japanese soldiery in the years from 1941 to 1945. They went further. They laid out with pain the sorrow that their own Anglican Church had connived with the regime in its imperialism and at least passively in concurrence with its cruelty. This was what they were laying before God in our presence on the anniversary of Hiroshima. Lament? Not the word used—but very near to it. That text is Sample 2 below.

Finally, I want to share with you a liturgical event—with, yes, a lament—in which I was involved personally. Three years ago there was an event in Jersey, one of the Channel Islands, that got high publicity. Part of a child's body had been found buried within the premises of a children's home there, and, when this was reported, people came forward to say they had been orphans there in years past and had been abused in various ways. There was a sense of horror in the fairly tight community, and the Anglican rector decided on the spot to hold a public service with leaders of the local community invited—and to do it the next day. He rang me up that afternoon, and I ran up some material during the afternoon and e-mailed it to him, and he adapted it and had his service ready the next day. The word "lament" was not used, I think, and the liturgical material did not focus the horror, but the context was one of lament. At any rate, Sample 3 is what I wrote, which he then adopted almost entire.

But I said I was simply asking questions. I think now I might have named the trouble more overtly, and the lament might then have been more clearly a lament. But, of course, the brief had not exactly been for a lament, but rather for a quest for a kind of merciful deliverance and communal distancing. These elements are not precisely lament—but the question arises as to whether pure lament, without any note of hope, can ever be appropriately rendered in liturgy. And the need for a service the next day raises very acutely the question as to *when* a lament is appropriate, and how the timing then affects the content.

I might suggest other possible occasions. Ones in my mind include:

- "Compassionate friends"—an organization in England for parents who have lost children, with an annual service in many places, on which I have on occasion preached.
- Anniversaries of tragedies, as we had, when I was Bishop of Woolwich, with the annual service to remember some twenty black teenage youths who had died twenty years before in a fire in a house where a party was being held (and it was strongly held among their grieving parents that the fire had not been properly investigated).
- The holocaust itself.

But, I emphasize again that this is not a discipline in which the liturgists are well experienced. The field is open to (sensitive) research and experiment.

SAMPLE 1: "A LITURGY FOR LAMENT"[2]

This liturgy can be adapted for use in two ways. The first is the culmination of a process of lament within a pastoral context, which may have taken place over a number of hours or even months. In this case there may only be two persons present, the person needing to lament and the minister facilitating that process. In this case the sections in ordinary type are for the minister, and those in bold for the other person to respond.

The second is a regular service within a worshipping community, which may or may not have a particular focus. The space for teaching may be important, and plenty of time needs to be given for those present to offer (in whatever way they choose) their complaint or lament,

In both cases the form of lament serves to bring into focus the feelings and complaints of the people.

Addressing God

Opening Hymn/Song

Invocation

Out of the depths I cry to you, O Lord:
O Lord, hear my cry.
Let your ears be attentive
to my cry for mercy.
We have come as the people of God
to voice our pain and assert our hope.
We have come as the people of God.
Where else can we go?
You have the words of eternal life.

Reading

One from the following: Gen 32:22–28; Job 2:1–10; Hab 1:12–21; Matt 14:22–33; John 11:17–37

Teaching on Lament *As appropriate*

Voicing Lament

Lament

People are now invited to express their lament—during this time individuals are encouraged to disclose their lament; this may take the form of a prepared written lament, or a picture, a poem, a clay model, an image, anything that gives expression to the individual's

2. Appended to Bradbury, *Sowing in Tears.*

pain and complaint, Time is given for any images or words to be given full explanation and meaning.

Petition

Prayers are said for the situation. The prayers end with the following responses:

I wait for the Lord, my soul waits
and in his word I put my hope.
My soul waits for the Lord
more than watchmen wait for the morning.

Silence

Reaffirming Praise

Praise

O Israel put your hope in the Lord,
for with the Lord is unfailing love
and with him is full redemption.
He himself will redeem Israel from all their sins.

Time is given for praise and thanks in view of God's faithfulness and mercy.
This may take the form of extemporary praise or sung worship.

Going out with Hope

Closing responses

My heart is not proud, O Lord,
my eyes are not haughty;
I do not concern myself with great matters
or things too wonderful for me.
But I have stilled and quieted my soul.
Like a weaned child with its mother
O Israel, put your hope in the Lord.
both now and for evermore.

SAMPLE 2: "LAMENT" OF THE JAPANESE BISHOPS AT THE 1998 LAMBETH CONFERENCE

The Japanese Bishops were responsible (as they had been in 1988) for the Conference Eucharist on the Feast of the Transfiguration, 6 August, a date which is also the anniversary of the dropping of the first atomic bomb on Hiroshima in 1945. The Eucharist was presented bilingually, with both languages set out on facing pages of the Conference worship book (*Lambeth Prayer*) which I edited, and the text below is the relevant part of the English-language version of the "Call to Worship" and the "Prayers of the People" within that Eucharist.

The point was emphasized within the rite by the invitation of the Japanese bishops to Susan Cole-King, a woman presbyter of The Episcopal Church (USA), to preach at the Eucharist, as her father, Bishop Leonard Wilson, had been Anglican Bishop of Singapore when the Japanese occupied Singapore in 1942, and they had interned him and tortured him. The choice of a Korean hymn to punctuate the intercessions was also significant. And the overall lament was also emphasized by a statement agreed in Japan which the bishops read separately to the Conference expressing deep remorse for their Anglican Church's backing of the imperialist regime in its pursuit of such a cruel war.

Call to Worship

On 6 August 1945 the world's first atomic bomb was dropped on Hiroshima.

In our Eucharist today, while we remember the victims of the atomic bombings of Hiroshima and Nagasaki, we also remember the many people in Asia and throughout the world who became victims of the Japanese army, as well as all victims of all wars.

We bring to mind and pray in solidarity with those who work for peace in the face of the threat of war and fear of nuclear destruction that continues to this day.

May our Lord who revealed to his disciples the brilliant light of his transfigured presence, transfigure our world too, into a world where all may live at peace.

Prayers of the People

Between each intercession we sing the Korean hymn:

"Come now, O Prince of peace."

O-so-so O-so-so
pyong-hwa-ui im-guma
U-ri-ga Han-mom i-ru-ga
ha-so-so.

Come now, O Prince of peace,
make us one body, O Lord,
Jesus reconcile your people.

God of peace:
We pray for all those who became victims of the incandescent fire, blast and radiation when the atomic bombs were dropped on Hiroshima and Nagasaki fifty-three years ago. We remember also the many victims of Japanese militarism, especially the people of Okinawa, women and children, and all who suffered at the hands of the Japanese Army. Help us always to keep in mind the sufferings of those who are still deeply wounded in body and spirit, and give us strength to work to bring about peace

O-so-so O-so-so . . .

God of forgiveness:
We mourn the more than 20,000 Koreans forcibly brought to Japan by the colonial government, who lost their lives through the atomic bombing of Hiroshima, and pray for those Korean victims who still live in suffering today, without ever having received compensation. We call to mind the sufferings of the victims of Japan's invasion and colonial rule in Asia and the Pacific, remembering those who still feel the pain of their wounds to this day, and we pray before you for forgiveness.

O-so-so O-so-so . . .

God of healing:
As we remember before you all people who experienced the cruelty of the Japanese Army during World War II, we confess that our own wartime church shared in the responsibility for those acts. We believe that you heard the voices of the women who through being forced into sexual slavery for the military had inflicted upon them unforgettable pain, in body and in mind, and the voices of those who cry out today for restoration of their human dignity. Pour out your healing fully upon them.

O-so-so O-so-so

God of reconciliation:
Even now, at this very moment the wars and horror of nuclear destruction that violate the dignity of humanity continue without cease. Bring

healing to the pain and suffering of all who are victims of nuclear contamination, and all who have driven from their homes by war.

O-so-so O-so-so

God of hope:
Strengthen and encourage all who work to bring about peace and reconciliation upon this earth. Bless all within the different religious and church communities who work to establish justice and human rights.

O-so-so O-so-so

[Confession followed, in fairly standard Anglican form]

SAMPLE 3: A SERVICE OF "LAMENT" IN JERSEY 2008

The rector's brief to COB: "to pray for the peace of all who are scarred by the tragic events of the past, to pray for the police in their ongoing investigation, and for all those responsible for the care of children in our Island today."

Draft suggestions by COB

Sketched possible outline order

(a) Brief welcome with clear statement of the event leading to the service with outline purpose of service.

(presumably including an awareness (i) that no identification of victims has happened, and (ii) that no allocation of responsibility has yet been possible—but that a cloud hangs over all).

(b) Possibly stand for one minute's silence

(c) Hymn—perhaps Psalm 23 as "The King of Love my shepherd is" or possibly Crimond.

(d) Sit for, say, Psalm 130

(e) Introduction to a litany (which, I suggest, could be strongly retrospective and circumstantial, but in which you ask for a clear response from the congregation). Here is a sample or two—I could write more, and so, I am sure, could you:

From all deceit of the world, the flesh and the devil

Good Lord, deliver us.

From all hauntings of memory and evil imagination in respect of the past

Good Lord, deliver us.

From all current fears and suspicions running on from the past

Good Lord, deliver us.

From over-inquisitiveness, false sensationalism, prurient curiosity, and pandering to media interest

Good Lord, deliver us

From all jumping to conclusions, irrational vengefulness, and misplaced accusations

Good Lord, deliver us.

Hear us, good Lord, and grant us peace as we live with this tragedy from the past

Hear us, good Lord.

Help us each day to trust in your mercy and love

Hear us, good Lord.

Help us to wait for your light as those who wait for the morning

Hear us, good Lord.

(You might want to go from the apotropaic to the almost exorcistic)

(f) Perhaps a two or three-verse Scripture passage about light, and light in the Lord (or Jesus calming storm?)

(g) Two-minute or three-minute homily

(h) Hymn—perhaps overt "What a friend we have in Jesus" (good for the fringe-people to sing?)

Forward-looking prayers for the stated purpose (perhaps again litanical, but note the selection in CW [the Church of England's *Common Worship*]*Pastoral Services* pp. 354ff)—including living victims, friends and supporters, police and judicial services

(i) I wonder whether a use of "Christ be with me" (from St Patrick's Breastplate, in CW *Pastoral Services* p. 346) printed out in full and to be said by all, but said slowly and deliberately quietly, would fit?

(j) Hymn—"Abide with me"

(k) Blessing (write a targeted one)

APPENDIX: RESPONDING TO THE CHRISTCHURCH TRAGEDY OF 22 FEBRUARY 2011

A. Christchurch Cathedral Lament

[Taken from the cathedral website by a New Zealander presbyter in England who had lost a school-friend in the earthquake. This was clearly composed with days, even hours, of the original quake]

A Prayer in Time of Need
Lord, at times such as this,
when we realize that the ground beneath our feet
is not as solid as we had imagined,
we plead for your mercy.

As the things we have built crumble around us,
we know too well how small we truly are
on this ever-changing, ever-moving,
fragile planet we call home.
Yet you have promised never to forget us.
Do not forget us now.

Today, so many people are afraid.
They still wait in fear of the next tremor.
They remember the cries of the injured amid the rubble.
They roam the streets in shock at what they see.
And they fill the dusty air with cries of grief
and the names of the missing dead.

Comfort them, Lord, in this disaster.
Be their rock when the earth refuses to stand still,
and shelter them under your wings
when homes no longer exist.

Embrace in your arms those who died so suddenly this week
Console the hearts of those who mourn,
and ease the pain of bodies on the brink of death.

Pierce too our hearts with compassion,
we who watch from afar,
find only misery upon misery.

Move us to act swiftly this day,
to give generously every day,
to work for justice always,
to pray unceasingly for those without hope.

And once the shaking has ceased,
and images of destruction have stopped filling the news,
and our thoughts return to life's daily rumblings
let us not forget that we are all your children
and they, our brothers and sisters.
We are all the work of your hands.

B. Christchurch City Lament

Drafted by COB in England in March 2011 at request of Tim Meadowcroft, who had been approached by people in Christchurch—and without any strong emotional involvement with the text as drafted.

God our Father, creator of heaven and earth and all that is in them;
you have given us a fruitful and beautiful land,
and we inhabit it as your creatures, dependent upon your goodness,
and yet knowing our own frailty.

Lord, the earth has shaken, the ground has quaked,
terror has struck, and our hearts are dismayed;
our buildings are down,
and friends, neighbours, and family-members have died;
much of the city we loved is in ruins;
people are missing, families are homeless, after-shocks continue,
and our easy confidence in life has gone.

Lord and Father, we lament the city's fate before you;
we who have trodden the ground in assurance,
and built our homes, and driven our cars,
and played our sports upon it,

we now mourn the city's loss, and grieve that we can trust
the ground no longer.

Yet, Lord, this is your world, and you are sovereign over it,
and even the hairs of our heads are numbered by you.

Let us learn of you, but give us space and time to do so;
help us to come to terms with disaster,
and yet find your hand of love within it.

And while we grieve, we thank you for the selfless labours
of rescue workers and volunteers,
we commend to you the bereaved, the injured, the homeless
and all who suffer;
we rejoice at the unstinting help of many from far and near;
and we seek from you the will and the way for the city to recover,
for life in it to flourish, for memories to be healed,
for every loss to be made good.

Lord, deal gently with us as we mourn; and so reveal yourself to us
that we may in time put darkness and loss behind us
and walk whole and healed.

Lord, we believe: but we have staggered at this earthquake
and all that it has done;
restore now our trust in you and lead us out of darkness
into your marvellous light.

PART THREE

Explorations

11

Learning to Lament in Aotearoa

Alistair Mackenzie

"Whakaakona ā koutou tamāhine ki te tangi,
ngā hoa hoki o tēnei, o tēnei, ki te uhunga."

"Teach your daughters how to wail;
teach one another a lament."[1]

This paper began as an interesting academic exercise, but became a much more personal journey as the author set about writing the final draft in Christchurch, New Zealand, after the earthquake on 22 February 2011. It is dedicated to Rhys Brookbanks, Don Cowie, Te Taki (Wally) Tairakena, Murray Wood, Owen Wright, and Stephen Wright who died in the earthquake.

INTRODUCTION

The grief that accompanies loss is a universal experience. Most cultures have developed mourning rituals to express this grief. Among these rituals are laments. Laments are common and take a variety of forms. Laments may be elaborate poems, or sung chants, or "tuneful weeping."[2] They usually involve mourning, but not just for the dead. There are

1. Jer 9:20b.

2. Holst-Warhaft, *Dangerous Voices*, 1.

laments about the fall of great cities, about emigration from the points of view of both those who leave and those who are left behind, and laments related to marriage rituals as a bride leaves to join her husband's household.

Since the mid-1960s there have been an increasing number of studies of rituals surrounding death and mourning by anthropologists, sociologists, and social historians. Herminio Martins, in his introduction to *Death in Portugal*, identifies four main reasons for this research into death in the Western world: (1) The hospitalization and medicalization of death, (2) the deritualization of death, (3) the decay of language or discourse about death, and (4) the meaninglessness of death.[3] For Holst-Warhaft, "the absence of lament has left us without language to express not only the grief but the rage of the living in the face of death."[4] Her argument is that the voices of the women who previously kept alive our lament traditions in the West have been suppressed, and we are the poorer for this. And, except where a strong tradition of folk-songs has continued, we are cut off from any vital opportunity to rediscover this. However, Holst-Warhaft suggests that women writers and singers are starting to rediscover elements of lament in their writings and songs. We also "sense its presence in the blues—perhaps the last great manifestation of lament to emerge in the west from a people more recently in touch with a folk tradition."[5] The author of this chapter wants to suggest that people connected to indigenous cultures, who have continued the practice of lamenting, also have a lot to teach others.

THE PURPOSE OF LAMENTS

Sociologists, such as Berger and Luckmann, see cultural forms built around regularized language as one way a community creates and maintains a life-world.[6] Laments provide examples of regularized language enabling anguish to be articulated so that its impact is not ignored or minimized, while at the same time also limiting the experience of

3. Quoted in Holst-Warhaft, *Dangerous Voices*, 7–8.

4. Ibid., 9.

5. Ibid.

6. See Berger, *The Sacred Canopy*; and Berger and Luckmann, *The Social Construction of Reality*. Brueggemann also draws on the observations of these sociologists in his essay "The Formfulness of Grief," 265.

suffering so that it can be accepted and coped with by the community according to its perceptions and resources. The lament form provides an acceptable way of giving expression to what might otherwise be unbearable and unmanageable for the community. And because this form offers a legitimate way for grieving deeply, the griever can be kept in the community, or offered a way back into the community without dismissing their grief. "The passion of grief is volatile. The rites of mourning . . . are society's means of performing and containing it."[7] In her exploration of laments in Papua New Guinea, Gillespie notes: "A death is usually a period of immense social upheaval for individuals, and often a whole community, and as such it becomes a fulcrum for cultural creativity, where the living have a forum for the expression of their feelings of tension and desire, and where they can make connections between the living and the dead, and the past, present and future."[8]

THE CHURCH AND LAMENTS

Observations about the lack of lamenting in Western culture as a whole also apply to Christian churches in the West. According to Walter Brueggemann, "in her songs, testimonies and prayers the church only knows of praise."[9] Billman and Migliore agree: "Psalms of lament are poorly represented in the worship books of most mainline denominations . . . it would appear that prayer and worship in many Christian congregations fail to make room for the experiences of lament, protest and remonstration with God."[10] John Leach makes a very similar observation about the worship of churches shaped by the charismatic renewal. According to Leach, "Charismatics are good at the high . . . but not so good at the lows."[11] Leach notes how James Hopewell, using Northrop Frye's four types of literature, identifies charismatic spirituality with the "Romantic" adventure, which overcomes a succession of trials, often with supernatural help, towards a happy ending.[12] Leach suggests that charismatics are often overzealous to rush to the happy ending, hence they

7. Holst-Warhaft, *The Cue for Passion*, 2.

8. Gillespie, *Steep Slopes*, n.p.

9. Brueggemann, *The Message of the Psalms*, 51.

10. Billman and Migliore, *Rachel's Cry*, 13.

11. Leach, *Renewing Charismatic Worship*, 23.

12. Hopewell, *Congregation: Stories and Structures*, n.p.

are frequently identified as "triumphalistic."[13] If mainline churches don't do lament well, it would seem charismatics hardly do it at all. Frederico Villanueva, making a more general observation, concludes that "there is no place for unanswered prayers in the church."[14]

In responding to this lack, Brueggemann claims that "[t]he Lament Psalms offer important resources for Christian faith and ministry even though they have been largely purged from the life of the church and its liturgical use. Such purging attests to the alienation between the Bible and church."[15] One notable exception to this is the historic Black churches in the USA, which developed a tradition of laments incorporated in Spirituals and Blues forms,[16] which have also impacted widely on other contemporary musical genres.[17]

Brueggemann is not the only one to claim that for the health of the church it is important that the lament psalms be rediscovered in helping to shape its life and faith. Paul A. Baglyos appeals for a recovery of lament in the liturgy of the church with a particular emphasis on the importance of this for rural churches, where telling the truth about suffering and the honest expression of lament in contexts where whole communities groan under stress seems not only very appropriate, but also very necessary.[18] Baglyos observes that every day there are people in rural America who have reason to wonder or ask, "My God, my God, why have you forsaken me, forsaken us?"[19] Villanueva emphasizes the importance of using the lament psalms in preaching as poetry (expressing the experiences of the psalmist), theology (pointing to God with a particular view of God and life), and prayer (inviting others to participate in this experience).[20] Paul Bradbury also encourages churches to use lament forms based on the Psalms in their worship.[21]

13. Leach, *Renewing Charismatic Worship*, 21.

14. Villanueva, "Preaching Lament," 65.

15. Brueggemann, "The Formfulness of Grief," 263.

16. See, e.g., Cone, *The Spirituals and the Blues*.

17. A series of essays and diagrams tracing the origins and influence of blues and Black gospel music can be found in Bogdanov et al., *The All Music Guide to the Blues*, 680–726. Numerous references to blues and gospel music related to laments can also be found in Lee, *Lyrics of Lament*.

18. Baglyos, "Lament in the Liturgy of the Rural Church," 253–63.

19. Ibid., 253.

20. Villaneuva, "Preaching Lament," 64–84.

21. Bradbury, *Sowing in Tears*.

TRADITIONAL LAMENTS IN AOTEAROA

Over a period of forty years the distinguished Māori leader and scholar Sir Apirana Ngata collected and recorded hundreds of songs and chants from the iwi of Aotearoa. This is the largest and most comprehensive collection of Māori waiata and became the four volumes of *Ngā Mōteatea*, with translations and annotations by Ngata and Pei Te Hurinui Jones. A completely redesigned and reset edition which preserves the original text has recently been published in four volumes, also including 136 songs on CD's accompanying each volume.[22]

There is ongoing discussion about the most appropriate terminology for Māori chants and waiata. Charles Royal expresses his preference to retain the word *mōteatea* for pre-existing traditional indigenous Māori chants (such as those collected by Ngata in *Ngā Mōteatea*), although Royal also expands this to include new expressions that are derived from, and remain faithful to, the classical conventions of this form.[23] This is in contrast to Mervyn McLean, who places emphasis upon the term waiata as a generic term for all Māori songs in all forms.[24] Ngata seems to place all "classical" waiata (as opposed to waiata hou,[25] which is the term for songs influenced or drawn from non-Māori culture) within the definition of *mōteatea*. Because we are quoting from a variety of sources in this chapter meanings may not coincide exactly, but this does not affect the chapter's main argument.

MĀORI LAMENTS

Of the 391 songs published in the four volumes of Ngata's *Ngā Mōteatea*, almost half are laments. In his 1929 introduction Ngata makes some general observations about the songs.[26] Firstly he notes that women as a group predominate as composers, particularly in the songs of love and lament, although men composed most of the priestly songs addressed to the gods themselves. However, not many of these priestly songs are

22. Ngata, *Ngā Mōteatea: The Songs*.

23. In a paper delivered to a conference entitled "Oceania, World Music Days, International Symposium and Festival Dialogue in Music," n.p.

24. See McLean, *Māori Music*, 110–11.

25. Literally, "new song," meaning a new song form.

26. This introduction can also be found in the preface to the 1961 edition, and is now included in *Ngā Mōteatea Part 2*.

published in Ngata's collection. Ngata also notes that a common technique is followed in each group of songs, as if they are based on one pattern. So Ngata's description of the pattern for laments, for example, includes these elements: "the pain of sorrow agitates the mind, and this finds expression in intense longing, complaining words, mournful lamentation and cries of anguish. This is accompanied by the scourging and lacerating of one's flesh, the gods are called upon, and a farewell tribute is paid to the dead; following this comes the cursing of the men or people who did the killing, and then the call is made to warrior relatives to go forth and seek revenge."[27] Ngata also notes that "among the songs of the Māori, laments are by far the most numerous, irrespective of the themes of the laments."[28]

There are many different sorts of laments. Ngata offers descriptions of the following groupings:

(a) Laments for warriors, for chiefs, or for a tribe defeated in battle fought in the light of day.

(b) Laments for men killed by treachery or murder.

(c) Laments for chiefs who die a natural death.

(d) Laments for death by misadventure or accident.

(e) Laments for a child, for a husband dead or gone away, for a husband who has been taken by another, or for a lover.

(f) A lament for a land deserted or the loss of a tribe, for a canoe wrecked or stranded, for seed lost through rot, for a diseased neck, for a plantation with a rotted crop.

(g) Laments by an invalid because of some affliction.

In his descriptions of waiata tangi, McLean notes that, "[A]lthough distinctions are made between laments (waiata tangi) and love songs (waiata aroha and waiata whaiāipo), the two classes of song are functionally and textually often identical; musically in common with other waiata, they are entirely so."[29] Best points out that although laments for the dead are called (waiata) tangi, so are songs bewailing lesser misfortune, even events as seemingly trivial as the loss of an eel pot or a fish hook.[30] According-

27. Ngata, *Ngā Mōteatea Part 2*, xxvii.

28. Ibid., xxviii.

29. McLean, *Māori Music*, 114.

30. Best, *The Māori as He Was*, n.p.; quoted in McLean, *Māori Music*, 114.

ing to McLean "because love songs are invariably about lost or unhappy love, the term waiata aroha becomes interchangeable with waiata tangi although the converse is not necessarily true."[31]

THE FORM OF MĀORI LAMENTS

According to Margaret Orbell, "[A]ll waiata take the form of complaints. Most of them are waiata aroha, 'songs of yearning' in which women complain about gossip, or unrequited love, or the way their husbands are treating them; and waiata tangi, which may bemoan an illness or some other trouble but usually lament the death of a relative."[32] Orbell states that waiata "were usually sung publicly on a marae or elsewhere to express the poet's feelings, convey a message and sway the listener's emotions. Their language is often elaborate, with specialised expression and complex allusions. They were sung very slowly, with melodies in which endlessly inventive use was made of a small range of notes."[33] Orbell claims that waiata tangi were composed equally by men and women (in contrast to Ngata's assertion that women predominate) and they were usually laments for the dead, although some were composed to lament the loss of land, or crops, or illness, or some other loss. They were usually composed to be sung by an individual or group at a tangi[34] and then were subsequently used on other occasions to remember and mourn the person who had died. Over time they would also be sung, sometimes in modified form, to mourn other deaths. Orbell suggests that between them, "the waiata tangi and waiata aroha lament and comment upon the experiences of separation through death and separation in life."[35] In describing the characteristic features of the waiata laments, Orbell identifies the following characteristics:

(a) the poets speak of their distress and of the separation from a person (or people) which has caused it

31. McLean, *Māori Music*, 114.

32. Orbell, *The Natural World of the Māori*, 58.

33. Orbell, *Waiata: Māori Songs in History*, 1.

34. The terms "tangi" and "tangihanga" refer to Māori approaches to funerals and the process of grieving for someone who has died.

35. Orbell, "My Summit Where I Sit," 191.

(b) they describe the circumstances that have caused the distress, often giving reasons for what has occurred (although these may be related in a highly elliptical narrative style)[36]

(c) frequently there is praise expressed for the person who has died

(d) frequently blame is expressed

- enemies who are considered responsible may be attacked and threatened
- the person who has died may be reproached for leaving
- the poet may blame himself or herself for not dying as well[37]

According to Orbell, the singing of laments, as well as paying tribute to those who were gone, reinforced ties that bound the living and provided a link with the past. Old laments are often used to reinforce connection with ancestors and old laments can also be used or adapted to fit new circumstances.[38]

RECURRING IMAGES IN THE LAMENTS

In Māori society, as in other oral traditions, language was part of lived reality. As Margaret Orbell says, "[w]hereas we, in our print culture, say that 'actions speak louder than words,' people living in oral cultures considered words to be a form of action. This is why it was believed that religious incantations influenced events, making gardens grow and enemies die, and why curses and insults . . . were taken so seriously."[39] This attitude is summed up in the Māori proverb:

> He tao rākau e karohia atu, ka hemo—
> Te kao kī, werohia mai, tū tonu.
> A wooden spear can be parried, and miss its mark—
> The spoken spear always pierces and wounds![40]

Many of the laments contain common themes. This conventional nature of the forms and language and themes allows poets to make

36. Orbell, *Māori Poetry: An Introductory Anthology*, 11.

37. Orbell, "My Summit Where I Sit," 190–91. These pages also include a comparison of the forms of waiata tangi and waiata aroha.

38. Orbell, *Waiata: Māori Songs in History*, 2.

39. Orbell, *Māori Poetry: An Introductory Anthology*, 6.

40. Cited in ibid.

cryptic and allusive remarks and still be understood by their hearers. Light, for example, is associated with life and success, and darkness with death and failure. The image of the setting sun is often associated with death, just as stormy water and strong winds and gathering clouds are associated with human strife. Lightning flashing in the sky, or a red glow in the sky, or mist drifting or hiding a mountain peak, or birds flying about in obvious distress are also ominous signs. Though not always symbols of death,[41] these elements may be a portent of death: "The lightning flashes and forks above the mountain peaks. It is the sign of death."[42] Biggs adds, "the grief occasioned by death is likened to rain, to the moaning of the sea, or to biting winds. And loneliness is a constantly recurring theme."[43]

Expressions of grief are often connected with images of both flowing tears and flowing blood associated with mourners lacerating themselves. Laments associated with death also often include some reference to the journey to the underworld. Mitcalfe notes how many laments open with a visual symbol—the shades of evening or a peak on the horizon—and move from there to recount the attributes of the one who has died.[44] The incorporation of mythological and ironic elements is also common.[45] The naming of mountain, river or lake is used to identify the people of that place and also the values that are attached to that symbol.[46]

According to Mead, differences are evident in the laments composed by males and females.[47] Those composed by women tend to emphasize the feelings of the composer more than the greatness of the deceased, and the composition is more likely to be a personal statement of grief rather than a statement made on behalf of the tribe. The composition is also usually shorter. Those composed by men tend to emphasize the loss to the tribe rather than the composer's own feelings. The imagery tends to be more dramatic, the chiefly attributes of the warrior are extolled, there are more references to natural phenomena, especially constellations and stars, and the compositions tend to be more formal and longer.

41. Mead, "Imagery, Symbolism and Social Values in Māori Chants," 384–85.

42. Biggs, "The Oral Literature of the Polynesians," 46, quoted in McLean and Orbell, *Traditional Songs of the Māori*, 15.

43. Biggs, "The Oral Literature of the Polynesians," 46, quoted in McLean and Orbell, *Traditional Songs of the Māori*, 15.

44. Mitcalfe, *Māori Poetry: The Singing Word*, 8.

45. Ibid., 11.

46. Mead, "Imagery, Symbolism and Social Values in Māori Chants," 378–404.

47. Ibid., 386–90.

Mead claims that the cultural values underlying the whole institution of tangihanga[48] and the associated significance of the laments are found in ancestor worship and the concern not to upset the spirits of the departed, nor disturb their safe journey to Hawaiki.[49] According to Orbell,

> At a tangihanga relatives and friends gather to honour the dead and affirm their ties with the living. It was thought that the wairua, the soul, remained with the body for three days and nights, and during this time mourners wept and addressed the deceased in oratory and song. They spoke of their grief, they offered praise, they recalled the past, if necessary they promised revenge, and they helped the person make the transition from this world to the next. Sometimes the wairua was believed to mount to the skies, where the left eye might become a star, but usually it was thought to make its way by water to Te Reinga, the entrance to the underworld in the Far North.[50]

While there is general agreement among Māori about events surrounding death, specific beliefs differ significantly from tribe to tribe.[51]

MĀORI LAMENTS AND THE PSALMS

Just as almost half Māori mōteatea contain elements of lament, so, according to Walter Brueggemann, "nearly half of the Psalms are songs of lament and poems of complaint."[52] It is interesting to compare the Māori lament forms we have described above with the way Brueggemann describes seven of the regular elements that are part of the laments in the Psalms.[53]

(a) Brueggemann calls them psalms of complaint, because elements of complaint are the most commonly recurring theme in these biblical laments

(b) The Psalmist usually begins by addressing God quite intimately: "My God" or "God of my fathers." This is not a complaint offered

48. See n. 34.

49. Mead, "Imagery, Symbolism and Social Values in Māori Chants," 391.

50. Orbell, *Waiata: Māori Songs in History*, 7.

51. See discussion in Mead, *Tikanga Māori*, 146–50.

52. Brueggemann, "Introduction," x.

53. Ibid., x–xii.

to a stranger, but a cry of pain aimed at a God who is believed to be listening.

(c) The Psalmist usually moves straight into the complaint. No particular niceties, just a straightforward statement of how troubled life is and quite specifically what this trouble is about. This often includes some exaggerated statements from the person in pain. Their world is caving in, everyone is against them and God is absent, silent, indifferent, and uncaring.

(d) These psalms usually come to focus on a clear request demanding that God take notice and turn and act to change things to rescue the Psalmist and their situation.

(e) The Psalmist usually goes on to heap up reasons why God must act, some honorable reasons, some less honorable.

(f) The Psalmist often talks about wanting vengeance and asking for God's help to make sure that something hurtful and punishing and destructive happens to the people who have caused their pain.

(g) When the anger and pain of the Psalmist has been expressed enough to allow for a turning, other more positive themes may be sounded. Sometimes a resolution is expressed in rejoicing and praise, at other times it is more muted than this, but a psalm usually expresses more hope at the end than at the beginning.

Michael Coogan provides a similar description of the typical structure of biblical laments: an address to God, description of the suffering/anguish from which one seeks relief, a petition for help and deliverance, a curse towards one's enemies, an expression of the belief of one's innocence or a confession of the lack thereof, a vow corresponding to an expected divine response, and lastly, a song of thanksgiving.[54]

There are clearly many elements that are common to Māori laments and biblical laments.

(a) The poetic form designed to be sung or chanted.

(b) The experience of separation from one who has previously been a source of consolation.

(c) The public expression of deep personal pain and grief and disappointment.

54. Coogan, *A Brief Introduction to the Old Testament*, 370.

(d) The rehearsing and analysis of events.

(e) The strong and raw expression of complaint and blame and anger.

(f) The desire for vengeance.

The lament Psalms in the Bible and the Māori laments express similar states of disorientation, deep longing and loss, complaints, cries of anguish and calls for revenge. The main difference that is apparent is that Māori laments are not generally so specifically addressed to God or the gods. They are usually complaints directed to people (both those who are present and those who have departed), and the elements (which in Māori cosmology are often identified with particular gods), rather than complaints to a God who is known to listen and is expected to act. It is also clear that Māori laments perform a different function to karakia, which are designed to influence events and sometimes include direct appeals to the gods. Karakia include charms, incantations, invocations, spells and prayers and usually involve a set formula of words chanted to obtain benefit or avert trouble. Different levels of karakia are used by children, laypeople, and tohunga in increasing order of importance. Yet, even in karakia, making a direct appeal to a god is a rare occurrence.[55] According to Elsdon Best, "[t]he infrequent occurrence of true invocations, of direct appeal to the gods, is a very remarkable feature in Māori ritual."[56] Generally, there seems to be a hesitancy to address deities directly. However, this writer has heard stories from Māori tribal traditions passed on orally of tribal chiefs and priests complaining strongly to God and the gods about particular events. Clarification of the relationship between laments and karakia (and also understanding of the relationship between the gods and the Supreme Being in pre-Christian Māori traditions) belong to other studies. Overall, though, it would seem that in very few Māori laments are the gods addressed directly, although sometimes the elements associated with them (earth, wind, sky, sea, etc) are addressed. This is a major difference between Māori laments and laments in the Psalms.

These differences warn us against any attempt to suggest that waiata tangi perform the same function for Māori that the Psalms do in the Judaeo-Christian tradition. The distinctive perspective of the lament Psalms is expressed well in Walter Brueggemann's response to the way that Elizabeth Kübler-Ross deals with death and dying. He notes that,

55. See Reed and Mikaere, *Taonga Tuku Iho*, 97.

56. Best, *Māori Religion and Mythology Part* 1, 307.

"[t]he responding partner in her form, that is a friend, relative, medical personnel . . . means that the move to the affirmation is not full and buoyant, because such responding agents cannot powerfully intrude to transform. The formfulness of the event is essentially and necessarily humanistic. What is lacking is the presence of a sovereign God who can authorize."[57] Kübler-Ross urges the acceptance of death with serenity, but for Brueggemann this is contrary to Israel's perception of death as a conquered enemy. For Israel, loss, grief, and death are both present realities and real dangers, but Yahweh deals with them. God is not apathetic and untouched by the cries of the people of God. God is moved by such address and responsive to those who address God. This sense of "the presence of a sovereign God who can authorize" and whose people are invited to lodge their complaints is a dimension we do not find explicitly named in the Māori laments. Nevertheless, the presence of so many other common elements suggests that there is still much that can be learned from these indigenous expressions of lament.

CONCLUSION

This essay has identified some important elements of the tradition of Māori laments. It is clear that this is an extensive and deeply rooted tradition in Aotearoa. We have also identified more superficially some characteristics of the biblical tradition of laments, particularly in the Psalms, and noted how these compare with Māori laments. How can we learn from these traditions and give appropriate contemporary expression where lament is needed today? Both Māori and biblical laments encourage honest expressions of grief, disappointment, alienation, and pain. In addition, the biblical laments invite us to deliberately place these expressions in "the presence of one who alone can address decisive word to those who suffer."[58] Funeral services,[59] Anzac Day commemorations[60] and public memorial services, such as those associated with the Pike River Mine disaster and the Canterbury earthquakes, are probably those parts of New Zealand culture that have come closest to combining these

57. Brueggemann, "The Formfulness of Grief," 272.

58. Ibid., 263.

59. Such as the public memorial service for the 29 Pike River Mine disaster victims in Greymouth, New Zealand, on 2 December 2010.

60. Taylor, "Scars on the Australasian Heart," 48–74.

elements recently in a public way. Further exploration of the indigenous Māori and biblical lament traditions could assist us and our communities to deal with death and the deep grief that accompanies it even more honestly and effectively.

12

Framing Lament

Providing a Context for the Expression of Pain

Jeanette Mathews

In this chapter I suggest that the form-critically identified laments of the Hebrew Bible can be understood via the performance concept of "framing." In art, drama, and literature the frame lifts the work or event to a heightened consciousness and provides a context for practitioners and audiences to interact. My interest is in the link between frame (form) and content. I argue that the lament form provides a literary framework for the expression of anguish by empowering those who are suffering to name their pain, despite the constraints of the form that generally culminate in a leaning towards hope. Comparison of biblical laments emanating from the experience of exile with lament poetry written by exiled Burmese Karen refugees in the twenty-first century will show that resonances exist between the disparate communities through their common framing of pain via lament.

BRINGING THE FRAME INTO VIEW

The concept of "framing" is most familiar in the visual arts—where a painting or artwork is set in a frame or on a pedestal. It is probably true to say that for the most part the frame is ignored—it is merely the supporting or defining structure that allows the artwork to be viewed. Even when ornate frames are used in galleries or private collections, there is a tendency for the frame to become invisible, or paid little heed.

The frame, of course, is a historical artifact. The earliest artworks were images drawn onto cave walls with rough surfaces and no set boundaries. In a seminal article on the frame as a boundary to the artwork, Meyer Schapiro notes that not until the creation of pottery and architecture with regular angles and smooth surfaces did the prepared field for art become normative.[1] Cultural evolution and societal norms mean that even the most primitive of children's drawings still take place on an artificial rectangular field and we frown upon graffiti or provide spaces in our public areas where such expression is sanctioned and controlled. By defining the parameters of the work, the frame has a *constraining* function on the artwork. In our modern world the frame is a given and in fact it is often taken for granted.

It has been argued, however, that the frame is the very thing that creates the space for the artwork to be viewed and interpreted. "Through the frame, the picture is never simply one thing to be seen among many: it becomes the object of contemplation."[2] The frame separates the artwork from its surrounding environment and lifts it to a heightened significance. Sallie McFague, commenting on a broad spectrum of the arts, states "paintings, poetry, novels, sculpture, dance, music help us look at colors, sounds, bodies, events, characters—whatever—with full attention. Something is lifted out of the world and put into a frame so that we can, perhaps for the first time, *see* it."[3] In relation to art as dramatization, Richard Shusterman also notes that putting an event or story in the frame of a theatrical performance "sets the work apart from the ordinary stream of life and thus marks it as art."[4] He speaks of dramatization as "the staging or framing of scenes" and recognizes the appropriateness of the French term *mis-en-scène*, often used as a synonym for framing or setting. This *heightening* aspect is a second important way the frame functions.

Shusterman's observation that dramatization provides a "greater vividness of experience and action"[5] echoes Schapiro's earlier claim that

1. Schapiro, "On Some Problems," 9.

2. Marin, "The Frame of Representation," 82. See also Duro, *The Rhetoric of the Frame*.

3. McFague, *Super, Natural Christians*, 29, emphasis original.

4. Shusterman, "Art as Dramatization," 367.

5. Ibid., 368.

the frame deepens the view of the object to be studied. Schapiro likens this phenomenon to that of a window frame through which a space may be seen beyond the glass. "The frame belongs then to the space of the observer rather than the illusory, three-dimensional world disclosed within and behind."[6] Thus, the frame not only encloses the artwork, it also shapes the way it is perceived. This *clarifying* function is a third aspect of the frame worth noting. It becomes evident when moving away from visual arts to a more inclusive analysis of framing as part of everyday communication and interaction. Erving Goffman claims that framing is used to make meaning out of everyday experience as well as unusual events. Fantastical or ridiculous scenarios are accepted if we know that we are being told a joke or a fictional story. For the most part, according to Goffman, frameworks are intuitive. An individual "is likely to be unaware of such organized features as the framework has and unable to describe the framework with any completeness if asked, yet these handicaps are no bar to his easily and fully applying it."[7]

THE IMPORTANCE OF THE FRAME IN PERFORMANCE

In the area of performance studies, not a great deal of attention has been given to the frame. In many respects, it is taken for granted in the performing arts as well as the visual arts. The "proscenium arch" is the term given to the architecture of traditional theatre, where the audience is separated from the stage by the proscenium ("in front of the scenery" in Latin). The physical structure thus provides a frame for viewing and emphasizes the separation between performers and audience. But even where this traditional separation is breaking down, such as in the more audience-inclusive nature of Performance Art, little attention has been paid to the way in which shifts in the frame through which audiences view performance changes their perception of the content.[8] Take the example of a woman posing as a model for a nude art class. During the drawing period the woman's body is a tool, if not a work of art in itself. As the class breaks for refreshment or even merely a change of pose, the model's nakedness is reframed through the change of context and she feels compelled to cover her nakedness until the next pose is required.

6. Shapiro, "On Some Problems," 11.
7. Goffman, *Frame Analysis*, 21.
8. See Spencer, "Disrupting the Boundaries."

The art student, likewise, is implicated in the vulnerability implied by nakedness and would perhaps evidence responses ranging from embarrassment to lechery that would otherwise not be evident in the modeling session. Elizabeth Grosz speaks of spectators being "protected" from this vulnerability "when nakedness is contained within a frame."[9] Thus the clarifying function of the frame in performance is critical for audience perception.

Performance Art involves experimentation with the roles of performers and their audience. The breadth of experience can be seen from just a few examples. "Invisible Theater," developed by Augusto Boal in Argentina as part of the Theater of the Oppressed, takes place in public spaces but aims to ensure the audience is ignorant of a theatrical event unfolding around them. Some artists have prepared installations or events where audience reaction is videotaped and placed on view as integral to the work. Experimental theatre characteristically draws audience members into the performance by asking them to participate in the action on stage or by being directly addressed by the performers. Each of these examples illustrates how the frame of the performance affects the way the work is perceived.

It is clear that both the composer of the artwork or theatrical experience and the audience member has a role in recognizing and interpreting the frame. A performer chooses the frame for presenting his or her work, and is constrained by the parameters of the form selected, but does have the freedom to manipulate the audience's experience. An audience's appreciation and understanding of the work will be enhanced by recognition of the frame in which it is presented.[10]

Shusterman's essay alludes to all three functions of the frame that have been identified: its constraining function is seen in that it demarcates what is framed from the rest of life; its heightening function is seen in the way it highlights and intensifies reality; and its clarifying function is seen in the context it gives for viewing the work or experience. He says: "As Aristotle already adumbrated in his theory of catharsis, art's frame permits us to feel even life's most disturbing passions more intensely,

9. Grosz, "Naked," 216.

10. An audience may choose to view a work through a frame other than intended by the artist, however; a phenomenon shown clearly in the controversy over the Henson photographic works in Australia in early 2008. A promotional leaflet depicting a naked pre-pubescent female body was variously perceived as "art" or "obscenity" in the ensuing public debate.

because we do so within a protected framework where the disruptive dangers of those passions can be contained and purged, so that neither the individual nor society will suffer serious damage."[11]

LAMENT AS A FRAME

The preceding discussion of the concept of framing and its value in the arts suggests that it is worthwhile raising the frame to greater consciousness. The frame lifts an event or artwork from everyday life to allow it to be experienced in a heightened manner. When focusing on lament literature, an important by-product of this heightening aspect of framing is the empowerment of those who suffer by providing a structure to express what might otherwise remain inexpressible.

In defining lament as "frame," the work of Louis Marin provides a helpful analysis of the terminology used in three different languages to speak of "frames." The French word *cadre* refers to the border of wood or other material in which one places an artwork. The Italian *cornice* has architectural overtones as it also is used for the edge of a building. It implies protection or perhaps projection, nuances that are not seen in the French word. The English "frame" refers to the structural element of the artwork's construction as well as its final encasing—a canvas is stretched onto a frame in order to be prepared for the product. In relation to the latter, Marin states "[r]ather than an edge or border, rather than an edging ornament, [the frame] supports the substructure and the surface of representation."[12] The nuances inherent in the English word "frame" allow for the provision of an environment that supports and contains an artistic expression of anguish.

Form-critical studies of biblical laments in a sense have identified the "frame" of the form by isolating a common structure and recognizing typical phrases across a variety of lament prayers.[13] Typical laments include a direct address to Yhwh, a complaint, words that reassure the speaker, motivation clauses for Yhwh to act, a petition for justice or vengeance, and a vow of praise anticipating Yhwh's intervention.[14] Such a

11. Shusterman, "Art as Dramatization," 370.

12. Marin, "The Frame of Representation," 82.

13. The *qinah* rhythm, often cited as the characteristic poetic metre of lament, could also be viewed as a framing device (see Gerstenberger, *Psalms*, 11).

14. Westermann, *Praise and Lament*, 64.

frame is evident in the observation that of the many lament psalms, Ps 88 is the only exception that does not end on a vow of praise or a note of hope. Although expressing the deep anguish of loss, sorrow, anger, pain, and death, the laments nonetheless generally have a structure that leans towards trust and hope for newness.

The constraining function of the frame is most clearly evidenced in the alphabetic acrostic poetry that characterizes the lament literature of the book of Lamentations. Acrostic poetry is used elsewhere in the Hebrew Bible (Pss 9–10; 25; 34; 37; 111; 112; 119; 145; Prov 31:10–31; Nah 1) but is striking in its concentration as the predominant form (with variations) that characterizes Lamentations. Of the five poems that make up Lamentations, the twenty-two letters of the Hebrew alphabet are used as the foundation for each poem. Chapters 1, 2, and 4 are twenty-two verse stanzaic acrostics, chapter 3 is a fuller three-line sixty-six verse stanzaic acrostic, and chapter 5 is a poem of twenty-two lines.[15] Norman Gottwald argues convincingly that the predominant motivation guiding the aesthetic constraint of the use of alphabetic acrostics in the book of Lamentations was the metaphorical force of totality and completeness that it suggests: "Those who entertain this idea of completeness, therefore, instinctively feel that in naming the whole alphabet one comes as close as man may to a total development of any theme or the complete expression of any emotion or belief."[16]

Gottwald is aware of the paradox of expressing deep emotion through a tightly controlled framework, evidence of the constraining function of framing, commenting that the "apparent contradiction between artificial literary form and spontaneity of emotion has attracted the attention of successive generations of commentators on Lamentations."[17] In his view, the function of the acrostic was "to encourage completeness in the expression of grief, the confession of sin and the instilling of hope."[18] Gottwald's analysis suggests that there is a congruency between form and intention such that the constraint of the form made room for the possibility of new horizons: "The acrostic may have hampered an unfettered

15. Note the inversion of the ayin-pe sequence in Lam 2, 3 and 4; an inversion that also occurs in the lament Ps 10 and the LXX of Prov 31:10–31, suggesting it is not a scribal error but, according to Will Soll, "adherence to different ordering conventions" (Soll, "Acrostic," 59).

16. Gottwald, *Studies*, 29.

17. Ibid., 24.

18. Ibid., 28.

emotionalism but it has greatly enhanced the expression of controlled feeling . . . reflection has already begun to bring calm into the midst of wild and irrational grief."[19]

FRAMING PAIN IN ANCIENT AND CONTEMPORARY CONTEXTS

Before moving too quickly to this resolution that follows the exposure of grief, I think it is helpful to dwell a little longer on the use of the form to allow expression of overwhelming emotion. Lamentations, while making extensive use of the lament form, also adapts it by minimizing positive features and expanding the complaints. Along with Gottwald,[20] Kathleen O'Connor recognizes that the third poem contains words of hope. But she also observes that the following two poems that return to the theme of despair and doubt reflect the "complex and uneven processes of coping with trauma in which hope flares up and fades."[21] Furthermore, since the voice of Yhwh is not one of the "multitude" of voices from many different perspectives, "the book honors voices of pain."[22] Cries of suffering and hopelessness are not denied.

O'Connor, along with others, stresses the importance of lament as a form of empowerment of the sufferer. Because lament is spoken into a pre-existing relationship between a believer and their God, it is a valid and necessary expression of faith when experience results in loss or pain. As O'Connor states: "The point of lamenting is not to confess sin . . . but to name injustice, hurt, and anger. . . . Laments empower sufferers to speak for themselves. . . . Naming suffering before God reclaims human dignity and power that has been trampled and violated. . . . Laments are the beginning of action, a rejection of passivity, and so they can invert despair."[23]

In contemporary situations of crisis and pain this expression of lament provides a framework for those who are powerless to express their pain and in so doing to ensure that their plight is neither ignored nor minimized. Nancy Lee and Carleen Mandolfo have edited a book of

19. Ibid., 32.

20. Ibid., 30.

21. O'Connor, *Lamentations*, 14.

22. Ibid., 15.

23. Ibid., 128–29.

essays entitled *Lamentations in Ancient and Contemporary Cultural Contexts* in which established scholars of the biblical lament literature engage in what Walter Brueggemann describes as the "critical" work of "connecting *ancient texts* to *contemporary crises*."[24] These essays recognize the commonality of the lament genre across cultural contexts both ancient and modern as a means to express pain and suffering. Some authors in this volume make specific links between biblical laments and contemporary expressions of lament, and the remainder of this paper continues in a similar manner, connecting several "lament poems" written by young Karen refugees in a Thai-Burmese border camp in 2006 to their counterparts in the lament literature of the Hebrew Bible.

FRAMING THE PAIN OF REFUGEES

In 2006 I was privileged to spend a fortnight in the Mae La Refugee Camp on the Thai-Burmese border together with three other members of my church congregation, teaching an intensive program to a group of tertiary age students in the Bible School run by Rev. Dr Saw Simon of the Karen (Kawthoolei) Baptist Church. The Karen made up a portion of the 50,000 Burmese refugees housed in the camp, one of several camps that nestle between the mountain range separating Thailand and Burma and Route 105 running north/south along the Western border of Thailand. Refugees housed in the camps have no passports and therefore are unable to travel beyond the camps. Many await visa applications to a third country such as Australia or Canada. The Kawthoolei Karen Baptist Bible School was brought to the Refugee Camp along with Dr Simon in 1990 and is described by him as a "displaced Bible School." Classes are taught in Karen, Burmese, and English languages, depending on the origin of volunteer teaching staff. The Bible School functions partly to occupy these young people following the basic education they receive in UN schools in the camp since they are restricted from the usual opportunities open to young people. But there is also an intention to train these young Christians for mission and evangelism amongst their own and other people groups. Dr Simon was awarded the Baptist World Alliance Human Rights award in 2000 for his work amongst refugees, but was unable to travel to the World Congress in Melbourne as, like others

24. Brueggemann, "Lament as Wake-up Call," 236, emphasis original.

in the camp, his own refugee status means he holds no citizenship and no passport.

While diligent and cooperative, I found the Karen students to be extremely shy and emotionally reserved, exemplified in discomfort with physical displays of affection and a lack of desire to linger over a meal, even on a special occasion. Despite connections with freedom-fighters and a daily hymn that exhorted "troops" and "leaders of troops" to revere God, the overall demeanor seemed more accepting than rebellious. Although most had left their homes in traumatic circumstances, citing burning villages, flight from Burmese soldiers and refuge in the forest before crossing the mountains to Thailand, their stories and experiences were told dispassionately. They cherished a hope that they would return to their country but waited with seeming unlimited patience for the more likely eventuality that they would be accepted as refugees in another nation.

Towards the end of the fortnight my Old Testament History class addressed the period of the Israelite exile. In an earlier sermon I had preached at one of the camp's Baptist churches, I had suggested that the story of the exodus community at the end of the book of Deuteronomy resonated with the experience of the Karen, poised on the edge of the land they believed they had been given as an inheritance, but not able to cross over and reap its benefits. There were also obvious connections with the exilic community at the other end of the Hebrew Bible: a community driven out of their land and forced to live as aliens in another land, yet holding onto their traditions and hopes for restoration.

As we studied the literature from the exilic period I gave the students an opportunity to make this connection for themselves. I asked them to write a lament poem, using their own experience as a basis. This was the last exercise of the class and it wasn't until after I had left the refugee camp that I read through their poems. As I did, I was staggered at the level of emotional outpouring that the poems evidenced. These quiet, reserved Karen students had been given a vehicle for expressing the pain of their experience and loss, and it was not until that moment that I had realized the depth of their passion and pain and their longing as displaced persons to return to their own place.

LAMENTING LOSS—RESONANCES AND CONTRASTS

Seven lament poems are reproduced in an appendix to this chapter. Although varied and individual, the most common theme addressed is the loss of the Kawthoolei traditional land and the fervent hope for a return home to this land. The first two poems speak directly to a personified land, evoking the "city-lament" genre that seems to form the foundation of the book of Lamentations.[25] The students had been members of small rural communities rather than a large capital city, but the descriptions of the destruction of their land and resulting devastation of communities and starvation are stronger images than the suffering of individual illness or sense of abandonment.

Nancy Lee speaks of common oral traditional elements in lament poetry across wide cultural and time spans, including personification of the land and the use of natural vegetation as a metaphor for human suffering.[26] It is striking to notice these elements in the Karen laments: the first two poems speak to Kawthoolei as if to a suffering parent and Poem 6 refers to the land as a fragile flower. Like the ancient Israelites and the communities involved in the Balkan conflicts discussed by Lee, the Karen people live close to the land, so natural imagery is understandably reflected in the poems.

Tod Linafelt, along with several other authors in the book edited by Lee and Mandolfo, speaks of laments as "survivor literature," a characteristic of which is metaphoric and symbolic descriptions of suffering rather than precise reports of events: "the book of Lamentations itself may be taken as an ancient example of survivor literature, a literature that is more about the *expression* of suffering than the meaning behind it, more about the contingencies of *survival* than the abstractions of sin and guilt, and more about *protest* as a religious posture than capitulation or confession."[27]

The Karen poems, too, are highly symbolic and provide a metaphorical rather than factual account. Writing this way heightens the emotional nature of the poems. This is an important observation in itself, given the habitual reticence of the Karen students in face-to-face encounters. As composers of survival literature they are freer to bring their pain to expression. According to O'Connor, the voice itself is a metaphor for

25. See Hillers, *Lamentations*, and Dobbs-Allsopp, *Weep O Daughter of Zion*.

26. Lee, "The Singers of Lamentations," 37.

27. Linafelt, "Surviving Lamentations," 62, emphasis original.

action. Because pain leads to silence, "to acquire a voice means to gain identity, to come into the truth of one's history, and to become a moral agent . . . voices are acts of survival."[28] In the case of the Karen students, of course, it was the written voice that brought their pain to expression. In expressing their feelings, a greater sense of Karen identity is portrayed. The Karen poems are written as individual voices, but when read together provide a cohesive canvas of suffering and hope, not unlike the literature of Lamentations in which multiple voices are heard.[29] My home country of Australia has experienced protesting asylum seekers gathered on the roof of a detention facility pleading to be heard via large banners. Such desperate action underscores the fact that refugee voices are seldom publicly heard on their own terms. Those who successfully navigate our "systems" of immigration are usually expected to speak a language that is different to their own, both literally and figuratively, as they prepare application forms that may require creation of non-existent identity papers and so forth. In these laments the exiled voices of refugees are allowed to speak for themselves, although it must be ironically acknowledged that these poems were written in English.[30]

Although the Mae La students were familiar with the Hebrew Bible traditions and had studied some lament psalms in class, only Poem 7 obviously borrowed from those traditions with its echoes of Ps 137. The striking imagery of a bird trapped in a cage (Poem 2) might have been influenced by a lecture describing Sennacherib's attempted invasion of Judah, but I am more inclined to view it as coincidence. Yet despite the historical and geographical separation of the Israelite and Karen communities, there is a familiarity between the Karen poems and the laments of the Hebrew Bible arising from similar experiences of oppression and abuse. Three poems ask the typical "why?" questions of lament literature (see the second stanza in Poem 2, the last stanza in Poem 3 and the last part of Poem 7). Poem 7 ends with the words "How long?"—a phrase

28. O'Connor, "Voices Arguing About Meaning," 28.

29. See Boase, *The Fulfilment of Doom* for a discussion of the dialogic nature of Lamentations.

30. Another irony that should be noted is that, despite their habitual reticence, the Karen people have a great love of singing and performance. While at Mae La I observed a sung rendition of Ps 137, with words modified to fit their own context and sung in their own language, and found it also to be a performance full of pathos. Perhaps music is another frame that allows a fuller emotional expression. We have been reminded in other essays in this volume that laments across a variety of cultures are frequently sung or chanted.

that is common in lament psalms.[31] The Karen poems are mostly written in the first person voice, but their subject matter is communal rather than individual loss: the individual voice represents the pain of the entire displaced community.

Some end on a note of faith, like the majority of lament psalms (see Poems 3 and 5 especially). But the overriding impression one is left with when reading them is an unresolved longing to return to the homeland. Tod Linafelt speaks of the open-endedness of the book of Lamentations with its final unanswered questions (Lam 5:20–22), and, in contrast to many lament psalms, its "refusal to move to praise."[32] A similar lack of resolution in the Karen poems reflects the seemingly irresolvable fate of the country of Burma that from time to time emerges in the consciousness of the Western media and conscience, but for the most part sinks back to oblivion as the world community throws up its hands and wonders if change will ever come.

Significant differences are also noticed when the Karen poems are contrasted with Hebrew Bible laments. They were written in the context of a "History of Israel" course in a Bible School, yet only one student included an invocation to God (Poem 7) and there was little complaining or accusation against God. In addition, the enemy that brought about destruction of their communities is largely absent from the poems—"the army" in Poem 4 and "SPDC"[33] in Poem 7 are the only references to a foe. One only gains a general sense of a land destroyed by war, suffering, poverty, hunger, and persecution. Nor is there any real appeal to justice or retribution; or any sense of sin or penitence, but only a strong sense of wanting to return to what once was. A strong impression of innocent suffering is given in the poems. But one is not left with the sense that these Karen students are part of a "victim culture" resulting in powerlessness. Rather, their expression of pain and longing is a form of empowerment that affirms the value of their Kawthoolei land and culture, as well as their own self-worth, seen especially in the metaphor of a flower to be protected in Poem 6. Like many laments, Poems 4 and 5 portray an expectation that any future justice will include drawing on God's power.

31. See Pss 6:3; 13:1; 35:17; 74:10; 79:5; 80:4; 82:2; 89:46; 94:3; 118:84. Note also the lament flavor of the opening poem in the book of Habakkuk (1:2–4).

32. Linafelt, "Surviving Lamentations," 58.

33. SPDC is a reference to the State Peace and Development Council, a somewhat euphemistic name for the military regime of Burma which seized power in 1988.

CONCLUSION: THE CONNECTION BETWEEN ANCIENT TEXTS AND CONTEMPORARY CRISES

This chapter has discussed the importance of the lament as a frame for the expression of suffering by Karen refugee students. Of the three aspects of framing that were identified: constraining, heightening and clarifying; it is the heightening aspect that is most at work in these Karen laments. The opportunity to create a personal lament within the context of a Christian Bible School subject allowed latent emotions to be lifted into consciousness and set apart as worthy of expression. The heightening function is further seen in the empowerment of students to give voice, albeit in written form, to the pain of their loss and their longing for a future restoration. The poems evoke the ancient city-lament form employed by the book of Lamentations by highlighting a personified land that has been ravished and left bereft of her children. The contemporary crisis of an unjust military rule in Burma that has resulted in large refugee populations fearful of oppression in their home country can find some echoes in the lament literature of the Judeo-Christian faith. One only hopes that these connections do not remain purely academic exercises but contribute to the ongoing protest against political injustice and its resultant suffering and in the re-creation of hope for a better future.

APPENDIX: KAREN LAMENT POEMS[34]

Poem 1. "My Beautiful Land"

Every night, in my dream I see you
Oh my beautiful land of Kaw Thoo lei

Wherever I go, wherever I live
I never forget you
Oh my beautiful land of Kaw Thoo lei

My tears shed for you every night
My heart aches for you every day
A land of war, a land of suffering

34. Where possible, the original authors of these poems have been contacted and permission has been gained to use the poems in this essay. All have now left Mae La Refugee camp and have been accepted as refugees in a variety of locations including Australia, USA, Canada, and Norway.

The woe of my people haunted me
And the poverty appalled me
My tears can never run dry as long as you are
Without hope to a new life.

Though I am in foreign land
You are always in my heart and mind
Without you I am a wretch, and without you
I am a slave in foreign lands.

Oh my beautiful Kaw Thoo lei
How I miss you so much
And how I long to be in your bosom again
Oh my land of glory and my land of riches
I'll never forget you, and never forsake you
The land I love and ready to sacrifice my life,
A land called Kaw Thoo lei, a land of Karen people,
A land for the freedom fighter.

—Daughter of Kaw Thoo lei
(Naw Tamla N'Ka Thwe Tun, Mae La Camp, September 2006)

Poem 2. "Back to You Again"

From my youngest age I knew
I was with you, enjoyed my life in you
I love your beauty and your dignity
I thought you are the best of all
Never want to stay far from you.

Later I saw the flowing tears on your face
As a result of forced labors and intimidation
I said why, but no answer from you
Step by step you led me far from you
I thought and felt that you forsook me
But you express your love and hope to my future life.

You did not tell me what you suffer
And how you felt
I couldn't see you with my own eyes, so I followed what you appointed

But later I realized what is in you
And I can read your mind.

Sometimes the heart can see what is invisible to the eyes
Now I know how great is your love
So I decide to return to you
And stay with you till the end of my age

But you will keep me temporarily in Siam
As an asylum seeker in it
As a little bird in Siam cage
I long for you and receive your love again
When can I return to you oh my mother land!
Every week in my dream I tell you
Back to you again, back to you again.

(Saw Jonathan, Mae La Camp, September 2006)

Poem 3. "I Search for Peace"

How wealthy on my eyes
Once a very famous time
Now the poorest in the world
Now full of fighting and the curse

I search for peace where I went
Can no one answer me?
Yes, some people had answers
which does not really fulfill what I need.

Justice, peace, love and kindness
Should be in everyone's mind
The most important way to build peace
Is the time when we really forgive!

Most people wandered all over the world
For this generation to survive
But some stay on this "Land"
Persecution to be their friend.

And the question still goes on
Why have we been born to this fate!
Not by human strength could I answer
For only in God comes the PEACE to all life's questions.

(Khu Pwo, Mae La Camp, September 2006)

Poem 4. "I Miss My Home Land"

I was born in a beauty land
Full of dignity and happiness
I wish to stay in our home forever
And I want to depart never.

The army entered my village
On a silent day.
Our fields were destroyed
And burnt the rice barn.

I was hungry
But no food to eat
I left my home land
Settled in another land.

I miss you every minute
Tears fall down on my feet
But still have hope
God will lead me home.

I miss my home land
Forever and never end.
I want to go back
To beautify our land again.

(Naw Htee Lah Hay Ku, Mae La Camp, September 2006)

Poem 5. "We are Hungry"

We are like the orphans
Without the nature parents

No home, no food, and naked
We always feel hungry.

Since 1949 we seized peace
We struggled for our freedom
Like a river the blood-shed
For 57 years revolution.

Into four parts we're separated
Kawthoolei and Refugees
Some in Burma and to foreign countries.
The Karen's blood always reveals.

But we are sure that one day
Our stomach will be fulfilled
With the strength of sovereignty Lord
Because we based our hope on him.

(Winber, Mae La Camp, September 2006)

Poem 6. "My Flower"

I'm holding a flower
The flower that I love
Hold it tightly in my hand
And will never let it fall.

If others take my flower
I will try to get it back
If others throw it away
Even tumble and wither
I will be picking it up
And put it into heart.

(Anonymous, Mae La Camp, September 2006)

Poem 7. "A Smile with an Aching Heart"

Unlike an Israel girl in Babylon
I could raise my voice in Thailand
I sing with a smile.

Though I sang
My heart never reach gladness
'Cause I smile without a heart
sang with an absent mind

I weep for her inside Karen State "Kaw Thoo Lei"
"She ran, ate, slept like animal
give birth to a baby boy in the jungle
a distance
not far away from home
the only thing that make her warm
was a 25 years old dirty blue blanket"

Kneeling down before Almighty
I cried,
"Why is it happen to her?
Why not enough clothes
and why SPDC chase her . . .
when she is innocent
without weapon
why no food nor milk
why not her home is hers . . . "

At last
"Why I couldn't visit her?"

We are now in Mae La Temporary Shelter
"Temporary" means 16 years
I lift my eyes to you, O Lord
How long will I smile with an aching heart!

(Naw Hsar K'Nyaw Htoo, Mae La Camp, September 2006)

13

Public Lament

ELIZABETH BOASE AND STEVE TAYLOR

INTRODUCTION

THERE HAS BEEN A surge of scholarship around lament in recent times. Although the initial impetus for this resurgence can be found in the works of both Westermann and Brueggemann, the focus on lament has moved beyond the boundaries of biblical studies and has taken on a particular urgency in light of global events since the turn of the millennium.[1] The first decade of the twenty-first century has seen tragedies which have touched the consciousness of people worldwide. Headline examples include the attack on the world trade centre in 2001, the wars in Afghanistan and Iraq, terrorist bombings in Bali and London, the attack in Mumbai, the Asian tsunami, Cyclone Katrina, and earthquakes in Haiti, China, and Pakistan. Millions of people have been displaced, forced into exile through the ravages of civil war. As we write this chapter, the world is still reeling from the impact of recent earthquakes in Christchurch and Japan.

Such events evoke responses at the communal level, and raise questions about how the pain and suffering of the community can be both

1. See, for example, Westermann, *Praise and Lament*; Brueggemann, "The Costly Loss of Lament," 67–81; Brueggemann, "Formfullness of Grief," 263–75; Brueggemann, "Necessary Conditions," 19–49; Brown and Miller (eds.), *Lament*; Swinton, *Raging with Compassion*; Lee and Mandolfo (eds.), *Ancient and Contemporary Contexts*; Lee, *Lyrics of Lament*; Harasta and Brock (eds.), *Evoking Lament*.

expressed and processed. Although the church may once have been the institution to which people turned in times of crisis, it no longer necessarily provides the physical or ritual space where expressions of lament occur when a community is gathered together in grief. One of the reasons for this may well be the long noted absence of lament as a regular practice in Western Christian tradition.[2]

In the ancient world, rituals which incorporated liturgical genres such as the communal lament provided opportunities for the community to name its pain and suffering and to publicly begin the process of healing. Evidence suggests that lament occurred in the context of temple worship in ancient Israel. In its biblical form, lament addresses God (invocation), describes and protests suffering, petitions God, and expresses confidence that God can and will act to address the current situation. Vows of praise are also common. Biblical lament holds together both despair and hope as it articulates pain alongside petition. The petition arises from the belief that God can and will act to bring about change. Lament is an ultimate expression of hope that suffering is not all that there is to life, and that meaning and coherence will one day be regained. As Westermann argues, the petition to God, which represents hope, defines biblical lament:

> There is not a single Psalm of lament that stops with lamentation. Lamentation has no meaning in and of itself. That it functions as an appeal is evident in its structure. What the lament is concerned with is not a description of one's own sufferings or with self-pity, but with the removal of the suffering itself. The lament appeals to the one who can remove the suffering.[3]

From a pastoral perspective, Polke identifies lament as a "galvanizing act that carries within itself the hope of transcending the contexts of suffering, death, guilt and hostility and to break new grounds for living."[4] Lament gives language through which loss and vulnerability can be embraced, and is able to give voice "to the meaninglessness and absurdity of the circumstances of life."[5]

2. Westermann, *Praise and Lament,* 274; Brueggemann, "The Costly Loss of Lament," 59–60.

3. Westermann, *Praise and Lament*, 266, 272–73. The cry to God is grounded in the salvific action of the God who hears the cries of God's people (Exod 3:7; Westermann, *Praise and Lament,* 271).

4. Polke, "God, Lament, Contingency," 50.

5. Ibid., 54.

If lament is not being practiced within the church, how, then, does a community come together to lament?

In order to address this question, this chapter conducts a search for lament, with a particular focus on public spaces. Lee suggests one possible venue, that of music concerts, large spaces in which people gather around music.[6] In the discussion which follows, two recent examples of public lament in the context of music concerts will be analyzed. The first example occurred in November 2011, when U2 played a concert in Auckland on a day of national mourning following the Pike River Mine disaster, which claimed twenty-nine lives. The second event comes from the *Sound Relief* benefit concert held in March 2009 in Melbourne in the wake of the Victorian bushfires on February 7, 2009 which claimed one hundred and seventy-three lives. While both concerts differed in purpose, they shared some commonality with regard to the provision of public spaces in which lament could be enacted.

In the discussion which follows, a two-fold analytical schema will be used.[7] The first will involve an analysis of live concert performance, using the categories of segue, history, lyrical adaptation, visual cues, production commentary and audience response.[8] The second will involve an analysis using the categories of biblical lament, including invocation, description of distress, petition, and expressions of confidence.

6. Lee notes that "[i]n modern western cultures, religious and secular realms are pushed apart from each other, and Christian communities often no longer sing laments for the dead and do not regularly sing lament prayers or songs. Nevertheless, it is ironic that it is the popular song writers and poets, often more powerfully than the crafters of religious liturgies, it might be argued, who have been most responsive and flexible to adapt and compose new songs to meet the emotional and spiritual needs of sorrowing people" (Lee, *Lyrics of Lament*, 11).

7. Analysis of the U2 performance will be based on video from news footage and YouTube. News concert video footage from "U2, Jay-Z wow Auckland crowd—Video," n.p. YouTube concert footage available at "One Tree Hill—U2—Live Auckland 25 Nov 2010—360° Tour (complete)," n.p. The Paul Kelly performance will be based on publicly released concert footage: *Sound Relief*, DVD.

8. This is based on the work of Mark Cunningham, who argues that to understand a U2 concert, you need to pay attention not only to lyrics, but also to lighting, design, video, theatrical gestures and audience participation (Cunningham, "A Short History of Rock Touring," 196).

PERFORMING CONTEMPORARY LAMENT: U2 AND THE PIKE RIVER MINING TRAGEDY

On Thursday 25 November 2010, U2, one of the best-selling music artists of all time, performed live in Auckland, New Zealand.[9] The buildup to the Auckland concert was over shadowed by one of New Zealand's worst mining disasters, an explosion, on 19 November 2010, inside the Pike River Mine, on the West Coast of New Zealand. Twenty-nine miners were declared missing and the nation hoped for a miracle. Sadly, on 24 November, a further explosion resulted in the official announcement that the miners were presumed dead, and the possibility that their bodies might never be recovered. The next day, 25 November, was declared a day of national mourning, with flags to be flown at half mast, church services to be held throughout New Zealand and bells to toll in memory.

That the U2 concert coincided with the day of mourning raises questions as to how a visiting band, booked to entertain over 45,000 people, might respond. Would there be any attempt to engage in public lament? These questions are all the more pertinent in the case of U2, given that U2 scholar Cogan argues that part of the appeal of U2 is their perceived vulnerability, emotionality, and spontaneity, and the way this is deployed to connect with audiences.[10]

This characteristic is evident in the live performance history of U2. As argued elsewhere, a live concert performance, and most particularly, a U2 concert, is one of only a few "public space experiences" left in contemporary culture.[11] By way of example, during the third leg of their 2001 Elevation Tour, playing in the United States immediately following 9/11, U2 took incredible live performance risks in connecting with their audience in acts of public lament. This included scrolling the names of those killed in 9/11 on video screens. As stated by Parra: "What their audience seem to want right now is a sense of community, of togetherness, which is

9. U2 have played over 1,249 concerts in at least thirty-two countries (Based on calculations from http://U2.interference.com/f304/how-many-shows-have-they-played-total-198370.html and http://en.wikipedia.org/wiki/U2_360%C2%B0_Tour#Tour_dates). Ten of their twelve studio albums have reached number one in charts, while their music has garnered twenty-two Grammy awards (Figures taken from Cogan, *U2: An Irish Phenomenon*. Updated from "List of Awards Received by U2," n.p.).

10. Cogan, *U2: An Irish Phenomenon*, see especially chapter 8.

11. Taylor, " 'Bullet the Blue Sky,' " 94, quoting De Oliveria et al., *Installation Art in the New Millennium*, 29.

something the band have always been good at delivering—and has been at the core of the Elevation Tour since its conception."[12]

As will become evident in the discussion below, there are many similarities between the way U2 publicly processed lament in the Elevation tour and in 2010 in New Zealand. These include listing the names of victims, taking performance risks, the willingness to lament in public space and the ability to engage communal memory.

Analysis

Segue

The first mention of the Pike River tragedy by U2 on November 25th occurred a third of the way into the live performance. By way of segue, U2's lead singer Bono offered a brief spoken commentary: "What a privilege it is to play for you in this week of all weeks. And, at time like this when your hearts must be so aching and so raw. People deal with grief in all sorts of ways. In Ireland, we sing. These are for your twenty-nine lost to this earth, but not to the eternal."[13] The band then launched into two songs from their 1987 *The Joshua Tree* album, "I Still Haven't Found What I'm Looking For," followed by "One Tree Hill." (The latter is a song rarely sung live, except when the band play in New Zealand).

The verbal introduction by Bono is spare, almost poetic in its quality. The short speech performed a number of functions. First, it alerted the crowd that despite this being a rock concert, U2 were about to reflect on the Pike River Mining disaster. Second, it named the pain ("your hearts must be so aching and so raw"). It affirmed that grief takes multiple forms ("People deal with grief in all sorts of ways"), a helpful pastoral perspective. Third, it also allowed U2 to speak ("In Ireland, we sing"), and to share their own unique expression of grief. Finally, it also placed U2 within a history of lament. They are seeking to name themselves implicitly not only as rock stars (which they are), but explicitly as Irish, part of a nation which has experience of hearts "so aching and so raw." Cogan notes that "'Irishness' in U2 is seen in a modern light. It isn't an old-fashioned concept."[14] It includes a sense of place, a desire

12. De La Parra, *U2 Live: A Concert Documentary*, 258.

13. Transcription from concert video footage "One Tree Hill—U2—Live Auckland 25 Nov 2010—360° Tour (complete)," n.p.

14. Cogan, *U2: An Irish Phenomenon*, 61.

for independence, spirituality, generosity, and creativity of musical tradition.[15] It is out of this tradition that U2 will deal with grief, in song. Perhaps this also suggests a way forward in tragedy, a way of acting in lament, to find one's voice.

History

The argument that a category of lament can be applied to the performance of U2, both in terms of their musical catalogue and in terms of their live concert performance, is not new. Christian Scharen has organized the musical catalogue of U2 around categories including psalms as thanksgiving and lament.[16] U2 songs that lyrically seem to invoke lament include "Waves of Sorrow," "Wake up Dead Men," "White as Snow," and "One Tree Hill."

Historically, "One Tree Hill" was written in response to the death of Greg Carroll, a New Zealander, who was tragically killed riding a motorcycle while working for U2. The band attended his funeral, held in Whanganui, New Zealand, in 1986. U2 band members provide the following account:

> Greg Carroll was killed in a motorcycle accident in Dublin. He was a very special guy, a Māori from New Zealand. We hooked up with him in Auckland during our [ ] tour. . . . His death really rocked us—it was the first time anyone in our working circle had been killed. . . . Greg was like a member of the family, but the fact that he had come under our wing and had travelled so far from home to be in Dublin to work with us made it all the more difficult to deal with. . . . "One Tree Hill," [was] a song for Greg Carroll.[17]

A number of explicit biblical references are evoked in "One Tree Hill," contributing to the interpretation of the song as a lament. The first line of the chorus articulates the inevitability of death as expressed in Eccl 1:7.[18] The subject changes from second person singular to first person plural by

15. Cogan, *U2: An Irish Phenomenon*, 61 ff.

16. Scharen, *One Step Closer*. The other categories include wisdom as desire and illusion; parables as offense and mercy; prophecy as judgment and hope; and apocalypse as ecstasy and healing.

17. McCormick et al., *U2 by U2*, 177–79.

18. "All streams run to the sea, but the sea is not full; to the place where the streams flow, there they continue to flow." (Eccl 1:7, NRSV).

the song's end, from "You" to "We." Death, and so by implication lament, is an inevitable finality.

The song takes the listener on a journey. It begins by naming the pain of death, including echoes of the Cain and Abel narrative of Gen 4:10.

Yet lament is not the last word, for the song ends with hope. This is not a naive belief that all will be well in this life (the singer declares their lack of belief in painted roses or bleeding hearts). Rather it offers an eschatology in which the world is changed at the end of time This is achieved through echoes of Revelation 6:12–13 and the biblical phrases including the moon turning blood red and the stars falling from the sky.[19] Lyrically, despite the need for lament in the midst of our present darkness, there will be reunion with those we love, and have loved, coupled with judgment on present evil.

Lyrical Changes

A feature of U2 is their ability to improvise lyrically. During the concert on 25 November, 2010, a number of lyrical adaptations were made that seem to reference the Pike River tragedy.[20]

In the first verse, a number of changes occur. The word "bright" is replaced by the word "cruel." The lyric thus becomes "sun so cruel it leaves no shadows." The word "stone" is replaced by the word "ground." The lyric thus becomes "scars, carved into ground." The word "on" is replaced by "under" and the word "it" with "earth." The lyric thus becomes "Under the face of earth."

In the second verse, "poets" is replaced by "workers." The lyric thus becomes "Where workers speak."[21] All these changes seem to reference directly the mining disaster. They speak to the cruelty of the tragedy, the fact it occurred underground while men were working.

19. "When he opened the sixth seal, I looked, and there came a great earthquake; the sun became black as sackcloth, the full moon became like blood, and the stars of the sky fell to the earth as the fig tree drops its winter fruit when shaken by a gale" (Rev 6:12–13, NRSV).

20. This is based on comparing the original song on *The Joshua Tree* with video footage of the concert, available at "One Tree Hill—U2—Live Auckland 25 Nov 2010—360° Tour (complete)," n.p. Italics are used to identify the lyrical adaptations that are enacted in this act of public lament.

21. The remainder of the phrase is hard to discern.

Finally, there is a significant adaption in the refrain. In the album, the lyric plays with an image of water, and how it runs to the sea. During the live performance, the word "tears" is added. The addition suggests a mingling of grief. Whether intentional or not, the water imagery also evokes the West Coast, where the tragedy happened and which is known for heavy rainfall.

The lyrical changes seem to deliberately reference the events at Pike River, adding to the poignancy of the moment and increasing the power of naming. A song written historically to lament the death of a New Zealander is contextualized to become a lament for the deaths of twenty-nine in New Zealand.

Visuals/Theatre

The twenty-nine miners were also named visually, their names being scrolled during the choruses on large video screens (in a manner similar to the Elevation tour in the United States following 9/11). The names, stark white on black, enhance the describing which is an important function in the category of lament.

During the choruses of "One Tree Hill," patterns in the shape of the "koru," the unfurling silver fern frond, spiraled on the screen. This is an important symbol in Māori culture, referencing new life, growth, and strength. Various comments on the internet noted how effective this was: "The korus on the screen reinforced what all kiwis know, this is our song."[22] This can be interpreted in two ways. First, this references the collective identity that can be created by the use of a local symbol. Second, this references the potential of music, which "offers the immediate experience of collective identity."[23] Symbol and sound work together, allowing identification, evoking solidarity, and, through the koru, referencing hope.

A further, more spontaneous visual element was evident as the crowd released red balloons during the chorus. One concert goer wrote of this:

> I was up against the rail of the inner stage, in the circle, and had been handed a red balloon beforehand by the Aus-NZ group,

22. Jan, "U2 and public lament for Pike River Miners," n.p.

23. Firth, *Performing Rites: Evaluating Popular Music*, 273, cited in Cogan, *U2: An Irish Phenomenon*, 1.

> U2 fanz [*sic*], who offered them to everybody in the circle. It was at the point that Bono sings the refrain [from the song "One Tree Hill"] that everyone let go of the red balloons, and a river of red flew toward and over the stage. Bono did look genuinely touched by the effect/moment.[24]

This led to an unscripted, but poignant moment in which Bono continued to sing while holding one of the balloons released by the crowd. This speaks of vulnerability and fragility and allowed interplay between band and audience.

Production Commentary

This public performance of lament appears to be deliberate, as is evident from the online dairy of Willie Williams, Show Director on the 360 Tour.

> The New Zealand mining disaster is filling the news media and indeed the entire atmosphere here. It's a terrible and far from optimistic situation, made all the harder by coming so hard on the heels of the Chilean mining rescue. Clearly we will have to acknowledge the miners during the show but it's a moment-by-moment situation at present.[25]

This suggests that U2, in preparation for the concert, were aware of the situation, struggling with how they might respond to a rapidly evolving situation and putting significant creative attention into how they might negotiate this moment of lament.

Audience Response

Reader (audience) response to this act of public lament seemed positive. Williams made the following observation: "The miners' tribute seemed to be very well received and the audience appreciative. One Tree Hill was beautiful."[26] One concert reviewer noted: "A special highlight would

24. Deane, "U2 and public lament for Pike River Miners," n.p. It is important to note that this part of the ritual was scripted by a group of fans, who organized the balloons and coordinated their moment of release without any knowledge of the part they might play in this moment of lament (Donnarful, "U2—One Tree Hill—Auckland 25 Nov 10—dedicated to our lost miners—may they RIP," n.p).

25. Williams, "Scarlet," n.p.

26. Williams, "Rockin' the House," n.p.

have to be the band's acknowledgement and tribute to the 29 [*sic*] miners who had lost their lives in the South Island this week. Having the miners' names appear on screen as they played One Tree Hill was moving."[27] Another commented that "it was so emotional in the inner circle lots of people with tears."[28] This suggests that what U2 did worked as lament. In the middle of a public concert, billed as entertainment, they had referenced a national tragedy in a way that enabled people to grieve.

Both songs sung at this point—"I Still Haven't Found What I'm Looking For" and "One Tree Hill"—are well known to the audience, making understandable another audience comment: "Bono stood back and let the crowd sing and it became our song of grief. One Tree Hill was more a watch and remember and reflect, rather than joining in."[29] Both songs worked together, enabling the audience to adopt a number of postures—participation and contemplation—suggesting that a sense of journey through lament was being provided. U2 crafted a time to grieve by singing and a time to "breathe," to collectively contemplate grief.

In sum, categories of performance analysis have been employed to argue that U2 deliberately created an act of public and communal lament. The crafting of the segue served to create a space for grief, while the choice of songs, along with Bono's lyrical adaptations, provided a connectivity with the Pike River Mine disaster. Concert visuals were deployed in ways that named the grief, while suggesting the possibility of a movement through grief. Analysis of audience feedback suggests that this moment of public lament was not only appropriate, but also helpful, playing an important pastoral role. In other words, the U2 concert was an occasion of effective lament, albeit occurring entirely outside the traditional boundaries of organized religion.

Further discussion as to how this conforms to biblical notions of lament is needed. But first, another act of lament at another concert is worth considering.

27. Bain, "U2 Concert Review: Auckland, New Zealand," n.p.

28. Citing a fan who uses the internet name of Donnarful, "U2—One Tree Hill—Auckland 25 Nov 10—dedicated to our lost miners—may they RIP," n.p.

29. Jan, "U2 and public lament for Pike River Miners," n.p.

PERFORMING CONTEMPORARY LAMENT: PAUL KELLY AND AUSTRALIAN BUSHFIRES

In February 2009, Australia faced the tragedy of lives lost to bushfires. A series of live music benefit concerts were held across Australia. Michael Chugg, the Managing Director of Chugg Entertainment said of the concerts:

> Around the world, some of the words that are used to describe Australians include "big hearted," "generous," "battlers and "troopers." These concerts will honour all of those characteristics of the Australian people, both those who have suffered so much through this terrible tragedy, but also saluting the heroes who fought against the fires, and the courageous people whose fight is just beginning. With the help of the Australian Music Community, these concerts hope to bring people together, not just on the hallowed turf of the MCG and SCG, but around the country as we share the joy of live music. We will remember those who have lost so much, and celebrate the heroes of this devastating story.[30]

The *Sound Relief* concerts attracted a showcase of Australian artists, including Paul Kelly, a renowned singer-song writer who has been described as the "poet laureate of Australia."[31]

Analysis

Segue

Paul Kelly played a set list of six songs, with the final song being "Meet Me in the Middle of the Air."[32] This ran for just over two minutes, and was sung unaccompanied.[33]

30. Seymour, "Sound Relief concert in Melbourne and Sydney," n.p.

31. Denton, "Enough Rope with Andrew Denton," n.p.

32. "Down To My Soul," "Dumb Things," "To Her Door," "Leaps and Bounds," "How to Make Gravy," "Meet Me in the Middle of the Air." ("Paul Kelly Concert Setlist at Melbourne Cricket Ground, Melbourne, Australia on March 14, 2009," n.p.).

33. "Paul Kelly only played a stripped-down acoustic set with Ash Naylor accompanying on electric guitar, but it was no less effective. Though not loud enough to keep the crowd talking over them, the audience mostly didn't—all seeing the brilliance of hearing Leaps and Bounds sung at the MCG itself. From Little Things Big Things Grow would've been nice, but we did get How to Make Gravy nine months early, and

The transition into the song was minimal. Kelly simply placed his guitar behind his back, and announced; "I'll sing you one more song." There was no specific connection made with the bushfires, or to establish this song as a lament. This segue was far more understated than that of Bono during the U2 concert. That the U2 concert was on the day of public lament was not planned: the concert would have been held whether or not the Pike River tragedy had occurred. As such, to reference the disaster it was necessary that the event be named specifically ("What a privilege it is to play for you in this week of all weeks. And, at time like this when your hearts must be so aching and so raw"[34]). In the case of Kelly's performance, however, the context—a benefit concert for victims of the bushfire—carried the potential that any or all of the music played might function as lament. This was a public space created for the purpose of remembrance which provided a means for people to come together in grief and as a way forward into the future. In this case, the possibility of the song functioning as a lament is suggested by the movement to unaccompanied voice, which both calls for a level of silence from the audience and creates a sense of vulnerability.

History

Paul Kelly has been described as both a poet and a storyteller. "For thirty years he has written songs of uncommon directness about everything from love and land rights to cricket and cooking."[35] "Meet Me in the Middle of the Air" was originally written for the Australian movie "Tom White,"[36] and draws heavily on Ps 23 in the King James Version. This is not unusual in Kelly's work. The influence of the Bible and biblical themes has long been noted in his songs. In reference to his song "God Told Me To," Kelly says: "*The Bible's always been there, it's always bubbling up in my songs, one way or another. The Bible's got everything. Tarantino*

the hymnal Meet Me in the Middle of the Air sung a cappella. Though great, I got the feeling his lack of a full band might've been the reason for his set's early timing" (Richoad, "Sound Relief—the (un)official review!" n.p).

34. Transcription from concert video footage "One Tree Hill—U2—Live Auckland 25 Nov 2010—360° Tour (complete)," n.p.

35. Kelly, *How to Make Gravy*, front cover.

36. A 2004 release about a middle aged, middle class man who becomes homeless (Kelly, *How to Make Gravy*, 312).

can't touch it—it's got violence and heroism and great pettiness, wisdom, whim, grandeur and vindictiveness."[37]

The title line of the song "Meet Me in the Middle of the Air" is not original to Paul Kelly. He notes that the title has been a part of blues, gospel, and spiritual genres for over one hundred years. It is perhaps most well known from the traditional gospel song "Ain't No Grave Can Hold My Body Down," associated with the Appalachian mountain region, and popularized in a 1953 recording by a Pentecostal preacher/singer, Brother Claude Ely.[38] One of the verses of the song is,

> Well meet me, Jesus, meet me
> Meet me in the middle of the air
> And if these wings don't fail me,
> I will meet you anywhere.

The line is used in a range of songs by other artists, including Johnny Cash, Bob Dylan, Willie Johnson, the Tea Party, and Led Zeppelin.[39]

In his discussion about the writing of this song, Kelly wrote "I was in a tight spot, and like desperate men through the ages I turned to the Bible, specifically to King David. . . . Psalm 23, attributed to David, is often recited at funerals, having been set to music many times."[40] Despite this association with funerals, Ps 23 is not a lament psalm according to form-critical categories, but a psalm of trust. In his discussion of the use of Ps 23 in contemporary song and film, Karl Jacobson notes that psalms of trust arise out of laments, given that most laments do contain expressions of trust or confidence. "In almost every case where the psalm is taken seriously, contemporary films and songs wrestle with the interplay of lament and trust, the exhortation to confident faith and the argument of present reality."[41] Given the common use of the psalm in the context of funeral services, it can be argued that Kelly is intentionally seeking to evoke lament.

37. Watt, "Hey Hey Hey My My: Music for Adults. Paul Kelly Interview," n.p.

38. The earliest recording of the song was in 1942, but it was popularized by Brother Claud Ely in 1953, and later again by Johnny Cash (Bluegrass Messengers, "Ain't No Grave—Johnny Cash," n.p).

39. The Alternative Hymnal, "Meet Me In The Middle of The Air by Paul Kelly," n.p.

40. Kelly, *How to Make Gravy*, 313.

41. Jacobson, "Through the Pistol Smoke Dimly: Psalm 23 in Contemporary Film and Song," n.p.

It is worth exploring at this point the significance of Ps 23 in a Christian context. This is a psalm which has been used widely in Christian hymnody. Some of the more well known settings of the psalm overtly overlay the words of the psalm with Christological and Eucharistic meanings. For example, in the popular Crimond version, Ps 23:6b translated in the NRSV "and I shall dwell in the house of the Lord *my whole life long*" is changed to "and in God's house *for evermore*, my dwelling place shall be."[42] The shift from "my whole life long" to "for evermore" introduces an expression of the Christian belief in eternal life with God after death which is absent from the original Hebrew psalm.[43]

A second biblical allusion in Kelly's song is found in the chorus line itself. First Thessalonians 5:16–17 reads: "For the Lord himself, with a cry of command, with the archangel's call and with the sound of God's trumpet, will descend from heaven, and the dead in Christ will rise first. Then we who are alive, who are left, will be caught up in the clouds together with them to meet the Lord in the air; and so we will be with the Lord for ever."

The allusion to 1 Thess 5:16–17 and the funeral associations of Ps 23 introduce an element of eschatological hope into Kelly's song. The song can, arguably, be heard as a promise that those who have died, in this case the victims of the bush fires, will meet God "in the middle of the air," that is, be taken into heaven. True to the lament form, Kelly's performance expresses confidence in a God who acts. Unlike the original lament psalms, however, this hope is inherently eschatological and Christological given the themes and associations that the biblical references evoke.

Lyrical Changes

As with U2, a number of lyrical changes occur and are important. In evoking Ps 23, Kelly changes the speaking voice from second person address to God to first speech of God. The lyrics name the suffering, with reference to "lonesome valleys" and "death's dark shadow." The use of divine voice introduces hope, as do references to souls being "restored"

42. eHymns.org, "The Lord's My Shepherd," n.p.

43. An example of an Eucharistic overlay can be found in Henry William Baker's "The King of Love My Shepherd Is," in the verse which reads "Thou spread'st a table in my sight; thy unction grace bestoweth; and O what transport of delight from thy pure chalice floweth!" which modifies Ps 23:5 "You prepare a table before me in the presence of my enemies; you anoint my head with oil; my cup overflows" (eHymns.org, "The King of Love My Shepherd Is," n.p).

and dwelling in God's house forever. As an eschatological vision it applies equally to victims and survivors.

Audience Response

Although many in the audience may not have been fully conversant with the origins of the lyrics sung by Kelly, the impact of the song was evident by the response in the crowd. As one reporter wrote,

> Despite the size of the Sound Relief event, Kelly says he felt strangely calm playing. One minute, 80,000 people were singing along with him to Leaps and Bounds: "I'm high on the hill/ Looking over the bridge to the MCG." The next minute, he brought the audience to silence with his beautiful, hymnal, a cappella song, Meet Me in the Middle of the Air. Singing "I will lay you down/ In pastures green and fair/ Every soul shall be restored," his voice echoed around the great stands.
>
> The crowd was all singing along and then doing the last song a cappella, they all went really quiet. Hearing 80,000 people suddenly go quiet—it was like the Anzac Day footy game when they do the Last Post before the game. It's a different quality of silence, like silence out of the desert or something. It was very powerful. It's a song of healing.[44]

Although much of the concert was a pitched at a more "high energy" level, Kelly's a cappella singing, alongside the lyrics, injected both theological content and an element of hope for survivors and victims alike. Kelly's song created a reflective space in which the audience was invited to acknowledge the presence of the pain and suffering in the community.

Visuals/Theatre

Kelly also used a number of gestures within the song, some of which had liturgical allusions. Accompanying references to anointing with oil and the preparation of a table, Kelly used two handed gestures, initially with the palms faced downwards, the movement suggesting an act of anointment, then in the shape of a table, but finishing with the palms facing upwards, suggesting an invitation to the table, or a form of blessing. Kelly's gift to the audience was shaped by Judeo-Christian words and gestures of invitation and hope. The song voiced the distress of the community, and,

44. Donovan, "Wanted man," n.p.

at the same time, evoked the divine responsiveness to those who suffered, expressing a sense of eschatological hope.

In sum, this use of performance analysis has once again led to the conclusion that Paul Kelly provided an opportunity for communal lament. This was provided by the context (a concert in response to tragedy) and achieved through the lyrics, the a cappella singing and the liturgical type gestures. The performance created a stillness, in which grief could be named, while the lyrics evoked hope.

CONVERSATIONS

In order to capture the data presented to date, a table is helpful. It allows the performances to be summarized, and placed against biblical categories of lament.

U2	Segue	History	Lyrical change	Visual theatre	Audience response
Structure – invocation	"What a privilege it is to play for you in this week of all weeks"				
Structure – description	"when your hearts must be so aching and so raw"; "People deal with grief in all sorts of ways. In Ireland, we sing."	Death of Greg Carroll, use of biblical references (Eccl 1:7; Gen 4:10.	"Sun so *cruel,*" "carved *into ground,*" "*Under* the face of *earth,*" "*workers*"	Names of miners, koru's unfurling, red balloons	Positive feedback on internet.
structure – petition					

U2	Segue	History	Lyrical change	Visual theatre	Audience response
structure – confidence		"I'll see you again When the stars fall from the sky/And the moon has turned red over One Tree Hill"; Rev 6:12-13			
Ritual – communal		A U2 concert is one of few "public space experience" in contemporary culture.		"The koru's on the screen reinforced what all kiwis know, this is our song."	
Ritual – naming				Names of miners on screen.	"Bono stood back and let the crowd sing and it became our song of grief."
Ritual – new beginnings				Koru's as a symbol of new life	

PAUL KELLY	Segue	History	Lyrical change	Visuals/ theatre	Audience response
Structure – invocation	"I'll sing one more song" I am your true shepherd …				Crowd became still and "silent"
Structure – description		Strong association with funeral services within Christian tradition; Draws on traditional blues/spiritual song "Ain't no grave"	"fear not death's dark shadow" – brings to mind the reality of suffering and death		
structure – petition					
structure – confidence		Psalm 23 – paraphrases the words	Change of voice – first person speech of God. Hope provided through promise of God's meeting "in the middle of the air"		
Ritual – communal				Gestures of anointing/ blessing and invitation to the table	

PAUL KELLY	Segue	History	Lyrical change	Visuals/ theatre	Audience response
Ritual – naming			Context of Sound Relief for victims of Black Saturday bushfires.		
Ritual – new beginnings			"every soul shall be restored," etc.	Gestures of invitation	

So are these two live concert performances lament? Clearly, the songs do not contain the same structural elements as biblical lament. As seen in the tables, neither have an invocation or a direct petition. This does not mean, however, that the performances were not experienced as lament. This suggests that lament cannot only be confined to structure.[45] Elements of performance hermeneutics, including categories such as mood, intent, and function need also to be taken into account. If a focus on performance rather than structure is employed, how might these two public concerts be understood as lament?

One way to approach this argument is to return to the insights of Westermann and Polke. For Westermann, lament is not a mere evoking, "not a description of one's own sufferings," but an appeal to "the one who can remove the suffering."[46] In both contemporary examples, such an appeal is present, albeit indirectly. Kelly sings of meeting in the middle of air, taking on the persona of a God who offers the restoration of relationship in the eternal. In using the words from a psalm of trust, Kelly's song in itself becomes a song of trust. It functions as an appeal to the God who is present in the psalm. Bono's suggestion that "twenty-nine are lost to this earth, but not to the eternal" is also an indirect appeal to eternal hope. Lyrically, "One Tree Hill" offers hope of a new heaven and new earth. In their inter-textual engagement with biblical texts, both examples are an appeal, even if implicitly, to the One who can remove suffering.

For Polke, lament is a galvanizing act that carries "hope" and the possibility of "new grounds for living," one that gives voice "to the meaninglessness and absurdity."[47] A bushfire and a mining disaster are

45. See the chapter in this volume by Boase.

46. Westermann, *Praise and Lament*, 266, 272–73.

47. Polke, "God, Lament, Contingency," 50, 54.

clearly acts of "meaninglessness and absurdity," and these contexts were acknowledged in both performances. U2 named the context of suffering explicitly, referring to the disaster, the day of mourning and the miners. The bushfires were the impetus for the Sound Relief concerts, whose purpose was to "remember those who have lost so much, and celebrate the heroes of this devastating story."[48] In their different ways, both performances occurred in a context in which a communal acknowledgment of suffering was being named, opening the potential for the movement towards new ways of being in community.

That the performances functioned as lament is supported by responses of those participating. Both performances created space for audience response. Bono facilitated audience singing in utilizing a well-known song ("I Still Haven't Found What I'm Looking For") and standing back from the microphone during the first verse, and in response the audience were allowed space to sing and could hear themselves sing. A number of the audience who attended the U2 concert, used words like "our song of grief," "lots of people with tears," yet the use of the koru clearly referenced hope and new possibilities.[49]

Kelly's strategy was different. He finished his set with a less known song, one that was more contemplative in tone. This seemed to draw silence as a response and so served to provide a space for reflection. Kelly, in the interview following his performance, claimed "Meet Me in the Middle of the Air" was "a song of healing."[50] There is hope in the possibility of meeting God "in the middle of the air." The quieting of the audience during the performance indicates, at the very least, that Kelly achieved a reflective atmosphere which allowed for the entry into a moment of grief.

The evocation of hope is strengthened by the argument of Stanley Hauerwas, who reflects on the silence wrought by suffering and the importance of lament in the naming of that silence, of providing language from which to move from that silence.[51] It is striking how both performances created silence, the audience taking time for reflection during "One Tree Hill" after the shared singing in "I Still Haven't Found What I'm Looking For," and the quietness that resulted during the a cap-

48. Seymour, "Sound Relief Concerts," n.p.

49. Citing a fan who uses the internet name of Donnarful, "U2—One Tree Hill—Auckland 25 Nov 10—dedicated to our lost miners—may they RIP," n.p. Citing also Jan, "U2 and public lament for Pike River Miners," n.p.

50. Donovan, "Wanted Man," n.p.

51. Hauerwas, *Naming the Silences*, 82.

pella performance by Paul Kelly. This silence, or silencing, created the atmosphere for lament, but in the same moment the songs provided a language, lyrical, visual and in mood, which moved beyond the silence of suffering and suggested hope.

As has been argued, the hope expressed in the performances alludes to or evokes a particularly Christian hope. Both singers utilize eschatological expressions, Bono in speaking of the eternal and Kelly through the presentation of a God who meets us "in the middle of the air."

Working from the insights from Westermann, Polke and Hauerwas, it can be argued that these performances did constitute moments of public lament. Despite this recognition, however, some caution is needed before too readily drawing parallels between these performances and the communal lament genre.

If communal lament provides an opportunity to name suffering publicly, and functions as a means through which new possibilities for living are opened up, how does the context of the large concert performance shape or limit the function of the lament? Concerts are occasional, in that the audience comes together for a short period of time to witness a live performance. Although the band or singer might offer an experience of lament, there is little possibility of ongoing exploration or relationship. The rock star is removed from the audience, made inaccessible by security and PR representatives. In contrast, while acts of public worship may also be occasional, especially in the context of services such as a funeral service, they provide more opportunity for ongoing relationship and exploration. The occasional nature of the concert experience makes even more intriguing the fact that lament can still occur, that people are willing to express emotion in public, with strangers and in response to the performance of a stranger.

Although the concert itself is occasional, the evolution of concerts and technology allows the generation of artifacts such as DVD, CD, or YouTube. This raises the question of how occasions of communal lament might be part of ongoing processes of individual lament. What happens when a person who attended the U2 concert in Auckland later hears "I Still Haven't Found What I'm Looking for"? What hope is remembered when "Meet Me in the Middle of the Air" is seen via DVD again? While a concert is occasional, technology allows the moments of lament to be remembered. This opens up a potential avenue for further research, in exploring how the artifacts of a concert, including DVD, CD, or YouTube, might be deployed in the process of grief. How do these communal processes feed into individual processes? How might this be the same, or different, from hearing again a hymn sung at a funeral of a parent?

Concerts are not only occasional, they are also transactional, placed within the context of revenue raising. This suggests a danger, that people's emotion and vulnerability are being commodified. Yet it is worth noting that funerals come at a price, including costs associated with the minister and organists. Further, ancient sacrificial systems relied on the community providing offerings. Even if a level of transaction and commodification are present, this does not make less authentic the experience of lament.

Finally, these concerts are operating in a context markedly different from that of Ancient Israel. In the world of biblical lament, church and state are fused. All public performance occurred in a world that employed language of the Divine. Elements of invocation and petition that address God are expected. Even when God is not evoked, the silences still evoke an expectation of Divine activity. Yet in a modern secular context, church and state, Divine and human can be separated. This makes more problematic any analysis of lament as contemporary. Echoes of Ps 23, Eccl 1, 1 Thess 5, and Rev 6 heard by biblical scholars are not necessarily heard by concert goers.

This contextual observation might suggest that the absence of direct invocation and petition is a natural consequence of a society moving from the Constantinian fusion of church and state to a multicultural plurality in which multiple worldviews are present.[52] Whether this is to be celebrated or not might depend on the perspective of the reader. What is undeniable is that despite the shifts in culture, public lament still continues in contemporary Western cultures.

Taylor has argued elsewhere that public concerts can create an experiential space that is introspective, immersive, and social.[53] They allow a "viewing of the self contemplating the external world."[54] The outcome is that in a culture which "mourns the loss of public space," a live concert is one of few "public space experiences" left in our culture.[55] Drawing on two recent examples of live public concerts, this chapter has argued that the performances of U2 and Paul Kelly provided a context in

52. "Constantinian" is a sociological term. See, for example Bosch, "God's Reign," 89–95.

53. Taylor, "Bullet the Blue Sky."

54. De Oliveria et al., *Installation Art in the New Millennium*, 53.

55. Ibid., 29.

which communal lament was made possible. The analysis of the concert performances has demonstrated that the context of lament was made possible through the intersection of a number of variables including the segue into the song/s, lyrical adaptations, visual cues and theatre, and audience response. A consideration of both the history of the performers—U2's past use of songs as memorial or lament works, and Kelly's frequent use of biblical allusions within his music—alongside the production commentary of the U2 concert, suggests that there was some intentionality in the creation of these lament contexts. In both cases, the lyrical wording and allusions introduced a markedly "Christian" expression of eschatological hope which potentially provided the language through which new beginnings might be made. These public laments may not resemble the typical biblical lament forms, but they do form a vehicle for the communal expression of suffering and grief.

14

Lament in an Age of New Media

STEPHEN GARNER

INTRODUCTION

"THERE IS NOTHING NEW under the sun," the Teacher remarks in the book of Ecclesiastes, and yet, the constant catch-cry in our contemporary technoculture is that everything is changing and everything is new. The promises of new technologies and media promotes slogans, such as Apple's "There's an App for That," that assert no matter what problem you face, technology can solve it. But even in this bright and shiny world the words of the Teacher still ring true, for there is much that is not new under the sun: bad things happen to good people; good things happen to bad people; and people have to live in a world shaped by human strengths and weaknesses. And in this world people experience and respond to the pairings of great joy and great sadness, of blessing and curse, and of wellbeing and distress.

Lament, complaint, and imprecation within the Hebrew Scriptures address some of the negative experiences of human life, and in this chapter, we will examine how those might be expressed in the spaces opened up by new media and digital technologies. What might be some of the ways in which things such as blogs, social networking, and video sharing provide contemporary spaces for the expression of lament and complaint? In what ways might they prove unhelpful? Indeed, in contemplating lament might we find that there is already "an App for that"?

COMPLAINT, LAMENT, AND IMPRECATION

Within the Hebrew Scriptures, and especially the Psalms, lament, complaint, and imprecation are recurring voices, expressed through individuals like Job (Job 3; 30; 31) or by communities in distress (Lamentations). Moreover, prophets lament, empathizing with and expressing the pain of God's people (Jer 8:18, 21–22), God laments over God's people (Isa 1:2; Jer 8:5; Hos 6:4), and personifications, such as Zion, lament their troubling situation (Lam 1:21–22).

It is in the Psalms that lament features as *a*, if not *the*, significant form of expression, and the moods and situations of human life are expressed in poetic language that conveys those experiences with depth and vitality.[1] Exact groupings of psalms into types is contested, but the categories of hymns, communal laments, royal psalms, individual laments, and individual thanksgiving psalms are helpful in alerting us to the presence of groups of laments.[2] These laments tend to fall into two general kinds: laments of the community and laments of the individual, though the differences between the two kinds can get blurred at times.[3]

Communal laments are psalms that lament a disaster or event that threatens the wider community or nation, and allow the community to express their distress about the situation in the midst of struggling with the affirmation that "God is with us."[4] As such, these laments consist mainly of complaints to God and pleas for deliverance in situations such as the destruction of the temple in Jerusalem (Ps 79) and the exile in Babylon (Ps 137). Typically structured around an introductory address and petition, followed by a lament and then a confession of trust, these psalms are generic enough to reuse on various occasions, especially the

1. Zenger, A God of Vengeance?, 76.

2. Day, *Psalms*, 11–12. Day gives a good, brief outline of the major categories of this approach. For completeness sake we note that hymns extol God's work or acts in history (e.g., Ps 33), royal psalms focus on God's ordained monarchy (e.g., Pss 2; 110), and examples of individual thanksgiving for God's saving work include Pss 34; 41.

3. Anderson and Bishop, *Out of the Depths*, 55–56. Anderson notes in Ps 129 Israel speaks in the first person, while in Ps 77 the individual seen as identifying with the state of Israel and cries out for and with the community.

4. Anderson and Bishop, *Out of the Depths*, 56. He note this fundamental conviction expressed in the word *Immanuel* "God with us" seen both in the OT (Isa 7:14) and the NT (Matt 1:22–23). Communal laments include Pss 12; 44; 58; 60; 74; 79; 80; 83; 85; 89:38–51; 90; 94; 123; 126; 129; 137; and also Lam 5.

cultic "fast" held in times of crisis—a time of community mourning and soul-searching (Judg 20:26; 1 Kgs 21:9–12; 2 Chr 20:3–19).[5]

Individual laments, the most common of psalms, concern the personal and specific situation of individuals as opposed to communities. These psalms are patterned on an invocation of Yhwh, followed by laments and pleas for help, and then sometimes a note of confidence at the end, though as with communal laments there is no absolute structure.[6] The superscription of Ps 102, "A prayer of one afflicted, when he is faint and pours out his complaint before the Lord," is an appropriate introduction to the genre as a whole.[7]

Laments cover the range of human suffering and affliction. Psalm 22, for example, opens with the heart-rending cry of "My God, my God, why have you forsaken me?" with the psalmist's darkest moment expressed as separation from God. Then, if that is not enough, the psalmist suffers rejection by his fellow human beings (Ps 22:6–11).[8] Lament also articulates human separation from God expressed through the language of guilt (Ps 51), and the psalmist's need to be restored into relationship with God's steadfast love (חסד).[9] The latter is also located in the feelings of depression and spiritual thirst where the writer "thirsts" for God as a "deer longs for flowing streams" (Ps 42:1). These psalms also capture the emotive cries for God to avenge injustices done against the psalmist and his people (Ps 79), and the sense of oppression felt by God's people in exile (Ps 137).

THE FUNCTION OF LAMENT

Claus Westermann's reflection upon the nature of lament in the Psalms highlights a wrestling with a threefold interplay between other people, God, and the individual. That initial invocation or accusation against the divine is coupled with complaints directed against other people, and then filtered through the experience of the individual or community.

5. Westermann, *Praise and Lament in the Psalms*, 52–64; Anderson and Bishop, *Out of the Depths*, 56–57.

6. Day, *Psalms*, 11–12. Examples of individual laments include: Pss 3–5; 7; 9–10; 13; 14; 17; 22; 25–28; 31; 35; 36; 39–43; 52–57; 59; 61; 63; 64; 69–71; 77; 86; 88; 109; 120; 139–42 and Lam 3.

7. Anderson and Bishop, *Out of the Depths*, 58.

8. Craigie, *Psalms 1–50*, 198–99.

9. Tate, *Psalms 51–100*, 5, 8.

The interrelationship of these three things—the divine, the social, and the personal—defines the lived experience of the person or people concerned. As Westermann puts it,

> The threefold character of the lamentation reveals an understanding of man in which the existence of an individual without participation in a community (a social dimension) and without a relationship with God (a theological dimension) is totally inconceivable.[10]

This is similar to Walter Brueggemann's understanding that lament functions in a way that seeks to be transformative, to restore the situation between the individual or community, God, and other parties to one that is just and whole. Using a structure of orientation, disorientation, and new orientation, Brueggemann seeks to show that lament (disorientation) serves as a bridge between the old world of relationships before the crisis (orientation) and the potential new world (new orientation) hoped for in the crisis' alleviation.[11]

This disorientation, the expression of the pain, suffering, alienation, incomprehension, and anger found in the current situation, can be used to challenge the assumptions that underpinned the previous understanding of the world and how one fitted into it. It seeks to ask the questions: "Is God responsible for this?" "Where is God in all of this?" and "What can I trust in this situation?" Moreover, lament functions in a realistic fashion, underscoring that everyone may, at some point in their life, find their foundational understandings of that life challenged. Brueggemann also notes that in a dominant culture that seeks to avoid pain and pursue success, the acknowledgment of this truth may find little space to be explored in both religious and secular contexts. He comments:

> I think that serious religious use of the lament psalms has been minimal because we have believed that faith does not mean to acknowledge and embrace negativity. We have thought that acknowledgment of negativity was somehow an act of unfaith, as though the very speech about it conceded too much about God's "loss of control."[12]

10. Westermann, *The Psalms*, 267.
11. Brueggemann, *The Message of the Psalms*, 19–21.
12. Ibid., 52.

THE LOSS OF LAMENT?

Both Carl Trueman and Paul Bradbury echo Brueggemann in their own respective experiences of worship within the Christian community. Trueman asserts that the Christian church in the Western world, and especially the evangelical church, has bought into a gospel of health, wealth, and happiness. The end result is a continual procession of positive hymns and songs that fail to recognize the negative dimensions of the human condition. The Christian life becomes "one long triumphalistic street party," a theologically and pastorally dangerous scenario in a world of broken people.[13] Trueman's challenge is for the language of lament in worship to be reclaimed because:

> By excluding cries of loneliness, dispossession, and desolation from its worship, the church has effectively silenced and excluded the voices of those who are themselves lonely, dispossessed, and desolate, both inside and outside the church.[14]

Similarly, Bradbury recounts his own experiences of being in churches where different situations should have lent themselves to the language of lament being used faithfully and constructively to allow people to express their emotions and faith struggles. That this didn't take place is indicative that the language of lament has been lost in some way, in part Bradbury argues, because "[l]ament makes faith more difficult, more complex and less straightforward, but it makes it more close to the truth of who we are and who God is."[15]

If, as some claim, the language of lament has been lost from various contemporary church communities, then has it been lost altogether? In late 2010, the deaths of twenty-nine miners in the Pike River mine accident on the West Coast of New Zealand created a deep sense of national mourning, generating a variety of lamentations and other responses. One of the most publicized of these was incorporated into the U2 concerts held just after the tragedy. Through the combination of lead singer Bono's short reflection on the tragedy, the performance of "One Tree Hill" (a song about loss with New Zealand connections), and the projection of the names of lost miners on video screens, the band created a space

13. Trueman, "What do Miserable Christians Sing?," 1.

14. Ibid., 2.

15. Bradbury, *Sowing in Tears*, 5.

where the audience could share in and express the rawness and grief that affected the nation at that time.

Perhaps U2's response at the time, of being able to create such a space for lament, is because they have an understanding of the power and role that lament has within human and religious experience. Certainly the band have used the Psalms to good effect in their music (e.g., their song "40" based on Ps 40 with the refrain "How long to sing this song?") and in his reflection on the book of Psalms as a whole Bono elaborates: "That's what a lot of psalms feel like to me, the blues. Man shouting at God—'My God, my God why hast thou forsaken me? Why art thou so far from helping me?'"[16] This ability to mix to popular culture with biblical material and themes drawn particularly from the Hebrew Scriptures is also highlighted in their 2000 album, *All That You Can't Leave Behind*. Here systematic injustice, and the evil it represents, is confronted in both prophetic utterance and lament, connected explicitly to the figure of the imprisoned Burmese leader Aung San Suu Kyi. From Michael Gilmour's perspective, these songs function in a manner similar to the lamenting prophet Jeremiah where "weapons in the struggle for justice—nonviolent, grassroots, political action (activism) and religious hope (prayer)—are held together beautifully in Bono's writing."[17]

U2's music is just one example of how lament and complaint might be expressed and made accessible to a wider public. Another pertinent example, connecting to the concept of psalms being like the blues, is the song "Strange Fruit" performed regularly by Billie Holiday, based on the 1936 poem by Jewish teacher Abel Meeropol about racism in the United States and the lynching of African Americans—the "strange fruit" found swinging from the trees. Its lament juxtaposes an idyllic pastoral picture of the "gallant South" against the "bulging eyes and the twisted mouth" of those hanged and the "sudden sweet smell of burning flesh."[18]

At its heart, lament and the cries of complaint raised against God, others, and self is rooted in the desire for justice; for the oppressors to be brought down and held accountable for their actions, and for the oppressed to be raised up and vindicated before God and community. Lament for the sake of lament and for the experience of self-pity does not allow the power of transformation hinted at in Brueggemann's possibility

16. Bono, "The Book of Psalms," 136.

17. Gilmour, "The Prophet Jeremiah," 43.

18. Margolick and Als, *Strange Fruit: The Biography of a Song*, 1.

of a new orientation leading to a life restored and renewed. As Westermann puts it,

> Lamentation has no meaning in and of itself. That it functions as an appeal is evident in its structure. What the lament is concerned with is not a description of one's own sufferings or with self-pity, but with the removal of the suffering itself. The lament appeals to the one who can remove suffering.[19]

Both of the examples drawn from popular culture above I believe seek that sense of transformation. The challenge to the contemporary situation has been laid down, an appeal made in some way for justice and healing, and now the space is present for some kind of response.

VIOLENCE IN LAMENT AND COMPLAINT

The rawness of lament and emotive complaint can lead to psalms of lament and similar writings being considered, in Brueggemann's words, "psalms of darkness." Some will see them as acts of unfaith and failure, while others as deeds of bold faith recognizing that there is no place for either self-deception about the situation or God being excluded from it.[20] The call for justice, and allowing the space for that call to be heard by God and others, recognizes the presence of the oppressed, persecuted, and voiceless within the community of faith and the wider community. Moreover, the silencing of those voices (or restricting them through some form of physical or institutional "kettling," to use a contemporary example)[21] puts the silencers firmly on the side of the oppressors.[22]

But if one allows the space for these and other forms of lament and complaint, how does one engage with the violence, both implicit and explicit, found within them? Within these psalms, we find imprecation, malediction, and cursing of those who oppress or abandon the speaker, as well as cries of vengeance for violence being perpetrated. In part, this language exists in the Hebrew Scriptures because it was a common speech form in the communities of the ancient Near East. It can be found in the sanctions for covenantal disobedience (e.g., Lev 26:14–39; Deut 27:11–26), prophetic contexts of judgment, and oaths which are linked to

19. Westermann, *The Psalms*, 266.

20. Brueggemann, *The Message of the Psalms*, 52.

21. Joyce, "Police 'Kettle' Tactic Feels the Heat."

22. Anderson and Bishop, *Out of the Depths*, 71.

negative consequences for the breaker of the oath, as well as the Psalms, but does it have a place in the contemporary world?[23]

The appeal for "vengeance" (נקם) seen in imprecatory psalms is a call for God to establish God's justice upon the earth where the overwhelming situation is placed into the hands of God, the ultimate judge. Imprecation at its very heart is a call for justice, and the establishment of God's kingdom through liberation and vengeance. Without it there is no justice and no hope (Ps 58:12; Ps 149:7–9). The presupposition is that when God entered into the covenant relationship, God took upon Godself the role of judge or vindicator defending and upholding justice. Erich Zenger frames it well when he says:

> These psalms are a form of human struggle against chaos—a struggle simultaneously *against* and *with* God. They are neither the result of dogmatic reflection nor the expression of higher or lower sensibility. They are the mirror and the articulation of fear and the state in which those who pray now find themselves and/or in which they see others. In this, they are the expression of a passionate conviction that this situation contradicts what they believe and hope about the reality of God.[24]

Thus the psalmists cry out for vindication and vengeance. In the situation that they find themselves in they only have one voice left to petition God with—lament. Lament's power is in its call for the redistribution of power in the world—for the claims of the powerless and the oppressed to be legitimated by God by his acting in the face of his rule being questioned.[25] This leads to a spirituality that is honest and plain, with all the platitudes thrown away in the pain of expression. It locates an individual's pain, and that of others, and cries out the recognition that things are not right, that they can and should be changed for the current situation is unacceptable, and it is God's obligation to change them. For the psalmist, the failure to articulate the terrors of the world before God leads to a passive and ultimately destructive acceptance of the *status quo*.

Therefore these texts and expressions serve a threefold role. Firstly, lament ensures that the voices of the oppressed are not lost, and demands that the apparently absent God act. Secondly, these laments and complaints highlight the potential violence present in the realities of human

23. Strawn, "Imprecation," 314–20.

24. Zenger, *A God of Vengeance?*, 74, emphasis original.

25. Brueggemann and Miller, *The Psalms and the Life of Faith*, 101.

community, calling for transformed relationships and new ways to live well. Lastly, the texts of vengeance and complaint exist within a wider canon that speaks against violence, urging non-violent responses and looking forward to a time, begun now, where *shalom* is restored in all its fullness.[26]

How then, might these themes be represented and uttered in the contemporary setting, and in particular in the world of new media and internet technologies?

NEW MEDIA AND DIGITAL TECHNOLOGIES

Digital technology is commonly associated with information and communication technologies, often exemplified in personal computers, digital audio/visual systems, and digital communications infrastructures. New media, though, is a more slippery term. For some, it is used is simply to describe anything related to technologies associated with that amorphous beast known as "the internet," while for others it is purely any new form of media that emerges, such as the codex or radio.[27] Email, social networks, web sites, blogs, electronic commerce, video production and sharing, and mobile communications often get lumped under the term "new media," regardless of how they function as mediated communication or if they bring something new to the mix. Moreover, new media also contains the sense of "cyberculture," where the focus is upon the different social phenomena that internet technologies engender and the ways in which these challenge, form, and reshape notions of human community.

Lev Manovich, in seeking to define the term "new media" more clearly, highlights that cyberculture tends to emphasize the social phenomenon, while new media, in his view, focuses more upon the use of computer/digital technology as a distribution platform. Creating a new film using digital technology does not count as new media, but distributing the film though a web site such as YouTube does. This is not a simple one-way transaction, though, because the way in which a cultural object, such as a film clip, computer game, or web site, is engaged with and manipulated by people in this networked environment creates a feedback loop that then shapes the way in which the technology develops. It is this feedback loop that puts the "new" in new media.[28]

26. Zenger, *A God of Vengeance?*, 85.

27. Campbell, *When Religion Meets New Media*, 9.

28. Manovich, "New Media from Borges to HTML," 13–28.

Bryan Murley likens this feedback loop to the theological changes emphasized in the Protestant Reformation, which challenged established teaching about the relationship between God and the Christian believer. Murley argues that just as Protestant Reformation diminished the role of priest as a sole intermediary between God and the believer (through Jesus Christ) by emphasizing a more direct relationship between believer and God, so too new media technologies change the rules around control and access to information. No longer do people have to consume media that has been packaged in a static form by a media company or other authority. Instead, they can access and manipulate that media and information more directly through new technologies, as well as producing their own media to distribute to an audience of any size.[29]

The authorities' roles in mediating and controlling information has been reduced, though not completely removed, as consumer-produced media may still be regulated in a number of different ways (e.g., by the license agreement on a video sharing site or government regulation relating to the content of the media produced). Playing off the Protestant idea of a priesthood of all believers, Murley coins this as the "mediahood of all receivers," with obvious parallels in the way in which both might be seen as "revolutionary" events.[30]

New media's potential for people at a grassroots level to become critical, discerning consumers and producers of media opens the door for the expression of religious lament, complaint, and imprecation in online environments. Whether in Facebook or Twitter, blogging, in collaborative work using wikis or Google Docs, through image and video sharing on Flickr and YouTube, or in basic email and text messaging, there are ample opportunities for responding to individual and community situations in public and private settings.

The trajectory for doing this is shaped by a number of factors. Firstly, there is the increasing pervasiveness of online connectivity coupled in turn with easy to use tools for the creation of online content and cheap online storage. Secondly, the ease of which online content can be accessed, created and interacted with leads, Peter Horsfield and Paul Teusner contend, to a diminished trust in those who hold control over

29. Murley, "Mediahood of All Receivers."

30. Similarly, for an examination of hyperbole around the iPhone as the "Jesus Phone," and the religious language and symbols being used to describe it see: Campbell and La Pastina, "How the iPhone became Divine: New Media, Religion and the Intertextual Circulation of Meaning," 1191–1207.

information. This diminished trust filters through into religion's interaction with the online world, with believers now able to access "spiritual" information and teaching from a wide range of online sources outside of other more traditional sources.

Moving beyond seeking doctrinal information, this has opened up into the translation of offline religious practice into the online world, as well as the creation of new kinds of religious ritual.[31] Thus new spaces for lament, outside of the control of institutional religion, emerge in the online world, offering alternative locations to spaces for lament within existing religious communities that may have become lost or unavailable. Furthermore, Horsfield and Teusner note additional factors such as new religious language, contextual theology, intentional communities, and "glocalization" are also influencing the mediation of religion in the online world.[32]

NEW LOCATIONS FOR LAMENT

New media allows both the emergence of new forms of discourse, as well as forums for more traditional expression. For example, in order to maintain their ethnic and religious identities, some Mountain Jewish communities in Azerbaijan perform their traditional forms of lament within their own physical communities, while at the same time using the internet share these laments across the region and around the world.[33] In a similar fashion we see other forms of lament and complaint sitting as carefully structured pieces of writing or liturgy for a physical worship context, while coexisting with examples that take advantage of new media.

This might include traditional biblical psalms of lament being performed on YouTube, perhaps with musical background or visual imagery added, or preached about in a local context but made available via the Internet.[34] Alternatively, original psalms of lament and complaint

31. Collins, "Network Church"; Horsfield and Teusner, "A Mediated Religion," 288–89; Bednar, "Blogging: Report from a Grassroots Revival," 24–30.

32. Horsfield and Teusner, "A Mediated Religion," 291–93.

33. Goluboff, "Communities of Mourning," 149–77.

34. Sermons from 21 March through 18 April 2011 at House of Providence, "Sermons." For "performed" psalms of lament and imprecation see SurfaceOfTheEye, "Psalm 137—Ian White"; Coeurigeuse, "Psalm 143 A Lament"; Etonick, "Psalm 10—A Complaint about Evil People."

might be performed or presented in new media formats, often mixing material from various sources into a final media product.[35] Sometimes these original compositions pick up on explicit political issues, from a personal psalm of lament composed about the nation of Kenya, through to a musical lament that explores grief over past events in El Salvador, or a personal reflection on the Guantanamo Bay detention camp.[36]

Lament is also explored through the internet and new media in the contexts of education and counseling. Mark Roncace and Patrick Gray describe how they explore the genre of psalms of lament and imprecation through having students engage with popular culture and new media. Students are asked to seek out aspects within those media that reflect the disorientation phase noted by Brueggemann, and to identify ways in which those media help or hinder the move to a new orientation.[37] The role of lament is also explored online through groups providing educational and spiritual resources for those involved in social work and/or counseling, or for those seeking a way of expressing their current experiences.[38] In each of these cases it is possible to see the intersection between lament, the internet and new media beginning to develop in intriguing ways.

Returning to the Pike River mining tragedy cited earlier, we noted how the U2 concert provided a space of lament. In the contemporary world this event is no longer an isolated incident, with both mainstream media and the wider public using new media to communicate that experience.[39] Video clips of U2's engagement with the tragedy were recorded on mobile devices and uploaded to sites like Facebook and YouTube with comments from both posters and viewers.[40] Not all comments were rel-

35. For an original psalm of lament set to tune of George Michael's "Careless Whisper" see eevee2hufflepuff, "Psalm of Lament." For another original lament see BearerOfChrist 35, "A Psalm-Lament of Christopher." For a musical reflection on Ps 22 see ProfessorJTan, "Lament, Grief, Hope: A Meditation on Psalm 22 (2010)."

36. Hurlocks, "Lament for Kenya"; Colon, "Violence, Lament, Redemption: A Composer's Journey"; Lee, "Psalms of Lament from Guantanamo Bay."

37. Roncace and Gray, *Teaching the Bible*, 198–206.

38. Seale, Everett, and Spiritual Care Collaborative, "The Power of Lament"; Smith and North American Association of Christians in Social Work, "Darkness is my Closest Friend"; Hammersley, "Psalm of Despair"; Hammersley, "Psalm of Disaster."

39. NZPA, "U2 pays tribute to lost miners"; Smith and Kara, "U2 pays tribute to Pike River miners"; SunriseOn7, "U2's tribute to the NZ Pike River miners."

40. E.g., Kiwistu72, "U2—One Tree Hill—Auckland 25 Nov 10—Dedicated to Our Lost Miners—May They RIP"; jetskifisher, "U2 Live in Auckland 25 Nov 2010—One Tree Hill in Memory of Westcoast Miners. R.I.P."

evant, but messages of sympathy, further lament, and a sense of being part of the community caught up in the tragedy were also communicated, and links to the clips and comments passed on to friends and others.

Explicit theological, pastoral, and personal reflection about the tragedy was also taking place on news sites and blogs. Theologian Steve Taylor used his blog to write a piece, "U2 and public lament for Pike River Miners," that explored the connection between the concert and lament in general, while also linking through others writing on similar themes. Space for others to comment was taken advantage of by readers of Taylor's material.[41] Similarly, the mainstream media made space for the wider public to express their feelings about the tragedy, with both the NZ Herald and Stuff (Fairfax Media) websites posting condolences and sentiments from the New Zealand public and those further afield.[42]

This kind of process involves a kind of contextual theology bringing the experience of the past, recorded in the sacred texts and traditions of the faith community, into dialogue with the experience of the present. This experience of the present includes not only personal and communal experiences, but also an understanding of how those experiences are shaped by the culture they occur within, the social location of the people involved, and any social changes presently taking place.[43] U2's and Taylor's deliberations, as well as those of others like the Azerbaijani Mountain Jews and the responses to various political situations, involve taking into account both past and present and with a potential future hoped for. Thus a movement from orientation to disorientation to reorientation might be observed taking place here.

Similarly, those seeking to understand how worship might take place within a culture saturated in new media are also carrying out contextual theology. For instance, UK musician, blogger, and "worship curator" Jonny Baker explains how lament was incorporated into the life of his London community of faith. Paying particular attention to lament, the tradition of the psalms in worship was mixed with contemporary video material in order to draw the congregation into creating their own psalms relating to their particular contexts. As this stands, this is technically not new media, but after the event Baker used his blog to communicate what

41. Taylor, "U2 and Public Lament for Pike River Miners."

42. "Your condolences for the families of Pike River miners"; "Condolences for the Pike River victims."

43. Bevans, *Models of Contextual Theology*, 3–7.

happened, link to resources used, and could receive feedback via the blog from others on the ideas presented there.[44]

These examples highlight Horsfield and Teusner's observation of religion in the online and new media environments conflating the local and the global. They assert that "[u]sers seek connections with people on the web regardless of their location, to build important relationships, find belonging and enhance their religious life in their own contexts."[45] The large number of people from around the world posting prayers, laments and petitions on the St Mary MacKillop web site prayer space in Australia is one illustration of this, as is the web site providing a collection of worship and prayer resources, including laments, drawn from natural disasters, and the lament of a mother who lost her son in the July 7 2005 bombing in London.[46]

THE DARKER SIDE OF LAMENT AND NEW MEDIA

For all the opportunities, however, the environment of new media presents a number of challenges for both producers and consumers of media around questions of the authenticity of communication, whether the process of lament is actually transitioning toward a new state of orientation and hopefulness, and if it is even possible to "perform" imprecation and lament in the public sphere of the internet.

Around the question of authentic online communication, particularly in the practice of people recording personal video messages on YouTube, anthropologist Michael Wesch observed the following about these messages:

> They are meant for anybody and everybody, or possibly nobody—not addressed to anyone in particular—or perhaps only vaguely addressed to "the YouTube community." They are videos of people sitting alone in front of their webcams and just talking to anybody and everybody who care to click on their video.

44. Baker, "Worship Trick 71." One of the resources created by a member of the congregation for the service was also distributed online, encouraging people to explore the different elements of the psalms outside of the context of the service. See Collins, "Psalm Structure Twister."

45. Horsfield and Teusner, "A Mediated Religion," 293.

46. The Sisters of Saint Joseph of the Sacred Heart, "Saint Mary MacKillop"; Jensen, "Pray . . . in 255 Characters or Fewer"; Woodard, "Worship and Prayer Resources Following a Natural Disaster"; Collins and Fatayi-Williams, "Straight from the Heart."

> These vloggers talk about their day, their problems, their accomplishments, their hopes, dreams, and fears. They represent less than 5% of the videos uploaded to YouTube, yet with YouTube bringing in more than 200,000 videos per day, their numbers are not insignificant, numbering in the thousands every day. A thriving community has emerged around such videos, one that some participate in and believe in with almost religious zeal.[47]

Wesch observes some producers of such video messages saying they have been able to express themselves intimately and personally, sharing both joy and trauma, without having to experience immediate personal interaction, thus overcoming social anxiety, and achieving deeper self-reflection and connection with their YouTube communities. Against that though, he remarks that messages can be taken out of context, put into other contexts, and a very real anxiety is expressed about how one should portray oneself. This, in turn, leads into questions as to the authenticity of the speaker or the message—for all the messages are performed in some way—and wider discourse about the tension between the search for community and maintaining a dominant individualism described as "community with constraint."[48]

Furthermore, there is also a danger that lament may itself be appropriated in a self-serving fashion both for individuals and communities, not seeking justice but rather the lamenter's own self-interest at the expense of all others. Westermann's comments noted earlier that lament should never be performed for its own sake or attached to self-pity are pertinent here. True lament is tied to the call for suffering to be alleviated and a new situation entered into, and to challenge hegemonic power in our society that seeks to remove or marginalize the voices of those who would question it.[49] Therefore, to lament and imprecate in order to paint those you oppose as monsters and less than human for one's own self interest, achieves nothing more than dehumanizing the lamenter and adding dysfunction to existing relationships. So too, does the use of lament used to support a psychological need fed by a sense of persecution and martyrdom.

A positive response to the online lament of others, and one that aimed to assist in the provision of hope in the face of trauma, occurred during the 2010 Queensland floods in Australia. Motivated by a Facebook

47. Wesch, "YouTube and You," 21.

48. Ibid., 25–28.

49. Brueggemann, "Lament as Antidote to Silence," 24–25.

conversation on the local radio station along the lines of "Where was God in all this?" a minister of the Uniting Church responded with the composition of a psalm-like song offering hope in the face of the disaster. The score, lyrics, and digital music file were the made available for download free to all.[50] Thus, the lament of the old situation passing away and leaving chaos in its place was met by a response, mediated by the internet, to offer hope and a way forward to a new orientation.

What new media opens up to the religious communities is the possibility of acts or performances of religious lament and imprecation that move from the private sphere within personal and institutional religious contexts into the wider digital public sphere. Of particular interest here is how the content and rituals of lament, and imprecation, might use new media in ways considered disturbing or transgressive in contemporary society. Earlier we observed that the space for lament is often missing with in church communities, whether through a lack of understanding of its role, a theological aversion to its perceived negativity, or its challenges to the institutional status quo. But is that space available in wider Western society, with liberal democratic principles arguing autonomous individuals and their communities are entitled to access to the public square to express their opinions?

In the New Zealand context human rights legislation asserts that is unlawful to publish, distribute, or broadcast matter that is threatening, abusive, or insulting, especially if that is,

> matter or words likely to excite hostility or ill-will against, or bring into contempt or ridicule, any such group of persons in New Zealand on the ground of the colour, race, or ethnic or national origins of that group of persons.[51]

As Gwilym Beckerlegge notes, this leads to societies promoting freedom of speech being caught in a deep ambivalence toward "offensive language directed towards ethnic and religious groups in order to offend, victimize or invite violence against them."[52] On the one hand, by defending the right of an individual or group to speak they can privilege a group attacking another, thereby marginalizing the addressed party. On the other hand, though, defending minority groups' rights to free speech may prevent criticism of the speakers by another party. The first and fourteenth

50. MacGregor, "Christ Shows his Face."

51. New Zealand Government, "Human Rights Act 1993 No 82," s 131.

52. Beckerlegge, "Computer-mediated Religion," 245.

amendments to the US Constitution, protecting free speech and equal protection under the law respectively, is an example of how "hate speech" might be reviled but at the same time protected.[53] This tension between the right to free speech and religious freedom, and the limits set for the preservation of the right to life and security in society, would seem to preclude the performance of some forms of lament and imprecation. Cries for vengeance to be enacted against a perceived oppressor, might be seen as crossing a line to incite or commit hatred and violence towards that group.

Societal guidelines, such as the (2007/2009) "Statement of Religious Diversity" and the (2010) "Freedom of Religion and Belief" draft report produced by the *New Zealand Human Rights Commission*, argue for the right of freedom of expression and the maintenance of religious difference, provided that is done within certain boundaries and assumptions.[54] One such assumption is the assertion in the "Freedom of Religion and Belief" draft that "[m]atters of religion and belief are deemed to be a matter for the private, rather than public, sphere."[55] Furthermore, while freedom of expression includes both the right to religious expression and the right to express views about religion, this is tempered by the call for "an appropriate balance between these freedoms and an awareness of what is sacred to people of different religions and cultures."[56] Where religious differences appear irreconcilable, the state may step in as the final arbiter to prevent violence or breaches of the law.

Thus, while lament and imprecation in private may be acceptable, moving those actions into the public sphere, whether in church or communicated to a wider audience via new media may be considered "beyond the pale," breaching standards deemed necessary for the smooth functioning of a modern pluralistic society. Furthermore, the public/private boundary is often unclear, with the unadulterated public reading or performance of a psalm of lament or imprecation perhaps being acceptable, while the reframing of that psalm to a contemporary context, community or person might not be.

53. Beckerlegge, "Computer-mediated religion," 245–47.

54. Human Rights Commission, *Freedom of Religion and Belief*; Human Rights Commission, *Religious Diversity in New Zealand: Statement of Religious Diversity*.

55. Human Rights Commission, *Freedom of Religion and Belief*, 2.

56. Human Rights Commission, *Religious Diversity in New Zealand: Statement of Religious Diversity*, 8.

From the perspective of those who are then silenced by the state, the power of lament as a challenge to hegemonic power in our society is perhaps then reinforced, rather than tempered.[57] Moreover, while members of Western societies may applaud the use of new media as a vehicle for individual and communities to lament, complain, and rail against the injustices perpetrated against them in places like the Middle East or Burma, they may be less comfortable when it is used for the same purposes in their own backyard.[58]

CONCLUSION

Digital technologies, and new media in particular, with their power to enhance communication and participation offer new spaces for lament, complaint, and imprecation. Moreover, new media offers the possibilities for much needed lament and complaint to occur in spaces that perhaps have been eliminated from traditional worshipping communities. As such, lament in the world of new media might offer that transitional place of moving from old orientation to new orientation, as well as serving to critique the lack of language and space within institutions, and perhaps, encouraging the reappropriation of lament.

However, new media also offers the darker potential of accentuating the power of this form of expression, and so should be treated with cautious respect and self-examination. While lament is an act of performance, the commoditization of lament in a new media world, perhaps in the form of a service or mobile device application to be purchased, could lead to it becoming a "sanitized" means to the end of making money and of feeding spiritual narcissism. In addition, lament that becomes disconnected from the Easter hope of transformation offered through the life, death, and resurrection of Jesus Christ becomes less than it might be, for ultimately transformation towards a new orientation is not found in "an App for that," but rather in the fullness of a new orientation arising from being in Christ, and from the future hope offered in God.

57. Brueggemann, "Lament as Antidote to Silence," 24–25.

58. Mackey, "June 22: Updates on Iran's Disputed Election"; Cellan-Jones, "Hi-tech Helps Iranian Monitoring."

PART FOUR

Refraction

15

In Search of the Shulamith in the State of Israel

A Lament

Yael Klangwisan

CAPO

I am black and beautiful, daughters of Jerusalem,
dark as the Bedouin tents of keder
Exotic as the tapestries of Shlomo
Do not see me as black: I have been pierced by the Sun's rays
The sons of my mother, their anger blazed.
My own vineyard I have not watched.

We arrived in Israel in the spring, C. and I. We were seeking the Shulamith. Together we would walk through the fields of wildflowers now springing up through the meadows in the north. We would camp in her forests and woodlands. We would walk through the villages on our way to the mountain. If there was something of her in the stream at Ein Gedi I would find her. If there was the echo of her steps in the streets of Jerusalem, then I would follow her. If there was the scent of her fragrance on the slopes of Hermon, then I would seek her out.

But I could not find her anywhere. And her fingerprints and traces had been covered. It was all wrong, caught in a carnival of the grotesque and her beautiful body was dismembered, chained, barricaded. She had faded away like Echo doomed to only repeat the last words anyone said. "Chains, fearful chains around me . . ." she said.

> This wall fortified by silver
> This door barricaded with a cedar beam

A YOUNG MAN IS STOPPED

You would have to walk on the streets of Jerusalem, to understand. The streets of Jerusalem are paved with new stones and old stones. It is a particular joy to walk on these stones; a particular joy to drink the strong, dark coffee, and eat tiny chocolate croissants from a brown paper bag while walking on these hewn stones early in the morning. There are new stones, sharply cut and glistening white in the sunshine. They are dazzling. We arrive in Jerusalem at dawn. The city glistens on top of its nest of hills. The city glistens like gold; Jerusalem of gold. My heart cries– take me there directly. Take me right to the top.

The guardians found me, the ones that surround the city . . .
Have any of you seen the one I love with all my breath?

There are watchers on the way and watchers everywhere. . . . There is no free run. We stop at checkpoints where there are blockades and guns. There are watchers at all the gates. "Have you seen her? Have you seen the Shulamith? She is a prince's daughter. She is a dark beauty. Have you seen her?" I say.

In the city the new stones surround the old. The old stones are in the old city. This old city is full of narrow streets. The streets all descend from Jaffa gate. We descend through the markets and plazas. From each side Arab merchants present their wares in the *souq*. Bags, scarves, coffee pots, spices, incense—buy, you must buy. Hey you! Yes, there are traces of her but I cannot take hold. I see a glimpse of her in the towers of spices and bowls of incense, in the honeyed sweets, and in the brightly colored cloths, and in the faces of the beautiful women with kohl lined eyes and framed by head scarves.

We rested on the street, the street that is at the intersection of the twelve stages of the cross, the street that leads also directly to the Kotel, and that street that lies mostly in the Arab quarter. We sat outside on a ground level terrace to drink minted lemon and eat a plate of hummus and pita. It is the best hummus in Israel they always say.

Across from us, C. and I, are a group of soldiers. They are young and brave—young men ought to be trying their hands at love. These almost-men handle machine guns, radios, and most of all it is their gaze that captures me. They are all eyes. Every gaze is the summation of threat. A teenage boy is stopped by the gaze. He is wearing jeans and sneakers. He has on a T-shirt. His dark hair is cropped short. He is the same height and same age of some of the young men dressed in military uniform who holding their rifles like one might hold the household cat. I can see he is angry to be stopped on this busy street that is his home. His cheeks flush red but he is silent and while his face speaks defiance he obeys every direction.

His body is stifled with rage but he is stock still.
His neck is taut. Taut like a tightly coiled spring that could burst or whip.

Up and down this street are these boys—or almost-men. He works in the street or his family live in this street, or his family has lived in this quarter for a hundred years or more. I knew the moment he had been stopped because all the eyes of the vendors in the street—the mobile phone salesmen, the coffee pot salesmen, the T-shirt salesmen, and the old men playing chess in the street wearing Arafat's checkered scarves. All eyes turned towards the young man. It was eerily silent even though the street still bustled and clanked.

"Give me your ID," said the young soldier. Give me your documents. Give me your name, your father's name. Give me the proof of who you are. Give me your credentials. And by the way, where are you going? What proof do you have you are going there? Now wait. Wait while I check your number against our database. Wait here and don't move. I am watching you. Remember that.

It is true they were watching. Because formerly there had not been cameras but now they are clear on every corner. Everyone is watching and being watched.

> Seize for us the jackals, vinespoilers! When our vines bud.

"Dark shadows, dark shadows all around us," Echo said.

SEDERS AND STATIONS

What to say . . . when too much speaking just sounds like a roar and achieves little!! Who can work it out. We are just sad.

Last night we went to visit a family in Nayot for the first night of Pesach when in the old days would have been the day of the slaughter of the lambs. In the late afternoon we walked from the Old City down through New Jerusalem. The high end retailers at Mamila, the cafes and bookshops on Rehavia's Derech Gaza were all closed. The city was silent apart from ubiquitous Arab taxis delivering the observant and the secular to seder dinners all over the city. Finally descending along Rabbi Herzog's street we saw the Botanical Gardens which identify the neighborhood of Nayot. To each side on our path are the wealthy stone apartments of New Jerusalem. The family we came to share the seder with are American and Polish. They are a modern observant family, modern educated citizens, at work towards building their country and having it survive. The father is an engineer, the mother a translator. They met at Hebrew University when they were young. Their sons are also educated civil workers, children of Israel, the hope and future. Their beloved and only daughter, beloved of her father, just finishing high school. She will go to the IDF soon. Chava says, "Listen to her pray, there is a native Israeli for you." Hebrew is her children's mother tongue and they raced through their prayers as only native speakers could—every word a child from their lips. Every word, a word of belonging. These are the new children of Israel.

At first we sat with the great grandmother of the family. She was a small, frail, dark-haired ninety year old woman. She told us how she lost her whole family in Poland in the Shoah. She stopped for a moment—her grief still palpable. Later her Israeli born son, the engineer, spoke about how Jewish people everywhere have always felt they had to fight to survive. It is an archaeological and historical phenomenon with which I could not disagree. We ate and sang and tried to follow the Haggadah with the super fast Hebrew. C. gallantly persevered through three hours of seder prayers. That night I heard the Song of Songs intertwined in the seder prayers. Was the Shulamith at the table, did she take Eliyahu's place? I did not see her. Perhaps she was in the desert or somewhere in the West Bank caught behind a high concrete wall.

This morning, the first great day of Pesach, we went down to another wall. The lion's share of the wall was awash in white prayer shawls and discordant chanting and singing. There appeared to be at least five shuls praying the Pesach morning service for the first day. Later we walked down to one of the Gethsemanes and revisited the 1000 year old olive trees. We went up to the Russian convent with the gold bell shaped spires. There was a cave in the convent garden where Mary Magdalene's tomb is full of decayed bodies and ossuaries. All the churches here pivot around death—the church of the Dormition, the Holy Sepulchre. In the tomb of the prophets a lone, pale, black-cloaked Russian priest looms out of the darkness as we creep down the stairs to join him in the underworld. The smell of death lingers on the dusty stone walls and dark grottos. I want to run back to those ever-living olive trees. I wondered if the kingdom on earth for which creation groans might be a kingdom of trees. Trees at least have done no wrong. There have been so many battles in Jerusalem. Some of these churches, ruins, and arches are as old as the genocidal crusaders. I can't see peace here when there are so many people who are ready to die over difference. Peace may only descend when we all go away, when human civilization reaches its apogee and then fades. Are those ancient olives waiting for the passing of the age of man?

Like a fruiting apricot among the woodland trees
This is my lover among sons . . .
Beneath the apricot tree I awoke you
It was there your mother travailed . . .
I would lead you, I would bring you
Into my mother's house . . .

In the valley between the old city and the churches of the Mount of Olives lie more famous tombs, falsely known as Pharoah's daughter's tomb shaped like a pyramid and Absalom's pillar, in between is the supposed tomb of Zechariah ben Jehoida. There are tombs and dank caves everywhere in this valley. I wonder about death. Seeing these tombs that are supposedly the last resting place of enigmatic characters of the sacred text, characters who seem to be ever running with their beautiful long hair flying in the wind, again and again in the text, and then caught by trees. But real life is a single gasp, a sudden intake of breath and then it is gone.

Where is the Shulamith? She is buried underneath the rubble of a thousand conquerings, razings, and decimations. She is entombed in rock, marked by plaques and pyramids. She is a victim of grave robbers. She is trodden upon by shield bearing legions. She is prostrated upon by hordes that weep and clutch. She is the holy grail of the Middle East peace process continually smashed. She is the fifteen year old Palestinian boy who died today on the Gaza Strip. She is the Israeli soldier who also died today, his pregnant widow wailing, both hands clutching her belly as she bends over in despair. She is a small, old woman who lost the entire world in 1939.

She has faded like Echo leaving only a whisper.

DRAGONS IN THE NEGEV

Yesterday, the wind changed and became the Sharuv. There were actually five days that became one long day. The day of the Sharuv. When the wind changes here in Jerusalem it becomes hot, and then dust comes with the hot wind. The hot, suffocating dust brought by the wind covers the whole city. I can barely see the sun. It becomes a dull, apocalyptic glow in the sky. I can't see the Mount of Olives or Mount Scopus from my rooftop, and I can barely see Mount Moriah. The dust laden wind is like a plague from Egypt, this wild, dry wind, its open and voracious mouth devouring any drop of water. It is a demon from the desert, which is where the wind comes from. The hot, devouring mouth of the desert, winding up from the depths of the Arabah, the great rift, the forbidding and rocky craters of the Negev, remnants of geological violence. This fire breathing dragon in the desert blows hot fumes on the city which is already burning from within.

Its passion relentless as Sheol
A flashing, flaming fire

This morning I needed to read and think about the Song of Songs. I got up but didn't want to go. C. was sleeping and he felt like peace. In the space of his breath the five days of Sharuv winds had dissipated leaving cool winds from the north, from Hermon, from the Lebanon. I got up to go but he said "stay with me" . . . so I stayed a little longer . . . but then I left to go to Mamila where I thought I could find a quiet warm place in a cafe overlooking the garden quarter outside Jaffa gate. I did. And then I read about Promethea, the last part where Cixous talks about love for Promethea, and the world with its bull's horns and heart moist like a river but torn together and apart. Something in the womb I had constructed in the cafe made the words of Promethea intense and I felt every one. I was torn by horns. And then the world tore again in the blast of the Yom HaShoah sirens. It was my heart and my eyes that were torn in two while the heart of the city stood still. My heart stopped and emptied. It emptied itself because of the collective memory of the deaths of six million children, six million who once were children but now ash. And every eye was touched with the pain of remembering and an old man stood in the cafe and cried. I stood but I drifted against the ceiling. My fingers stung and my emptied heart gaped mercilessly. And because at that moment I was already undone by Promethea, words on a page, a book, but a book of books, the siren and the eye unblinking and the silence and the blast and the stop pierced me and I felt entirely broken. And I can't really reconcile the depth of feeling because my soul is not pure enough for noble pain nor for the traumatic memories of the world. Afterwards I left and went to buy stamps. And the woman from whom I bought the stamps offered me a phone card. And I wanted to be sick because my heart was still in my throat and I couldn't breathe at all.

Bare me as a seal upon your heart
A seal upon your arm
For love is as vehement as death . . .

It was a little while after that that I found myself with C. in the botanical gardens in Nayot. We saw the yellow green bark of the pistachio, the brave and sturdy oak, the towering cypress, the torqued branches of the olive grove, the dry fingers of the balsam, the lotus drifted in pools and red poppies climbed through cracks in the rock. Like the ancient Olives of the Church of Gethsemane I was brought again to calm. With courage gained from the trees we caught a bus to Ein Kerem and went into Yad Vashem. It was for C. that we had gone, for I had already seen Yad Vashem and I had not survived it. When we came out of that dark space the sun was setting over the pine forest of Ya'ar Yerushalayim. I can't say any more about the memorial and the images and stories and recountings, and what I saw and heard and felt, the room of books full of names. The images of children, the paintings, the journals, the ribbons from their clothes, the mothers holding their children, the tears, shoes, spectacles, emerald necklaces, and the dark valley beyond tears. And the faces that turned away, and the very few faces who turned towards and the very many more evil hands. Some things can't be adequately written down.

And my Shulamith, where is she. At the bottom of a pit? Transmuted into ash? Emaciated, cradling her child at the last? As for me, a Sharuv had blown me into the Negev and I took shelter amongst the rocks.

EIN GEDI

We took a bus early this morning down to Ein Gedi in the desert. We walked up to Nahal David and then took a rickety path up the steep side of the wadi to the Dodim Cave—the cave of lovers! A beautiful peaceful pool and cave high above the lower waterfalls with a view over the Dead Sea which was a stunning crystal blue and the mountains of Jordan like immense spice towers stretched out beyond. Shulamith spring, cave of love, a wadi of peace. An oasis for thirsty travelers, a refuge for lovers, a watering hole for deer. Surely she is here. Look at the stately date palms. The ibex high up on the steep rocky outcrops of the wadi. The buzzing life in and around the fresh water stream.

My musk-scented nard, its fragrance breathes
A parcel of myrrh is my lover to me between my breasts
A spray of henna is my lover to me in the vineyards of Ein-Gedi

I slept all night but in and out of nightmares. Maybe it was the wind change, the fever that has clung to me since Yad VaShem. The heat of the desert, the cold nights in the mountains. The cool swim at Ein Gedi, and the hot walk high on the sides of the wadi. I dreamed of a colorless world. The blue of sea exchanged for the darkness of night. I was trapped for eternity in the Lovers' Cave, high in the wadi guarded by a stone man. I dreamed of cold, windswept mountains high up and near Syria. I dreamed in black and white of cavernous dwelling places, and striped rough cotton cushions, rams' horns, rocks piled into rows, and circles marking out ruins, chipped and broken mosaics. All this whirled around me as I peered wildly out of the Dodim Cave watched by the bearded Semitic king carved into the cliff by the wind. This morning I am exhausted as if I walked across the Negev in my sleep with the images of the Shoah walking with me, dread companions. Tired and throbbing in my temples. There were no little crayfish, conies, or ibex in these dreams, no doves, canaries, swallows. No black ants, and no red dragonflies alighting on clear pools.

Who is that?
She rises from the desert
like a pillar of cloud
like the smoke of myrrh and frankincense …

BESIDE A BULLET RIDDLED MOSQUE

Jerusalem. Jerusalem. We have left your streets and your shuttered windows which look so sad in the moonlight. We have left behind the paired archetypes of the silent violence of your streets still engaged in a combat of silences. The two almost-men are eternally silhouetted on that street corner engaged in a combat that requires the speaking of no true words. Each one is a caricature of his own perspective of the world; each one not articulating the truth of the encounter. Each one with his particular silence. But while the two almost-men are the same height as the other, one towers over the other and looks down at his bowed, flushed, defiant head.

The Egged bus whisked us away up into the North and there we had a dream that we slept in a tent high up in the mountain where clouds and storms and winds of both the natural and political world swept across overhead. The clouds surge past on gigantic waves of wind. She looks down upon us from Hermon, here is her power seat. But is it love or primordial frustration that swoops down from Hermon. We are shaken, and spend the night fitfully in our fragile tent. We woke feeling we hadn't slept at all. The mountain was disquieted as if it sought to rouse itself and rise from its northern throne and strike at the noise of mankind below.

Descend to me from your white mountain …
From this snow clad mountain come down
Look down from Amana
From the summits of Senir and Hermon
From the mountain caves of lions
From the leopard's alpine habitat

Along the flank of the mountain down the north-eastern side of the country is the land of Amos, and angry prophets condemning injustice would match the mood of the wind-swept, wild north with well chosen words of rebuke. But now the eastern Golan Heights are a barren no-man's land caught between Israel and Syria. The land of Bashan. No fool would venture into the fields either side of this lonely road. Ubiquitous signs warn of landmines, cruel and barbaric devices, taunting child shepherds. Taunting the children who run and walk in fields, and skip in the beautiful, wild hills on the mountain. Such beauty tormented by the grotesque device that lies in wait.

C. and I stopped at a bullet riddled Mosque on the lonely road. It was a cement brick Mosque with gaping holes in its side. It lay upon its side, a slaughtered goat with all its intestines bulging out. A carcass. The minaret still stood with its spire into the sky leaning at a precarious angle like Pisa. I said to C., "don't go in there, it might fall on you and besides there is a Muslim family here and they are eating a picnic." But he went anyway. He is better than me.

In this far flung and unlikely wilderness, pock-marked by a savage war, like the ravaged body that has a cancer in remission, a small family was eating a picnic beside the ruined mosque. It was a seder of difference and no less sacred than the one in Nayot. They were a Palestinian family. And the image created by the filial seder beside the broken mosque was incongruous. One half the image spoke of health, a future generation, a loving family, while the other half—that of the mosque—spoke only of destruction, the end of dreams, the denial of difference.

When my gaze was met by the family I hesitated as did they. We, in that moment, wondered silently about the other. What do they think? What do they want? What of anger? What of positioning? What of politics and/or grief? And I wondered what right had I, to look upon this tottering mosque, as some kind of site of interest at a road side stop. It was no place for a view. And no place for taking pictures. It was a place to tear one's clothes and to cry at the world, to cry at the stupidity of war. To cry at the rape of cultures, lands, and peoples.

Flee my lover!
And be like a gazelle or young stag on mountains . . .

C. spoke to the small family and the father. They sat at the gates of the mosque in the rubble as if it was a loved family home. The father motioned for C. to go in, to appreciate what remained of its tower, and ceiling, and the graffiti-covered walls. It was a magnificent and generous kindness. "Allah Akbar," he said. C. went in, but I don't know how he replied to the Palestinian father of the small family when he came out, but I saw that they smiled and shook hands. We left the family there at the damaged mosque. Had I known, I would have watched the Shulamith through the rearview mirror until she disappeared from sight.

CODA

. . . "Fearful chains around me" Echo said.
And then no more. She was turned away.
To hide her face, her lips, her guilt, among the trees.
Even their leaves, to haunt caves of the forest,
to feed her love on melancholy sorrow,
which sleepless turned her body to a shade,
first pale and wrinkled and then a sheet of air,
then bones which some say turned to thin-worn rocks,
then at last her voice remained. Vanished in forest.
Far from her usual walks in hills and valleys.
She's heard by all who call; her voice has life.[1]

1. Excerpts from the legend of Echo are taken from the English translation of Ovid, *The Metamorphoses*, translated by Horace Gregory (New York: Signet Classic, 2001). All translations of the Song of Songs are the author's own.

Bibliography

Anderson, Bernhard W., and Steven Bishop. *Out of the Depths: The Psalms Speak for Us Today*. 3rd ed. Louisville, KY: Westminster John Knox, 2000.

Auvray, P. "The Psalms." In *Introduction to the Old Testament*, edited by A. Robert and A. Feuillet, translated by Patrick W. Skehan et al., 2:367–404. Garden City, NY: Image, 1970.

Baglyos, Paul A. "Lament in the Liturgy of the Rural Church: An Appeal for Recovery." *CurTM* 34.4 (2009) 253–63.

Bain, Michael. "U2 Concert Review: Auckland, New Zealand." No pages. Online: http://www.u2tours.com/displayfan.src?ID=20101125&XID=12389.

Baker, Jonny. "Worship Trick 71." No pages. Online: http://jonnybaker.blogs.com/jonnybaker/2004/02/worship_trick_7.html.

Bakhtin, M. M. *Problems of Dostoevsky's Poetics*. Edited and translated by Caryl Emerson. Minneapolis, MN: Minnesota University Press, 1984.

Balentine, Samuel E. "Afterword." In *Seeking the Favor of God: The Origins of Penitential Prayer in Second Temple Judaism*, edited by M. J. Boda, D. K. Falk, and R. A. Werline, 1:193–204. EJIL 23. Atlanta: SBL, 2006.

———. "I was Ready to Be Sought Out by Those Who Did Not Ask." In *Seeking the Favor of God: The Origins of Penitential Prayer in Second Temple Judaism*, edited by M. J. Boda, D. K. Falk, and R. A. Werline, 1:7–8. EJIL 21. Atlanta: SBL, 2006.

———. *Job*. Smyth & Helwys Bible Commentary. Macon, GA: Smyth & Helwys, 2006.

Bandura, Albert. "Social Cognitive Theory of Mass Communication." *Media Psychology* 36 (2001) 265–99.

Bandura, Albert et.al. "Transmission of Aggression through Imitation of Aggressive Models." *Journal of Abnormal and Social Psychology* 63 (1961) 575–82.

Barth, Karl. *The Epistle to the Romans*. Translated by Edwin C. Hoskyns. London: Oxford University Press, 1933.

Bartholomew, Craig G., and Michael W. Goheen. "Story and Biblical Theology." In *Out of Egypt: Biblical Theology and Biblical Interpretation*, 172–84. Scripture and Hermeneutics Series 5. Carlisle, UK: Paternoster, 2004.

Bauer, Jonas. "Enquiring into the Absence of Lament: A Study of the Entwining of Suffering and Guilt in Lament." In *Evoking Lament: A Theological Discussion*, edited by Eva Harasta and Brian Brock, 25–43. London: T. & T. Clark, 2009.

Bauks, Michaela. *Die Feinde des Psalmisten und die Freunde Ijobs: Untersuchungen zur Freund-Klage im Alten Testament am Beispiel von Ps 22*. Stuttgart: Katholisches Bibelwerk, 2004.

Baumgartner, W. *Die Klagegedichte Jeremias und die Klagenpsalmen*. BZAW 32. Giessen: Töpelmann, 1917.

Bautch, Richard J. *Developments in Genre Between Post-Exilic Penitential Prayers and the Psalms of Communal Lament*. Academia Biblica. Atlanta: SBL, 2003.

BearerOfChrist35. "A Psalm—Lament of Christopher." No pages. Online: http://www.youtube.com/watch?v=ZXg40onLAqY.

Becker, J. *Israel deutet seine Psalmen*. Stuttgart: Katholisches Bibelwerk, 1966.

Beckerlegge, Gwilym. "Computer-Mediated Religion: Religion on the Internet at the Turn of the Twenty-First Century." In *From Sacred Text to Internet*, edited by Gwilym Beckerlegge, 219–64. Aldershot, UK: Ashgate, 2001.

Bednar, Tim. "Blogging: Report from a Grassroots Revival." *Stimulus* 12.3 (2004) 24–30.

Benczes, Réka. *Creative Compounding in English: The Semantics of Metaphorical and Metonymical Noun-Noun Combinations*. Amsterdam: Benjamins, 2006.

Bergant, Dianne. *Lamentations*. Abingdon Old Testament Commentaries. Nashville: Abingdon, 2003.

Berger, Peter L. *The Sacred Canopy: Elements of a Sociological Theory of Religion*. Garden City, NY: Doubleday, 1968.

Berger, Peter L., and Thomas Luckmann. *The Social Construction of Reality: A Treatise in the Sociology of Knowledge*. Garden City, NY: Doubleday, 1966.

Bergler, Siegfried. "Threni V—Nur ein Alphabetisierendes Lied? Versuch einer Deutung." *VT* 27.3 (1977) 304–20.

Berlin, Adele. *Lamentations*. OTL. Louisville, KY: Westminster John Knox, 2002.

Berridge, John Maclennan. *Prophet, People and the Word of Yahweh: An Examination of Form and Content in the Proclamation of the Prophet Jeremiah*. Zürich: EVZ, 1970.

Best, Elsdon. *Māori Religion and Mythology Part* 1. Wellington, NZ: Museum of New Zealand/Te Papa Tongarewa, 1995.

Bevans, Stephen B. *Models of Contextual Theology*. Maryknoll, NY: Orbis, 2002.

Bier, Miriam J. " 'Perhaps There Is Hope': Reading Lamentations as a Polyphony of Pain, Penitence, and Protest." PhD diss., University of Otago, 2012.

Billman, K. D., and D. L. Migliore. *Rachel's Cry: Prayer of Lament and Rebirth of Hope*. Eugene, OR: Wipf & Stock, 1999.

Black, Max. "Metaphor." In *Philosophy Looks at the Arts: Contemporary Readings in Aesthetics*, rev. ed., edited by Joseph Margolis, 451–68. Philadelphia: Temple University Press, 1978.

———. *Models of Metaphors: Studies in Language and Philosophy*. New York: Cornell, 1964.

Blank, S. "'And All Our Virtues.' An Interpretation of Isaiah 64:4b–5a." *JBL* 71 (1952) 149–54.

Blenkinsopp, J. *Ezra-Nehemiah*. OTL. London: SCM, 1988.

———. *Isaiah* 40–55. AB 19A. New York: Doubleday, 2000.

———. *Isaiah* 56–66. AB 19B. New York: Doubleday, 2003.

Bluegrass Messengers. "Ain't No Grave—Johnny Cash." No pages. Online: http://www.bluegrassmessengers.com/aint-no-grave--johnny-cash.aspx.

Boase, Elizabeth. "Constructing Meaning in the Face of Suffering: Theodicy in Lamentations." *VT* 58 (2008) 449–86.

———. "The Fulfilment of Doom? The Dialogic Interaction between the Book of Lamentations and the Pre-exilic Early Exilic Prophetic Literature." PhD diss., Murdoch University, 2003.

———. *The Fulfilment of Doom? The Dialogic Interaction between the Book of Lamentations and the Pre-Exilic/Early Exilic Prophetic Literature*. LHB/OTS 437. London: T. & T. Clark, 2006.

Boda, Mark J. "Confession as Theological Expression: Ideological Origins of Penitential Prayer." In *Seeking the Favor of God: The Origins of Penitential Prayer in Second Temple Judaism*, edited by M. J. Boda, D. K. Falk, and R. A. Werline, 1:21–50. EJIL 21. Atlanta: SBL, 2006.

———. "Form Criticism in Transition: Penitential Prayer and Lament, Sitz im Leben and Form." In *Seeking the Favor of God: The Origins of Penitential Prayer in Second Temple Judaism*, edited by M. J. Boda, D. K. Falk, and R. A. Werline, 1:181–92. EJIL 21. Atlanta: SBL, 2006.

———. "From Complaint to Contrition: Peering through the Liturgical Window of Jer 14,1—15,4." *ZAW* 113 (2001) 196–97.

———. *Praying the Tradition: The Origin and Use of Tradition in Nehemiah* 9. BZAW 277. Berlin: de Gruyter, 1999.

———. "The Priceless Gain of Penitence: From Communal Lament to Penitential Prayer in the 'Exilic' Liturgy of Israel." *HBT* 25 (2003) 51–75.

———. "The Priceless Gain of Penitence: From Communal Lament to Penitential Prayer in the 'Exilic' Liturgy of Israel." In *Lamentations in Ancient and Contemporary Cultural Contexts*, edited by Nancy C. Lee and Carleen Mandolfo, 81–101. SBLSymS. Atlanta: SBL, 2008.

———. *A Severe Mercy: Sin and its Remedy in the Old Testament*. Siphrut 1. Winona Lake, IN: Eisenbrauns, 2009.

———. "Theological Commentary: A Review and Reflective Essay." *MJTM* 11 (2009–10), 139–50.

Bogdanov, Vladimir et al. *The All Music Guide to the Blues*. 3rd ed. San Francisco: Backbeat, 2003.

Bono. "The Book of Psalms." In *Revelations: Personal Responses to the Books of the Bible*, edited by Richard Holloway, 135–40. Edinburgh: Canongate, 2005.

Bosch, David J. "God's Reign and the Rulers of This World: Missiological Reflections on Church-State Relationships." In *The Good News of the Kingdom: Mission Theology for the Third Millennium*, edited by Charles Van Engen et al., 89–95. Maryknoll, NY: Orbis, 1993.

Boswell, D. A. "Metaphoric Processing in the Mature Years." *Human Development* 22 (1979) 373–84.

Bracke, John. *Jeremiah 30–52 and Lamentations*. WBC. Louisville, KY: Westminster John Knox, 2000.

Bradbury, Paul. *Sowing in Tears: How to Lament in a Church of Praise*. Grove Worship Series 193. Cambridge: Grove, 2008.

Braiterman, Zachary. "Lamentations in Modern Jewish Thought." In *Great is Thy Faithfulness? Reading Lamentations as Sacred Scripture*, edited by Robin A. Parry and Heath A. Thomas, 92–97. Eugene, OR: Pickwick, 2011.

Braude, William Gordon. *The Midrash on Psalms*. Yale Judaica Series 13. New Haven: Yale University Press, 1959.

Bright, John. *Jeremiah*. Garden City, NY: Doubleday, 1965.

Brown, Francis, S. R. Driver, and Charles A. Briggs. *Hebrew and English Lexicon*. Peabody, MA: Hendrickson, 1996.

Brown, S. A., and P. D. Miller, editors. *Lament: Reclaiming Practices in Pulpit, Pew and Public Square*. Louisville, KY: Westminster John Knox, 2005.

Brown, S. A. "When Lament Shapes a Sermon." In *Lament: Reclaiming Practices in Pulpit, Pew, and Public Square*, edited by S. A. Brown and P. D. Miller, 27–37. Louisville, KY: Westminster John Knox, 2005.

Broyles, C. C. *The Conflict of Faith and Experience in the Psalms*. Sheffield: Sheffield Academic Press, 1989.

Brueggemann, Walter. "The Costly Loss of Lament." *JSOT* 36 (1986) 57–71.

———. "The Formfulness of Grief." *Int* 31 (1977) 263–75.

———. Forward to *Psalms of Lament*, by Anne Weems, ix–xiv. Louisville, KY: Westminster John Knox, 1995.

———. "Lament as Antidote to Silence." *The Living Pulpit* 11.4 (2002) 24–25.

———. "Lament as Wake-up Call (Class Analysis and Historical Possibility)." In *Lamentations in Ancient and Contemporary Cultural Contexts*, edited by Nancy C. Lee and Carleen Mandolfo, 221–36. Atlanta: SBL, 2008.

———. *The Message of the Psalms: A Theological Commentary*. Minneapolis, MN: Augsburg, 1984.

———. "Necessary Conditions for a Good Loud Lament." *HBT* 25 (2003) 19–49.

———. "A Shape of Old Testament Theology, II: Embrace of Pain." *CBQ* 47 (1985) 395–415.

———. "Theodicy in a Social Dimension." *JSOT* 33 (1985) 3–25.

———. *Theology of the Old Testament: Testimony, Dispute, Advocacy*. Minneapolis, MN: Fortress, 2005.

Brueggemann, Walter, and Patrick D. Miller. *The Psalms and the Life of Faith*. Minneapolis, MN: Fortress Press, 1995.

Burnett, J. S. *Where Is God? Divine Absence in the Hebrew Bible*. Minneapolis, MN: Fortress, 2010.

Calvin, Jean. *Commentary on the Book of Psalms*. Translated by James Anderson. Calvin Translation Society Publications 6. Edinburgh: Calvin Translation Society, 1845–49.

Cameron, Lynne. "Operationalising Metaphor for Applied Linguistic Research." In *Researching and Applying Metaphor*, edited by Lynne Cameron and Low Graham, 3–27. Cambridge: Cambridge University Press, 1999.

Campbell, Heidi A. *When Religion Meets New Media*. London: Routledge, 2010.

Campbell, Heidi A., and Antonio C. La Pastina. "How the iPhone Became Divine: New Media, Religion and the Intertextual Circulation of Meaning." *New Media & Society* 12.7 (2010) 1191–1207.

Cellan-Jones, Rory. "Hi-Tech Helps Iranian Monitoring." No pages. Online: http://news.bbc.co.uk/2/hi/technology/8112550.stm.

Cernuschi, Claude. *Not an Illusion but the Equivalent: Cognitive Approach to Abstract Expressionism*. London: AUP, 1997.

Childs, Brevard. *Introduction to the Old Testament as Scripture*. Philadelphia: Fortress, 1979.

———. *Isaiah*. OTL. Louisville, KY: Westminster John Knox, 2001.

———. "Toward Recovering Theological Exegesis." *Pro Ecclesia* 6 (1997) 16–26.

Clines, David J. A. *Ezra, Nehemiah, Esther*. NCBC. London: Marshall, Morgan & Scott, 1984.

———. *Job* 1–20. WBC 17. Dallas: Word, 1989.

Coeurigeuse. "Psalm 143 a Lament." No pages. Online: http://www.youtube.com/watch?v=Uv6fkGMMXUY.

Cogan, Višna. *U2: An Irish Phenomenon*. Cork, Ireland: Collins, 2006.

Cohen, A. "Lamentations 4:9." *AJSL* 27.2 (1911) 190–91.

Cohn-Sherbok, Dan. *The Crucified Jew: 20 Centuries of Christian Anti-Semitism*. Grand Rapids: Eerdmans, 1992.

Collins, Steve. "Network Church." No pages. Online: http://www.emergingchurch.info/reflection/stevecollins/index.htm.

———. "Psalm Structure Twister." No pages. Online: http://www.freshworship.org/zine/psalmtwister.html.

Collins, Tim, and Marie Fatayi-Williams. "Straight from the Heart." No pages. Online: http://www.guardian.co.uk/uk/2005/jul/13/july7.uksecurity23.

Colon, Carlos. "Violence, Lament, Redemption: A Composer's Journey." No pages. Online: http://www.transpositions.co.uk/2011/09/violence-lament-redemption-a-composer%E2%80%99s-journey/.

"Condolences for the Pike River Victims." No pages. Online: http://www.stuff.co.nz/national/pike-river-mine-disaster/4382258/Condolences-for-the-Pike-River-victims.

Cone, James H. *The Spirituals and the Blues: An Interpretation*. 2nd ed. Maryknoll, NY: Orbis, 1992.

Conway, M. L. "From Objective Observation to Subjective Participation: How the Speaking Voices in Lamentations Lead from Suffering Toward Redemption." MTS diss., McMaster University, 2008.

Coogan, Michael. *A Brief Introduction to the Old Testament*. Oxford: Oxford University Press, 2009.

Cook, Stephen L. "Relecture, Hermeneutics, and Christ's Passion in the Psalms." In *The Whirlwind: Essays on Job, Hermeneutics and Theology in Memory of Jane Morse*, edited by Stephen L. Cook, Corrine L. Patton, and James W. Watts, 181–205. JSOTSup 336. Sheffield, UK: Sheffield Academic Press, 2001.

Craigie, Peter C. *Psalms* 1-50. Waco, TX: Word, 1983.

Cunningham, M. "A Short History of Rock Touring, in U2." In *U2 Show*, edited by D. Scrimgeour, 196–99. London: Orion, 2004.

Davis, Ellen F. "Exploding the Limits: Form and Function in Psalm 22." *JSOT* 53 (1992) 93–105.

Day, John. *Psalms*. Sheffield, UK: Sheffield Academic Press, 1992.

De La Parra, Pimm Jal. *U2 Live: A Concert Documentary*. London: Omnibus, 2003.

De Oliveria, Nicolas et al. *Installation Art in the New Millennium: The Empire of the Senses*. London: Thames and Hudson, 2003.

Deane. "U2 and public lament for Pike River Miners." No pages. Online: http://www.emergentkiwi.org.nz/archive/u2-and-public-lament-for-pike-river-miners/#comments.

Delitzsch, Franz. *Biblical Commentary on the Psalms*. Translated by Francis Bolton. Clark's Foreign Theological Library 29–31. Edinburgh: T. & T. Clark, 1893.

Denton, A. "Enough Rope with Andrew Denton." No pages. Online: http://www.abc.net.au/tv/enoughrope/transcripts/s1147867.htm.

DeVaux, Rolland. *Single Combat in the Old Testament, in The Bible and the Ancient Near East*. Translated by Damian McHugh. New York: Doubleday, 1971.

Diamond, A. R. *The Confessions of Jeremiah in Context: Scenes of Prophetic Drama*. Sheffield, UK: Sheffield Academic Press, 1987.

Dion, Paul-Eugène. "Formulaic Language in the Book of Job: International Background and Ironical Distortions." *SR* 16 (1987) 187–93.

Dobbs-Allsopp, F. W. *Lamentations*. Interpretation. Louisville, KY: John Knox, 2002.

———. *Weep, O Daughter of Zion: A Study of the City-Lament Genre in the Hebrew Bible*. Rome: Pontifical Biblical Institute Press, 1993.

Donnarful. "U2—One Tree Hill—Auckland 25 Nov 10—Dedicated to Our Lost Miners—May they RIP." No pages. Online: http://www.youtube.com/watch?v=2c1BLn7-bsY&feature=related.

Donovan, P. "Wanted man." No pages. Online: http://www.theage.com.au/news/entertainment/music/stories-of-me/2009/05/14/1241894089133.html.

Driver, Samuel Rolles, and George Buchanan Gray. *Job*. 2nd ed. ICC. Oxford: T. & T. Clark, 1971.

Duggan, Michael W. *The Covenant Renewal in Ezra-Nehemiah (Neh* 7:72*B*—10:40*): An Exegetical, Literary, and Theological Study*. SBLDS 164. Atlanta: SBL, 1996.

Dunn, James D. G. *Romans* 1–8. WBC 38A. Dallas: Word, 1988.

Duro, Paul, editor. *The Rhetoric of the Frame: Essays on the Boundaries of the Artwork*. Cambridge: Cambridge University Press, 1996.

Eevee2hufflepuff. "Psalm of Lament." No pages. Online: http://www.youtube.com/watch?v=Lyr4vWWFMVk.

eHymns.org. "The Lord's My Shepherd." No pages. Online: http://www.ehymns.org/viewInfoDetail.php?recordID=684.

Eissfeldt, Otto. *The Old Testament: An Introduction*. Translated by Peter R. Ackroyd. New York: Harper & Row, 1965.

Emerson, Caryl. "The Outer World and the Inner Speech: Bakhtin, Vygotsky, and the Internalisation of Language." In *Introduction to Vygotsky*, edited by Harry Daniels, 123–42. London: Routledge, 1996.

Emerton, John A. "The Meaning of *ʾabnê qōdeš* in Lamentations 4:1." *ZAW* 79/2 (1967) 232–36.

Etonick. "Psalm 10—A Complaint about Evil People." No pages. Online: http://www.youtube.com/watch?v=jLrBEET3Xwc.

Evans, Vyvyan, and Melanie C. Green. *Cognitive Linguistics: An Introduction*. Edinburgh: Edinburgh University Press, 2006.

Fahnestock, Jeanne. *Rhetorical Figures on Science*. Oxford: Oxford University Press, 1999.

Falk, D. K. "Scriptural Inspiration for Penitential Prayer in the Dead Sea Scrolls." In *Seeking the Favor of God: The Development of Penitential Prayer in Second Temple Judaism*, edited by M. J. Boda, D. K. Falk and R. A. Werline, 2:127–57. Atlanta: SBL, 2007.

Fee, Gordon. *God's Empowering Presence: The Holy Spirit in the Letters of Paul*. Peabody, MA: Hendrickson, 1994.

Firth, Simon. *Performing Rites: Evaluating Popular Music*. Oxford: Oxford University Press, 1998.

Fisher, L. R. "Betrayed By Friends: An Expository Study of Psalm 22." *Int* 18 (1964) 20–38.

Fitzgerald, Aloysius. "BTWLT and BT as Titles for Capital Cities." *CBQ* 37.2 (1975) 167–83.

Fletcher, Banister, and Dan Cruickshank. *Sir Banister Fletcher's A History of Architecture*. Oxford: Architectural, 1996.

Frank, A. David., "Arguing with God, Talmudic Discourse, and the Jewish Countermodel: Implications for the Study of Argumentation." *Argumentation and Advocacy* 41 (2004) 71–86.

Frevel, Christian. "'Eine kleine Theologie der Menschenwürde': Ps 8 und seine Rezeption in Buch Ijob." In *Das Manna fällt auch heute noch: Beiträge zur Geschichte und*

Theologie des Alten, Ersten Testaments, edited by Frank-Lothar Hossfeld and Ludger Schwienhorst-Schönberger, 244–72. HBS 44. Freiburg: Herder, 2004.

Frymer-Kensky, Tikva. "Zion, the Beloved Woman." In *In the Wake of the Goddesses: Women, Culture, and the Biblical Transformation of Pagan Myth*, 168–78. New York: Free, 1992.

Fyall, Robert S. *Now My Eyes Have Seen You: Images of Creation and Evil in the Book of Job*. Leicester, UK: Apollos, 2002.

Gabriel, A. Richard. *The Military History of Ancient Israel*. Westport, CN: Praeger, 2003.

Galambush, Julie. *Jerusalem in the Book of Ezekiel: The City as Yahweh's Wife*. Atlanta: Scholars, 1992.

Gentner, Dende, et al. *The Analogical Mind: Perspectives from Cognitive Science*. Cambridge: MIT, 2001.

Gerstenberger, Erhard S. *Der Bitte Mensch*. Neukirken-Vluyn: Neukirken, 1980.

———. *Psalms, Part 1 with an Introduction to Cultic Poetry*. FOTL 14. Grand Rapids: Eerdmans, 1988.

———. *Psalms, Part 2, and Lamentations*. FOTL 15. Grand Rapids: Eerdmans, 2001.

Gillespie, Kirsty. *Steep Slopes: Music and Change in the Highlands of Papua New Guinea*. Acton, ACT: Australian National University E Press, 2010. No pages. Online: http://epress.anu.edu.au/.

Gillmayr-Bucher, Susanne. "The Psalm Headings: A Canonical Relecture of the Psalms." In *The Biblical Canons*, edited by J. M. Auwers and H. J. De Jonge, 249–54. Leuven: Leuven, 2003.

Gilmour, Michael J. "The Prophet Jeremiah, Aung San Suu Kyi, and U2's All that You Can't Leave Behind." In *Call Me the Seeker: Listening to Religion in Popular Music*, edited by Michael J. Gilmour, 34–43. New York: Continuum, 2005.

Gitay, Yehoshua. *Prophecy and Persuasion: A Study of Isaiah* 40–48. FTL 14. Bonn: Büttgemanns, 1981.

Goffman, Erving. *Frame Analysis: An Essay on the Organization of Experience*. Cambridge: Harvard University Press, 1974.

Goldembeerg, Robert. "Law and Spirit in Talmudic Religion." In *Jewish Spirituality from the Bible through the Middle Ages*, edited by Arthur Green, 232–53. New York: Crossroad, 1998.

Goldingay, John, and David Payne. *Isaiah* 40–55. *Vol.* 2. ICC. London: T. & T. Clark, 2006.

Goluboff, Sascha L. "Communities of Mourning: Mountain Jewish Laments in Azerbaijan and on the Internet." In *Religion, Morality and Community in Post-Soviet Societies*, edited by Mark D. Steinberg and Catherine Wanner, 149–77. Bloomington, IN: Indiana University Press, 2008.

Gordis, Robert. *The Book of God and Man: A Study of Job*. Chicago: University of Chicago Press, 1978.

———. "The Conclusion of the Book of Lamentations (5:22)." *JBL* 93.2 (1974) 289–93.

Gottlieb, Hans. *A Study on the Text of Lamentations*. Translated by John Sturdy. Acta Jutlandica Teologisk 12. Arhus, Denmark: Aarhus Universitet, 1978.

Gottwald, Norman. *Studies in the Book of Lamentations*. Studies in Biblical Theology. London: SCM, 1954.

Gous, Ignatius G. P. "Mind over Matter: Lamentations 4 in the Light of the Cognitive Sciences." *SJOT* 10.1 (1996) 69–87.

Grady, Joseph E. "Images Schemas and Perception: Redefining a Definition." In *From Perception to Meaning: Image Schemas in Cognitive Linguistics*, edited by Beate Hampe and Joseph E. Grady, 29:35–57. Berlin: de Gruyter, 2008.

Green, Arthur, "Introduction." In *Jewish Spirituality from the Bible Through the Middle Ages*, edited by Arthur Green, xiii–xv. New York: Crossroad, 1998.

Green, Douglas J. "The Good, the Bad and the Better: Psalm 23 and Job." In *The Whirlwind: Essays on Job, Hermeneutics and Theology in Memory of Jane Morse*, edited by Stephen L. Cook, Corrine L. Patton, and James W. Watts, 69–83. JSOTSup 336. Sheffield, UK: Sheffield Academic Press, 2001.

Grosz, Elizabeth. "Naked." In *Impossible Presence: Surface and Screen in the Photogenic Era*, edited by Terry Smith, 209–21. Chicago: University of Chicago Press, 2001.

Guillaume, Philippe. "Lamentations 5: The Seventh Acrostic." *Journal of Hebrew Scriptures* 9 (2009) 2–6.

Gunkel, Hermann. "Klagelieder Jeremiae." In *Die Religion in Geschichte und Gegenwart*, 2nd ed., 1049–52. Tübingen: Mohr Siebeck, 1929.

———. *The Psalms: A Form-Critical Introduction*. Philadelphia: Fortress, 1967.

Gunton, Colin E. *The One, the Three, and the Many: God, Creation, and the Culture of Modernity*. Cambridge: Cambridge University Press, 1993.

Habel, Norman C. *The Book of Job*. Philadelphia: Westminster, 1985.

Hammersley, John. "Psalm of Despair." No pages. Online: http://www.psalmsoflife.com/psalm68.htm.

———. "Psalm of Disaster." No pages. Online: http://www.psalmsoflife.com/psalm71.htm.

Hanson, P. D. *Isaiah* 40–66. Interpretation. Louisville, KY: John Knox, 1995.

Harasta, Eva, and Brian Brock, editors. *Evoking Lament: A Theological Discussion*. London: T. & T. Clark, 2009.

Hartley, John. E. *The Book of Job*. 2nd ed. NICOT. Grand Rapids: Eerdmans, 1988.

Hauerwas, Stanley. "Carving Stone or Learning to Speak Christian." In *Living Out Loud: Conversations about Virtue, Ethics, and Evangelicalism*, edited by Luke Bretherton and Russ Rook, 60–79. Milton Keynes, UK: Paternoster, 2010.

———. "How We Lay Bricks and Make Disciples." In *Living Out Loud: Conversations about Virtue, Ethics, and Evangelicalism*, edited by Luke Bretherton and Russ Rook, 39–59. Milton Keynes, UK: Paternoster, 2010.

———. *Naming the Silences: God, Medicine and the Problem of Suffering*. Grand Rapids: Eerdmans, 1990.

Hayes, K. "When None Repents Earth Laments: The Chorus of Lament in Jeremiah and Joel." In *Seeking the Favor of God: The Origins of Penitential Prayer in Second Temple Judaism*, edited by M. J. Boda, D. J. Falk, and R. A. Werline, 1:119–43. Atlanta: SBL, 2006.

Hays, Richard B. *Echoes of Scripture in the Letters of Paul*. New Haven: Yale, 1989.

Heim, Knut M. "The Personification of Jerusalem and the Drama of Her Bereavement in Lamentations." In *Zion, City of Our God*, edited by R. R. Hess and G. J. Wenham, 129–69. Grand Rapids: Eerdmans, 1999.

Hillers, Delbert. *Lamentations: A New Translation with Introduction and Commentary*. AB. New York: Doubleday, 1972.

———. *Lamentations: A New Translation with Introduction and Commentary*. 2nd ed. AB 7A. New York: Doubleday, 1992.

Hogewood, J. "The Speech Act of Confession: Priestly Performative Utterance in Leviticus 16 and Ezra 9–10." In *Seeking the Favor of God: The Origins of Penitential Prayer in Second Temple Judaism*, edited by M. J. Boda, D. J. Falk and R. A. Werline, 1:69–82. Atlanta: SBL, 2006.

Holladay, William. *The Architecture of Jeremiah 1–20*. Lewisburg, PA: Bucknell University Press, 1975.

Holst-Warhaft, Gail. *The Cue for Passion: Grief and its Political Uses*. Boston: Harvard University Press, 2000.

———. *Dangerous Voices: Women's Laments and Greek Literature*. London: Routledge, 1992.

Hopewell, J. *Congregation: Stories and Structures*. London: SCM, 1987.

Horsfield, Peter G., and Paul Teusner. "A Mediated Religion: Historical Perspectives on Christianity and the Internet." *Studies in World Christianity* 13.3 (2007) 278–95.

House, Paul R. *Lamentations*. WBC 23B. Nashville: Thomas Nelson, 2004.

House of Providence. "House of Providence: Sermons." No pages. Online: http://www.houseofprovidence.com/media.php?pageID=5.

Human Rights Commission. *Freedom of Religion and Belief*. Wellington, NZ: New Zealand Government, 2010.

———. *Religious Diversity in New Zealand: Statement of Religious Diversity*. 2nd ed. Wellington. NZ: New Zealand Government, 2009.

Hurlocks. "Lament for Kenya." No pages. Online: http://www.youtube.com/watch?v=oRmoihkIWu4.

Hyatt, J. Jeremiah. *Prophet of Courage and Hope*. New York: Abingdon, 1958.

Interference.com. No Pages. Online: http://u2.interference.com/f304/how-many-shows-have-they-played-total-198370.html.

Jacobson, K. "Through the Pistol Smoke Dimly: Psalm 23 in Contemporary Film and Song." No pages. Online: http://www.sbl-site.org/publications/article.aspx?articleId=796.

Jahnow, Hedwig. *Das Hebraïsche Leichenlied im Rahmen der Völkerdichtung*. BZAW 36. Giessen: Töpelmann, 1923.

Jan. "U2 and public lament for Pike River Miners." No pages. Online: http://www.emergentkiwi.org.nz/archive/u2-and-public-lament-for-pike-river-miners/#comments.

Janzen, J. Gerald. *Job*. Interpretation. Atlanta: John Knox, 1985.

Jensen, Erik. "Pray . . . In 255 Characters or Fewer." No pages. Online: http://www.stuff.co.nz/technology/digital-living/4296624/Pray-in-255-characters-or-fewer.

Jerome, and Siegfried Risse. *Commentarioli in Psalmos*. Turnhout: Brepols, 2005.

Jetskifisher. "U2 Live in Auckland 25 Nov 2010—One Tree Hill in Memory of Westcoast Miners. R.I.P." No pages. Online: http://www.youtube.com/watch?v=hMnycViozoU.

Joyce, Julian. "Police 'Kettle' Tactic Feels the Heat." No pages. Online: http://news.bbc.co.uk/1/hi/uk/8000641.stm.

Keil, C. F., and Franz Delitzsch. *Job*. In *Commentary on the Old Testament, Vol. 4*. Grand Rapids: Eerdmans, 1980.

Keith, Graham. *Hated Without a Cause? A Survey of Anti-Semitism*. Carlisle, UK: Paternoster, 1997.

Kellum, L. Scott. *The Unity of the Farewell Discourse: The Literary Integrity of John 13:31—16:33*. London: T. & T. Clark, 2004.

Kelly, P. *How to Make Gravy*. Camberwell, UK: Hamilton, 2010.

Kinzer, Mark. *Postmissionary Messianic Judaism: Redefining Christian Engagement with the Jewish People*. Grand Rapids: Brazos, 2005.

Kiwistu72. "U2—One Tree Hill—Auckland 25 Nov 10—Dedicated to Our Lost Miners—May They R.I.P." No pages. Online: http://www.youtube.com/watch?v=2c1BLn7-bsY.

Koehler, Ludwig et al. *The Hebrew and Aramaic Lexicon of the Old Testament*. Leiden: Brill, 2001.

Koenen, Klaus. *Ethik und Eschatologie im Tritojesajabuch: Eine Literarkritische und Redaktionsgeschichtliche Studie*. WMANT 62. Neukirchen: Neukirchener Verlag, 1990.

Kövecses, Zoltan. *Metaphor: A Practical Introduction*. Oxford: Oxford University Press, 2002.

Kramer, Samuel N. *Lamentation over the Destruction of Ur*. Assyriological Studies 12. Chicago: University of Chicago Press, 1940.

Krašovec, Jože. "The Source of Hope in the Book of Lamentations." *VT* 42.2 (1992) 223–33.

Krennmayr, Tina. "Using Dictionaries in Linguistic Metaphor Identification." In *Selected Papers from the 2006 and 2007 Stockholm Metaphor Festivals*, edited by N.-L. Johannesson and D. C. Minugh, 97–115. Stockholm: Department of English, Stockholm University, 2008.

Kynes, William J. *"My Psalm Has Turned Into Weeping": Job's Dialogue with the Psalms*. BZAW. Berlin: de Gruyter, 2012.

Lakoff, George, and Mark Johnson. *Metaphors We Live By*. Chicago: Chicago University Press, 2003.

———. *Philosophy in the Flesh: The Embodied Mind and Its Challenge to Western Thought*. New York: Basic, 1999.

Lakoff, George, and Rafael Nuñez. *Where Mathematics Comes From*. New York: Basic, 2000.

Lambert, Wilfred G. "A Further Attempt at the Babylonian 'Man and His God.'" In *Language, Literature, and History: Philological and Historical Studies Presented to Erica Reiner*, edited by Francesca Rochberg-Halton, 187–202. American Oriental Series 67. New Haven: American Oriental Society, 1987.

Lanahan, William F. "The Speaking Voice in the Book of Lamentations." *JBL* 93.1 (1974) 41–49.

Lapsley, Jacqueline E. "Shame and Self-Knowledge: The Positive Role of Shame in Ezekiel's View of the Moral Self." In *The Book of Ezekiel: Theological and Anthropological Perspectives*, edited by M. S. Odell and J. T. Strong, 143–73. SBLSymS 9. Atlanta: SBL, 2000.

Larner, Daniel. "Trucking Systems from Greece to America: Metaphorai, The Bacchai, and the Problem of Vision in the Contemporary Theatre." *Journal of Religion and Theatre* 3 (2004) 70–85.

Laytner, Anson. *Arguing with God: A Jewish Tradition*. New York: Aronson, 1990.

Leach, John. *Renewing Charismatic Worship*. Grove Renewal Series 10. Cambridge: Grove, 2009.

Lee, J. Barrett. "Psalms of Lament from Guantanamo Bay." No pages. Online: http://streetpastor.wordpress.com/2011/02/22/psalms-of-lament-from-guantanamo-bay/.

Lee, Nancy C. *Lyrics of Lament: From Tragedy to Transformation*. Minneapolis: Fortress, 2010.

———. "The Singers of Lamentations: (a)Scribing (De)Claiming Poets and Prophets." In *Lamentations in Ancient and Contemporary Cultural Contexts*, edited by Nancy C. Lee and Carleen Mandolfo, 33–46. Atlanta: SBL, 2008.

Lee, Nancy C., and Carleen R. Mandolfo, editors. *Lamentations in Ancient and Contemporary Contexts*. SBLSymS 43. Atlanta: SBL, 2008.

Leezenberg, Michiel. *Context of Metaphor*. Amsterdam: Elsevier, 2001.

Lefkowitz, Mary. *Greek God, Human Lives: What We Can Learn From Myths*. Willard, OH: Yale University Press, 2003.

Levenson, Jon D. *Creation and the Persistence of Evil: The Jewish Drama of Divine Omnipotence*. Princeton: Princeton University Press, 1988.

Linafelt, Tod. "The Refusal of a Conclusion in the Book of Lamentations." *JBL* 120.2 (2001) 340–43.

———. "Surviving Lamentations." In *A Feminist Companion to Reading the Bible: Approaches, Methods, and Strategies*, edited by Athalya Brenner and Carole Fontaine, 344–57. Sheffield, UK: Sheffield Academic Press, 1997.

———. *Surviving Lamentations: Catastrophe, Lament, and Protest in the Afterlife of a Biblical Book*. Chicago, IL: University of Chicago Press, 2000.

———. "Surviving Lamentations (One More Time)." In *Lamentations in Ancient and Contemporary Cultural Contexts*, edited by Nancy C. Lee and Carleen Mandolfo, 57–63. Atlanta: SBL, 2008.

Lipschitts, O. *The Fall and Rise of Jerusalem*. Winona Lake, IN: Eisenbrauns, 2005.

"List of Awards Received by U2." No pages. Online: http://en.wikipedia.org/wiki/List_of_awards_received_by_U2.

Longman III, Tremper. *Jeremiah, Lamentations*. NIBC 14. Peabody, MA: Hendrickson, 2008.

Luckmann, Thomas. *The Invisible Religion*. New York: Macmillan, 1967.

Macchia, Frank. "Sighs Too Deep for Words: Toward a Theology of Glossolalia." *Journal of Pentecostal Theology* 1 (1992) 47–73.

MacCormac, Earl R. *A Cognitive Theory of Metaphor*. Cambridge: MIT, 1985.

McCormick, Neil, et al. *U2 by U2*. London: Harper Collins, 2006.

McFague, Sallie. *Super, Natural Christians: How Should We Love Nature?* London: SCM, 1997.

MacGregor, David. "Christ Shows His Face . . . a Flood Reflection." No pages. Online: http://dmacgreg1.wordpress.com/2011/01/21/christ-shows-his-face-a-flood-reflection/.

Mackay, John L. *Lamentations: Living in the Ruins*. Mentor Commentary. Fearn, UK: Mentor, 2008.

Mackey, Robert. "June 22: Updates on Iran's Disputed Election." No pages. Online: http://thelede.blogs.nytimes.com/2009/06/22/latest-updates-on-irans-disputed-election-3/.

McLean, Mervyn. *Māori Music*. Auckland: Auckland University Press, 1996.

McLean, Mervyn, and Margaret Orbell. *Traditional Songs of the Māori*. 3rd ed. Auckland: Auckland University Press, 2004.

Maier, Christl. *Daughter Zion, Mother Zion: Gender, Space, and the Sacred in Ancient Israel*. Minneapolis: Fortress, 2008.

Mandolfo, Carleen R. *Daughter Zion Talks Back to the Prophets: A Dialogic Theology of the Book of Lamentations*. SemeiaSt 58. Atlanta: SBL, 2007.

Manovich, Lev. "New Media from Borges to HTML." In *The New Media Reader*, edited by Noah Wardrip-Fruin and Nick Montfort, 13–28. Cambridge, MA: MIT, 2003.

Margolick, David, and Hilton Als. *Strange Fruit: The Biography of a Song*. New York: HarperCollins, 2001.

Marin, Louis. "The Frame of Representation and Some of Its Figures." In *The Rhetoric of the Frame: Essays on the Boundaries of the Artwork*, edited by Paul Duro, 79–95. Cambridge: Cambridge University Press, 1996.

Mayer, Richard E. "The Instructive Metaphor: Metaphoric Aids to Students' Understanding of Science." In *Metaphor and Thought*, edited by Andrew Ortony, 561–78. Cambridge: Cambridge University Press, 2003.

Mays, James L. "Prayer and Christology: Psalm 22 as Perspective on the Passion." *ThTo* 42 (1985) 322–31.

———. *Psalms*. Louisville, KY: Westminster John Knox, 1994.

Mead, Hirini Moko. *Tikanga Māori: Living by Māori Values*. Wellington, NZ: Huia, 2003.

Mead, S. M. "Imagery, Symbolism and Social Values in Māori Chants." *The Journal of the Polynesian Society* 78.3 (1969) 384–85.

Meek, Theophile J. "Lamentations." In *The Interpreter's Bible*, edited by George Arthur Buttrick, 6:3–38. New York: Abingdon-Cokesbury, 1956.

Melugin, Roy F. *The Formation of Isaiah* 40–55. BZAW 141. Berlin: de Gruyter, 1976.

Menn, Esther M. "No Ordinary Lament: Relecture and the Identity of the Distressed in Psalm 22." *HTR* 93 (2000) 301–41.

Michalowski, Piotr. *The Lamentation over the Destruction of Sumer and Ur*. Winona Lake, IN: Eisenbrauns, 1989.

Middlemas, Jill. *The Troubles of Templeless Judah*. Oxford Theological Monographs. Oxford: Oxford University Press, 2005.

Milgrom, J. *Cult and Conscience: The ASHAM and the Priestly Doctrine of Repentance*. Leiden: Brill, 1976.

Miller, Charles William. "Poetry and Personae: The Use and Functions of the Changing Speaking Voices in the Book of Lamentations." PhD diss., The Iliff School of Theology and University of Denver, 1996.

Miller, N. E. and J. Dollard. *Social Learning and Imitation*. New Haven: Yale University Press, 1941.

Miller, P. D. "Heaven's Prisoners: The Lament as Christian Prayer." In *Lament: Reclaiming Practices in Pulpit, Pew, and Public Square*, edited by S. A. Brown and P. D. Miller, 15–26. Louisville, KY: Westminster John Knox, 2005.

Mitcalfe, Barry. *Māori Poetry: The Singing Word*. Wellington, NZ: Victoria University Press, 1974.

Mitchell, C. "Power, Eros, and Biblical Genres." In *Bakhtin and Genre Theory in Biblical Studies*, edited by Roland Boer, 31–42. Atlanta: SBL, 2007.

Mitchell, Mary Louise. "Reflecting on Catastrophe: Lamentations 4 as Historiography." In *Function of Ancient Historiography in Biblical and Cognate Studies*, edited by Patricia G. Kirkpatrick and Timothy D. Goltz, 78–90. LHB/OTS 489. New York: T. & T. Clark, 2008.

Morrow, W. "Affirmation of Divine Righteousness in Early Penitential Prayers: A Sign of Judaism's Entry into the Axial Age." In *Seeking the Favor of God: The Origins of*

Penitential Prayer in Second Temple Judaism, edited by M. J. Boda, D. J. Falk, and R. A. Werline, 1:101–17. Atlanta: SBL, 2006.

Morson, G. S. "The Aphorism: Fragments from the Breakdown of Reason." *New Literary History* 24 (2003) 409–29.

Mowinckel, Sigmund. "Some Remarks on Hodayot 39.5–20." *JBL* 75 (1956) 272–73.

Muilenburg, James. "Form Criticism and Beyond." *JBL* 88 (1969) 1–18.

Mumford, David B. "Emotional Distress in the Hebrew Bible." *British Journal of Psychiatry* 160 (1992) 92–97.

Muraoka, T. *A Greek-English Lexicon of the Septuagint: Chiefly of the Pentateuch and the Twelve Prophets*. Louvain: Peeters, 2002.

Murley, Bryan. "The Mediahood of All Receivers: New Media, New 'Church' and New Challenges." Paper presented at the Second Annual Civitas Conference, Cornerstone University, Grand Rapids, 21 May 2005.

Nasuti, Harry P. *Defining the Sacred Songs: Genre, Tradition and the Post-critical Interpretation of the Psalms*. JSOTS 218. Sheffield, UK: Sheffield Academic, 1999.

Newsom, Carol A. "The Book of Job." In *NIB* 4:318–637. Nashville, TN: Abingdon, 1996.

———. *The Book of Job: A Contest of Moral Imaginations*. Oxford: Oxford University Press, 2003.

Ngata, A. T., et al. *Ngā Mōteatea: The Songs*. 4 vols. Auckland: Auckland University Press, 2004–7.

NZPA. "U2 Pays Tribute to Lost Miners." No pages. Online: http://www.stuff.co.nz/entertainment/music/4392642/U2-pays-tribute-to-lost-miners.

O'Brien, Julia. *Challenging Prophetic Metaphor: Theology and Ideology in the Prophets*. Louisville, KY: Westminster John Knox, 2008.

O'Connor, Kathleen M. "Lamentations." In *NIB* 6:1013–72. Nashville: Abingdon, 2001.

———. *Lamentations and the Tears of the World*. Maryknoll, NY: Orbis, 2002.

———. "Voices Arguing about Meaning." In *Lamentations in Ancient and Contemporary Cultural Contexts*, edited by Nancy C. Lee and Carleen Mandolfo, 27–32. Atlanta: SBL, 2008.

O'Neil, Shaleph. *Interactive Media: Semiotics of Embodied Interaction*. London: Springer, 2008.

"One Tree Hill—U2—Live Auckland 25 Nov 2010—360° Tour (complete)." No pages. Online: http://www.youtube.com/watch?v=phAKu4yWZqw.

Opacki, I. "Royal Genres." In *Modern Genre Theory*, edited by David Duff, 118–26. Harlow: Pearson Education, 2000.

Orbell, Margaret. *Māori Poetry: An Introductory Anthology*. Auckland: Heinemann Educational, 1978.

———. "'My Summit Where I Sit': Form and Content in Māori Women's Love Songs." *Oral Tradition* 5.2–3 (1990) 184–204.

———. *The Natural World of the Māori*. Auckland: Collins, 1985.

———. *Waiata: Māori Songs in History*. Auckland: Reed, 1991.

Ovid. *The Metamorphoses*. Translated by Horace Gregory. New York: Signet Classic, 2001.

Parris, David Paul. *Reception Theory and Biblical Hermeneutics*. Princeton Theological Monograph Series 107. Eugene, OR: Pickwick, 2009.

Parry, Robin A. *Lamentations. Two Horizons*. Grand Rapids: Eerdmans, 2010.

———. "Lamentations and the Poetic Politics of Prayer." *TynBul* 62 (2011) 65–88.

———. "The Trinity and Lament." In *In Praise of Worship: An Exploration of Text and Practice*, edited by David J. Cohen and Michael Parsons, 143–61. Eugene, OR: Pickwick, 2010.

Parry, Robin A., and Heath A. Thomas, editors. *Great is Thy Faithfulness? Reading Lamentations as Sacred Scripture*. Eugene, OR: Pickwick, 2011.

Pioske, D. "Isaiah's Lament for the Hidden God." *Lutheran Forum* 43 (2009) 18–21.

Polan, Gregory J. *In the Ways of Justice towards Salvation: A Rhetorical Analysis of Isaiah 56–59*. American University Studies 7. Theology and Religion 13. Frankfurt am Main: Lang, 1986.

Polke, C. "God, Lament, Contingency: An Essay in Fundamental Theology." In *Evoking Lament*, edited by Eva Harasta and Brian Brock, 44–57. Edinburgh: T. & T. Clark, 2009.

Pragglejaz Group. "MIP: A Method for Identifying Metaphorically Used Words in Discourse." *Metaphor and Symbol* 22 (2007) 1–39.

Pritzker, Sonya. "Thinking Hearts, Feeling Brains: Metaphor, Culture, and the Self in Chinese Narratives of Depression." *Metaphor and Symbol* 22 (2007) 251–74.

ProfessorJTan. "Lament, Grief, Hope: A Meditation on Psalm 22 (2010)." No pages. Online: http://www.youtube.com/watch?v=kryQeMupAqY.

Provan, Iain W. *Lamentations*. NCB. London: Marshall Pickering, 1991.

———. "Reading Texts against a Historical Background: The Case of Lamentations." *SJOT* 1 (1990) 130–43.

Pyeon, Yohan. *You Have Not Spoken What Is Right About Me: Intertextuality and the Book of Job*. Studies in Biblical Literature 45. New York: Lang, 2003.

Rashi and Mayer I. Gruber. *Rashi's Commentary on Psalms*. Leiden: Brill, 2004.

Reed, A. W. *Taonga Tuku Iho*. 2nd ed. Revised by Buddy Mikaere. Auckland: New Holland, 2002.

Re'emi, S. Paul. "The Theology of Hope: A Commentary on the Book of Lamentations." In *Amos and Lamentations: God's People in Crisis*, by R. Martin-Achard and S. Paul Re'emi, 73–134. ITC. Edinburgh: Handsel, 1984.

Renkema, Johan. *Lamentations*. HCOT. Leuven: Peeters, 1998.

Renn, Stephen, D. *Expository Dictionary of Bible Words: Word Studies for Key English Bible Words Based on the Hebrew and Greek Texts; Coded to the Revised Strong's Numbers*. Peabody, MA: Hendrickson, 2005.

Reno, R. R. "Biblical Theology and Theological Exegesis." In *Out of Egypt: Biblical Theology and Biblical Interpretation*, edited by Craig Batholomew et al., 385–404. Carlisle, UK: Paternoster, 2004.

Richoad, "Sound Relief—The (Un)official Review!" No pages. Online: http://www.last.fm/user/Richaod/journal/2009/03/15/2kfz7k_sound_relief_-_the_%28un%29official_review!.

Ricoeur, Paul. "Between Rhetorics and Poetics." In *Essays on Aristotle's Rhetorics*, edited by Amélie Oksenberg Rorty, 325–85. London: University of California Press, 1996.

———. *The Rule of Metaphor: The Creation of Meaning in Language*. London: Routledge, 2003.

———. *Time and Narrative*. Vol. 1. Translated by Kathleen Blamey and David Pellauer. Chicago: Chicago University Press, 1984.

Rocca, Samuel, and Hook Adams. *The Fortifications of Ancient Israel and Judah 1200–586 BC*. Oxford: Osprey, 2010.

Rom-Shiloni, Dalit. "Socio-Ideological Setting or Settings for Penitential Prayers?" In *Seeking the Favor of God: The Origins of Penitential Prayer in Second Temple Judaism*, edited by M. J. Boda, D. K. Falk, and R. A. Werline, 51–68. EJIL 21. Atlanta: SBL, 2006.

Roncace, Mark, and Patrick Gray. *Teaching the Bible: Practical Strategies for Classroom Instruction*. Atlanta: SBL, 2005.

Royal, Charles. "Oceania, World Music Days, International Symposium and Festival Dialogue in Music." No pages. Online: http://www.charlesroyal.com/assets/moteateatraditionalsongpoetry.pdf.

Rudolph, David J. "Messianic Jews and Christian Theology." *Pro Ecclesia* 14 (2005) 58–84.

Ryken, Leland, et.al., editors. *Dictionary of Biblical Imagery: An Encyclopaedic Exploration of the Images, Symbols, Motifs, Metaphors, Figures of Speech and Literary Patterns of the Bible*. Downers Grove, IL: InterVarsity, 1998.

Ryken, Philip Graham. *Jeremiah and Lamentations: From Sorrow to Hope*. Preaching the Word. Wheaton, IL: Crossway, 2001.

Salters, Robert B. "Text and Exegesis in Lamentations 4:21–22." *In Shai le-Sara Japhet: Studies in the Bible, Its Exegesis and Its Language*, edited by Moshe Bar-Asher et al., 327–37. Jerusalem: The Bialik Institute, 2007.

Schaefer, Konrad. *Psalms*. Collegeville, MN: Liturgical, 2001.

Schapiro, Meyer. "On Some Problems in the Semiotics of Visual Art: Field and Vehicle in Image-Sign." *Simiolus: Netherlands Quarterly for the History of Art* 6.1 (1972–73) 9–19.

Scharen, C. *One Step Closer: Why U2 Matters to those Seeking God*. Grand Rapids: Brazos, 2006.

Scheuer, Blaženka. *The Return of YHWH: The Tension between Deliverance and Repentance in Isaiah* 40–55. BZAW 377. Berlin: de Gruyter, 2008.

Schramm, Brooks. *The Opponents of Third Isaiah: Reconstruction of the Cultic History of the Restoration*. JSOTS 193. Sheffield, UK: Sheffield, 1995.

Seale, Pat, Deborah Everett, and Spiritual Care Collaborative. "The Power of Lament to Create a Village of Care." No pages. Online: http://www.spiritualcarecollaborative.org/docs/workshop_handouts/M2.9%20Seale%20and%20Everett.pdf.

Seitz, Christopher. "Isaiah 40-66." In *NIB* 6: 309–522. Nashville, TN: Abingdon, 2001.

Seybold, Klaus. *Die Psalmen*. Tübingen: Mohr, 1996.

Seymour, M. "Sound Relief Concert in Melbourne and Sydney." No pages. Online: http://www.markseymour.com.au/forum/index.php?topic=195.0.

Shaffer, A. "Mesopotamian Background of Lamentations 4:9–12." *Er-Isr* 8 (1967) 246–50.

Shea, William H. "The Qinah Structure of the Book of Lamentations." *Bib* 60.1 (1979) 103–7.

Shusterman, Richard. "Art as Dramatization." *The Journal of Aesthetics and Art Criticism* 59.4 (2001) 363–72.

Smith, Jacqueline, and Scott Kara. "U2 Pays Tribute to Pike River Miners." No pages. Online: http://www.nzherald.co.nz/nz/news/article.cfm?c_id=1&objectid=10690162.

Smith, James K. A. *Desiring the Kingdom: Worship Worldview and Cultural Formation*. Cultural Liturgies 1. Grand Rapids: Baker, 2009.

Smith, Paul A. *Rhetoric and Redaction in Trito-Isaiah: The Structure, Growth and Authorship of Isaiah* 56–66. VTSup 62. Leiden: Brill, 1996.

Smith, Terry L., and North American Association of Christians in Social Work. "Darkness Is My Closest Friend: Using the Psalms of Lament to Address Grief Issues." No pages. Online: http://www.nacsw.org/Publications/Proceedings2007/SmithTDarkenessClosestFriendE.pdf.

Smith-Christopher, Daniel L. *A Biblical Theology of Exile*. OBT. Philadelphia: Fortress, 2002.

Solish, Gary, D. *The Law of Armed Conflict: International Humanitarian Law in War*. Cambridge: Cambridge University Press, 2010.

Solove, Daniel J. *The Digital Person: Technology and Privacy in the Information Age*. New York: New York University Press, 2004.

Sommer, Benjamin D. *A Prophet Reads Scripture: Allusion in Isaiah* 40–66. Stanford, CA: Stanford University Press, 1998.

Soskice, Janet. *Metaphor and Religious Language*. Oxford: Oxford University Press, 1985.

Soll, Will. "Acrostic." In *ABD* vol. 1, edited by David Noel Freedman, 58–60. New York: Doubleday, 1992.

Soulen, R. Kendall. *The God of Israel and Christian Theology*. Minneapolis, MN: Fortress, 1996.

Sound Relief. DVD. Sound Relief (Fund Raising Enterprise) Australia: Liberation Music, 2009.

Southgate, Christopher. *The Groaning of Creation: God, Evolution and the Problem of Evil*. Louisville, KY: Westminster John Knox, 2008.

Spencer, Sherryl. "Disrupting the Boundary between Art and Obscenity." Honours diss., Curtin University of Technology, 2010.

Sperling, David. "Israel's Religion in Ancient Near East." In *Jewish Spirituality from the Bible through the Middle Ages*, edited by Arthur Green, 5–32. New York: Crossroad, 1998.

Spieckermann, Hermann. *Heilsgegenwart: Eine Theologie der Psalmen*. FRLANT 148. Göttingen: Vandenhoeck & Ruprecht, 1989.

Stead, Michael R. *The Intertextuality of Zechariah* 1–8. LHB/OTS 506. New York: T. & T. Clark, 2009.

Steck, Odil H. *Studien zu Tritojesaja*. BZAW 203. Berlin: de Gruyter, 1991.

Stern, Elsie. "Lamentations in Jewish Liturgy." In *Great is Thy Faithfulness? Reading Lamentations as Sacred Scripture*, edited by Robin A. Parry and Heath A. Thomas, 88–91. Eugene, OR: Pickwick, 2011.

Stern, Judah Joseph. *Metaphor in Context*. Cambridge, MA: MIT, 2001.

Sternberg, Robert. J., and Jeff Mio. *Cognitive Psychology*. Belmont, CA: Wadsworth, 2008.

Stinespring, William Franklin. "No Daughter of Zion: A Study of the Appositional Genitive in Hebrew Grammar." *Enc* 26.2 (1965) 133–41.

Stokes, Ryan E. "I, Yhwh, Have Not Changed? Reconsidering the Translation of Malachi 3:6; Lamentations 4:1; and Proverbs 24:21–22." *CBQ* 70.2 (2008) 264–76.

Stolz, Fritz. "Psalm 22: Alttestamentliches Reden von Menschen und Neutestamentliches Reden von Jesus." *ZTK* 77 (1980) 129–48.

Strawn, Brent A. "Imprecation." In *Dictionary of the Old Testament: Wisdom, Poetry & Writings*, edited by Tremper Longman and Peter Enns, 314–20. Downers Grove, IL: InterVarsity, 2008.

Strong, John T. "Verb Forms of 'MM in Ezekiel and Lamentations." *Bib* 88.4 (2007) 546–52.

SunriseOn7. "U2's Tribute to the NZ Pike River Miners." No pages. Online: http://www.youtube.com/watch?v=zH8rCCoxfdk.

SurfaceOfTheEye. "Psalm 137—Ian White." No pages. Online: http://www.youtube.com/watch?v=IpXFaMupmRQ.

Sweeney, Marvin Alan. *Isaiah 1–39: With an Introduction to Prophetic Literature*. FOTL 16. Grand Rapids: Eerdmans, 1996.

Swinton, John. *Raging with Compassion: Pastoral Responses to the Problem of Evil*. Grand Rapids: Eerdmans, 2007.

Szlos, M. B. "Body Parts as Metaphor and the Value of a Cognitive Approach." In *Metaphors in the Hebrew Bible*, edited by Pierre Van Hecke, 185–95. Leuven: Leuven University Press, 2005.

Tanner, Beth LaNeel. *The Book of Psalms through the Lens of Intertextuality*. Studies in Biblical Literature 26. New York: Lang, 2001.

Tate, Marvin E. *Psalms 51–100*. WBC. Dallas, TX: Word, 1990.

Taylor, Steve. "'Bullet the Blue Sky': The Evolving Live Concert Performances." In *Exploring U2: Is This Rock'n'Roll?*, edited by Scott Calhoun, 84–97. Landam, MD: Scarecrow, 2011.

———. "Scars on the Australasian Heart: Anzac Day as a Contextual Atonement Image." *New Zealand Journal of Baptist Research* 6 (2001) 48–74.

———. "U2 and Public Lament for Pike River Miners." No pages. Online: http://www.emergentkiwi.org.nz/archive/u2-and-public-lament-for-pike-river-miners/.

Terrien, Samuel L. *The Psalms: Strophic Structure and Theological Commentary*. Grand Rapids: Eerdmans, 2003.

Tertullian. *Adversus Marcionem* 3.19. In *Tertullianus Against Marcion*. Vol. 7 of *Ante-Nicene Christian Library: Translations of the Writings of the Fathers Down to A.D. 325*. Edited by Alexander Roberts and James Donaldson. Edinburgh: T. & T. Clark, 1868.

The Alternative Hymnal. "Meet Me In The Middle of The Air by Paul Kelly." No pages. Online: http://alternativehymnal.digitalorthodoxy.com/?s=meet+me+in+the+middle.

The Earth Bible Team. "The Voice of Earth: More Than Metaphor?" In *The Earth Story in the Psalms and the Prophets*, edited by Norman C. Habel, 23–28. London: Continuum, 2001.

The Sisters of Saint Joseph of the Sacred Heart. "Saint Mary Mackillop." No pages. Online: http://www.marymackillop.org.au.

Thomas, Heath A. "Poetry and Theology in Lamentations: An Investigation of Lamentations 1–3 Using the Aesthetic Analysis of Umberto Eco." PhD diss., University of Gloucestershire, 2007.

———. *"Until He Looks Down and Sees": The Message and Meaning of the Book of Lamentations*. Grove Biblical Series 53. Cambridge: Grove, 2009.

Thompson, John A. *The Book of Jeremiah*. NICOT. Grand Rapids: Eerdmans, 1980.

Tidwell, N. L. "Holy Argument: Some Reflections on the Jewish Piety of Argument, Process, Theology and the Philosophy of Religion." *Religious Studies* 32 (1996) 477–88.

Tiemeyer, Lena-Sofia. *For the Comfort of Zion: The Geographical and Theological Location of Isaiah 40–55*. VTS 139. Leiden: Brill, 2011.

———. "Isaiah 40–55: A Drama of Judahite Voices." In *Daughter Zion: Her Portrait, Her Response*, edited by M. J. Boda, C. J. Dempsey and L. Snow Flesher. Atlanta: SBL, 2012.

———. "Lamentations in Isaiah 40–55." In *Great is Thy Faithfulness? Reading Lamentations as Christian Scripture*, edited by Robin A. Parry and Heath A. Thomas, 55–63. Eugene, OR: Pickwick, 2011.

———. *Priestly Rites and Prophetic Rage: Post-Exilic Prophetic Critique of the Priesthood.* FAT II/19. Tübingen: Mohr Siebeck, 2006.

———. "The Question of Indirect Touch: Lam 4,14; Ezek 44,19 and Hag 2,12–13." *Bib* 87.1 (2006) 64–74.

———. "Two Prophets, Two Laments, and Two Ways of Dealing with Earlier Texts." In *Die Textualisierung der Religion*, edited by J. Schaper, 187–89. FAT 62. Tübingen: Mohr Siebeck, 2009.

Tigay, Jeffery Howard, Alan Cooper, and Bathja Bayer. "Lamentations, Book of." In *Encyclopaedia Judaica*, 2nd ed., edited by Fred Skolnik and Michael Berenbaum, 12:446–51. Detroit: Macmillan, 2007.

Tisdell, Elisabeth J. *Exploring Spirituality and Culture in Adult and Higher Education.* San Francisco: Jossey-Bass, 2003.

Tregelles, Samuel Prideaux. *Gesenius's Hebrew and Chaldee Lexicon to the Old Testament Scriptures.* Grand Rapids: Baker, 2000.

Trueman, Carl. "What Do Miserable Christians Sing?" *Themelios* 25.2 (2000) 1–3.

Tostengard, Sheldon. "Psalm 22." *Int* 46 (1992) 167–70.

Tsumura, David Toshio. *The First Book of Samuel.* NICOT. Grand Rapids: Eerdmans, 2007.

"U2, Jay-Z Wow Auckland crowd—Video." No pages. Online: http://www.3news.co.nz/U2-Jay-Z-wow-Auckland-crowd/tabid/368/articleID/188038/Default.aspx.

U2. "One Tree Hill." On *The Joshua Tree.* CD. Island, 1987.

———. "Wake Up Dead Men." On *Pop.* CD. Island, 1997.

———. "Waves of Sorrow." On *The Joshua Tree.* CD. Universal Records, 2007 20th anniversary edn.

———. "White as Snow." On *No Line On the Horizon.* CD. Interscope/Mercury, 2009.

Vall, Gregory. "Psalm 22: Vox Christi or Israelite Temple Liturgy?" *The Thomist* 66.2 (2002) 175–200.

Vanhoozer, Kevin. *The Drama of Doctrine: A Canonical Linguistic Approach to Christian Theology.* Louisville, KY: Westminster John Knox, 2005.

Villanueva, Frederico G. "Preaching Lament." In *He Began with Moses: Preaching the Old Testament Today*, edited by Grenville J. R. Kent et al., 64–84. Nottingham, UK: InterVarsity, 2010.

von Rad, Gerhard. *Das Formgeschichtliche Problem des Hexateuchs.* Stuttgart: Kohlhammer, 1938.

———. "Die Konfessionen Jeremias." *EvT* 3 (1936) 265–96.

Vygotsky, Lev Semenovich. *Mind in Society: The Development of Higher Psychological Process.* Edited by Michael Cole et al. 14th ed. Cambridge: Harvard University Press, 1978.

Watt, A. "Hey Hey Hey My My: Music for Adults. Paul Kelly Interview." No pages: Online: http://www.heyheymymy.com.au/2008/12/01/paul-kelly-interview/.

Way, Eillen Cornell. *Knowledge Representation and Metaphor.* Oxford: Intellect, 1994.

Welch, A. C. "The Source of Nehemiah IX." *ZAW* 47 (1929) 130–37.

Werline, Rodney A. "Lament Regained in Trito-Isaiah's Penitential Prayer." In *Seeking the Favor of God: The Origins of Penitential Prayer in Second Temple Judaism*, edited by M. J. Boda, D. K. Falk, and R. A. Werline, 83–99. EJIL 21. Atlanta: SBL, 2006.

———. *Penitential Prayer in Second Temple Judaism: The Development of a Religious Institution*. Early Judaism and its Literature 13. Atlanta: Scholars, 1998.

Wertsch, J. V. *Vygotsky and the Social Formation of the Mind*. Cambridge: Harvard University Press, 1985.

Wesch, Michael. "Youtube and You: Experiences of Self-Awareness in the Context Collapse of the Recording Webcam." *Explorations in Media Ecology* 8.2 (2009) 19–34.

Westermann, Claus. *Basic Forms of Prophetic Speech*. Louisville, KY: Westminster John Knox, 1991.

———. *Isaiah* 40–66. OTL. London: SCM, 1969.

———. *Die Klagelieder: Forschungsgeschichte und Auslegung*. Neukirchen-Vluyn: Neukirchener, 1990.

———. *Lamentations: Issues and Interpretation*. Translated by Charles Muenchow. Minneapolis, MN: Fortress, 1994.

———. *Praise and Lament in the Psalms*. Translated by K. R. Crim and R. N. Soulen. Atlanta: John Knox, 1965.

———. *Praise and Lament in the Psalms*. Edinburgh: T. & T. Clark, 1981.

———. *The Psalms: Structure, Content, and Message*. Minneapolis, MN: Augsberg, 1980.

———. *The Structure of the Book of Job: A Form-Critical Analysis*. Translated by Charles A. Muenchow. Philadelphia: Fortress, 1981.

Whybray, R. N. *Isaiah* 40–66. Grand Rapids: Eerdmans, 1981.

Wikipedia. "U2 360° Tour." No pages. Online: http://en.wikipedia.org/wiki/U2_360%C2%B0_Tour#Tour_dates.

Williams, Willie. "Rockin' the House." No pages. Online: http://www.u2.com/news/title/rockin-the-house/12.

———. "Scarlet." No pages. Online: http://www.u2.com/news/title/scarlet/14.

Williamson, H. G. M. *Ezra-Nehemiah*. Waco, TX: Word, 1985.

———. "Isaiah 63,7—64,11: Exilic Lament or Postexilic Protest?" *ZAW* 102 (1990) 48–58.

———. "Structure and Historiography in Nehemiah 9." In *Studies in Persian Period History and Historiography*, 282–83. FAT 38. Tübingen: Mohr Siebeck, 2004.

Wolterstorff, Nicholas. *Lament for a Son*. Grand Rapids: Eerdmans, 1987.

Woodard, Jenee. "Worship and Prayer Resources Following a Natural Disaster." No pages. Online: http://www.textweek.com/response/natural_disaster.htm.

Wright, G. H. Bateson. *The Book of Job*. London: Williams & Norgate, 1883.

Würster, Eugen. "The Structure of the Linguistic World of Concepts and its Representation in Dictionaries." *Terminology* 10 (2004) 281–306.

"Your Condolences for the Families of Pike River Miners." No pages. Online: http://www.nzherald.co.nz/nz/news/article.cfm?c_id=1&objectid=10689824.

Yü, Ning. *Human Cognitive Processing*. Amsterdam: Benjamins, 1998.

———. "Metaphor, Body, and Culture: The Chinese Understanding of Gallbladder and Courage." *Metaphor and Symbol* 18 (2003) 13–31.

———. "The Chinese Heart as the Central Faculty of Cognition." In *Culture, Body, and Language: Conceptualisations of Internal Body Organs Across Culture and Languages*, edited by Sharifian Farzad et al., 131–68. Berlin: de Gruyter, 2008.

Zenger, Erich. *A God of Vengeance? Understanding the Psalms of Divine Wrath.* Translated by Linda M. Maloney. Louisville, KY: Westminster John Knox, 1996.

Zinken, Jörg, et al."Discourse Metaphors." In *Cognitive Linguistics Research: Body Language and Mind, Sociocultural Situatedness*, edited by M. Roselyn Frank et al., 363–86. Berlin: de Gruyter, 2008.

www.ingramcontent.com/pod-product-compliance
Lightning Source LLC
LaVergne TN
LVHW010934100826
845153LV00001B/35